English Renaissance Tragedy: Ideas of Freedom

RELATED TITLES

Othello: *The State of Play* edited by Lena Orlin
Macbeth: *The State of Play* edited by Ann Thompson
Emotional Excess on the Shakespearean Stage, Bridget Escolme
Essential Shakespeare, Pamela Bickley and Jennifer Stevens
Doing Shakespeare, Simon Palfrey

English Renaissance Tragedy

Ideas of Freedom

Peter Holbrook

Bloomsbury Arden Shakespeare
An imprint of Bloomsbury Publishing Plc

B L O O M S B U R Y
LONDON • NEW DELHI • NEW YORK • SYDNEY

Bloomsbury Arden Shakespeare

An imprint of Bloomsbury Publishing Plc

Imprint previously known as Arden Shakespeare

50 Bedford Square	1385 Broadway
London	New York
WC1B 3DP	NY 10018
UK	USA

www.bloomsbury.com

BLOOMSBURY, THE ARDEN SHAKESPEARE and the Diana logo are trademarks of Bloomsbury Publishing Plc

First published 2015

British Library Cataloguing-in-Publication Data
A catalogue record for this book is available from the British Library.

ISBN:	HB:	978-1-4725-7281-3
	PB:	978-1-4725-7280-6
	ePDF:	978-1-4725-7283-7
	ePub:	978-1-4725-7282-0

Library of Congress Cataloging-in-Publication Data
A catalog record for this book is available from the Library of Congress.

Series: Shakespeare and Theory, 1234567X, volume 2

Typeset by Fakenham Prepress Solutions, Fakenham, Norfolk NR21 8NN
Printed and bound in India

For Annie, William, and Eloise

CONTENTS

ACKNOWLEDGEMENTS

Heartfelt thanks to Margaret Bartley at Bloomsbury for her assistance and encouragement, and, above all, patience during the writing of this book. Xanthe Ashburner, my postgraduate student at the University of Queensland, read the manuscript closely, saving me from many errors and suggesting numerous improvements. Thanks also to Richard Newman, for help with proofs, and to Chris Tiffin, who prepared the Index. Finally, I acknowledge the support of the Australian Research Council in providing me with the necessary time to concentrate on writing.

PREFACE

This book explores a key genre of English literature – the tragic drama produced in and around the lifetime of William Shakespeare. English Renaissance tragedy is one of the most remarkable bodies of literature in English ever created. The book aims to demonstrate why we should still bother with texts created 400 years ago – why we should read them and see them performed. I have avoided specialist issues, some of which have in recent years become highly technical (for instance, scholars are now using computational techniques to refine our knowledge of the authorship of particular dramatic works). Instead I have concentrated on some key themes that the plays take up, and explored how these relate to the social, political and cultural conditions of early modern England. Of course, historical context can be overdone: these plays, indeed, are vital documents still. One reason for this is that many of the problems tragedies addressed – tyranny, injustice and inequality – are, alas, all too familiar today.

My particular focus is on the ways English Renaissance tragedy was invested in ideas of freedom. Speaking broadly, I argue that writers of tragedy in this period are opposed to tyranny, slavery and injustice. But, as we will see, this commitment by no means excludes a sharp awareness of how complex the question of freedom is in itself. Tragedy addresses this complexity. To what extent are we free? What factors enable or constrain freedom? Are they a matter of fate or necessity, or somehow of our own choosing? And what, when it comes down to it, *is* freedom? Does the word refer simply to the absence of coercion or restraint, or does it entail more than that?[1] Does it involve some notion of obeying reason, or is it simply a matter of being able to do what one wishes?

What is the relation between freedom and order, and tyranny and order? Is freedom always a good, or does it depend on what one is free for? These kinds of questions were alive in the political and social climate of Renaissance England and are taken up in the work of the dramatists I consider in these pages.

What follows is not intended as an exhaustive treatment of the plays (a task beyond the scope of a book of this length – indeed, a book of any length). It is not even an exhaustive treatment of the theme of freedom in these plays. Rather, what I present is an illustration of just a few of the ways in which we can approach these texts as saying something that is of importance now.

The book's first part discusses the genre of tragedy and makes a case for its preoccupation with ideas of freedom. Here I also explore some attitudes towards freedom in the political, social and intellectual worlds of Renaissance England. This section includes a discussion of the ways in which the institution of the theatre at the time fostered the kind of critical thinking we might consider central to our capacity to conceive of ourselves as free persons or citizens.

Part Two consists of a series of short, discrete readings of plays by, in particular, Christopher Marlowe, William Shakespeare, John Webster, Thomas Middleton and John Ford. I have chosen here to focus on works that I feel most compellingly take up the question of human freedom, but many other plays from the period might have been considered. It is important to note that the selection of plays represented in this second section of the book is by no means indicative of the breadth of English Renaissance tragedy as a whole. Some other works, for example *The Tragedy of Mariam*, one of the few surviving English Renaissance plays written by a woman, are briefly touched upon in Part One. Although certain themes do recur across my discussions of the plays, the readings presented in Part Two are intended to function independently of one another; those making use of this book may choose either to read it through from beginning to end, or simply to consult the section relevant to their particular interests.

CHRONOLOGY OF AUTHORS AND WORKS

The following is a timeline of the major authors and plays discussed in this book, in addition to a few other significant dates. Birth and death dates are taken from the *Oxford Dictionary of National Biography*. Dates of works are taken from the sources listed in the Note on the Texts.

1558	Accession of Elizabeth
1561	First performance of Sackville and Norton's *Gorboduc*
1564	Births of Shakespeare and Marlowe
1570	Excommunication of Elizabeth I by Pius V
1576	Founding of The Theatre by James Burbage
c. 1578–80	Birth of Webster
c. 1580	Birth of Middleton
c. 1586	Birth of Ford
1587	Composition of Marlowe's *Tamburlaine* Parts One and Two
1588–9	Composition of Marlowe's *Faustus*
c. 1590	Composition of Marlowe's *Jew of Malta*
1592	Composition of Marlowe's *Edward II*; printing of *Arden of Faversham*
1593	Death of Marlowe
1599	Founding of The Globe theatre
c. 1600–1	Likely composition of *Hamlet*

NOTE ON THE TEXTS

For Shakespeare, I have relied upon the sixth edition of
The Complete Works of Shakespeare, ed. David Bevington
(New York, 2009). I have frequently called upon Bevington's
glosses of particular words in the texts discussed. Quotations
from Christopher Marlowe are from the edition of the plays
prepared by Bevington and Eric Rasmussen (Oxford, 1995).
For *Gorboduc*, I have used William Tydeman's edition in
Two Tudor Tragedies (London, 1992). For *The Revenger's
Tragedy*, I have relied upon *Thomas Middleton: The Complete
Works*, eds Gary Taylor and John Lavagnino et al. (Oxford,
2007). For *Arden of Faversham*, I have relied upon Keith
Sturgess's edition in *Three Elizabethan Domestic Tragedies*
(Harmondsworth, 1969). For *The White Devil*, *The Duchess
of Malfi*, *The Changeling* and *'Tis Pity She's A Whore*, I have
used *English Renaissance Drama: A Norton Anthology*, eds
David Bevington, Lars Engle, Katharine Eisaman Maus and
Eric Rasmussen (New York, 2002). Old-spelling texts have
been modernized. References to the Bible are to the King
James Version.

PART ONE

Tragedy and Freedom

... the high and excellent Tragedy, that openeth the greatest wounds, and showeth forth the ulcers that are covered with tissue; that maketh kings fear to be tyrants, and tyrants manifest their tyrannical humours ...

SIR PHILIP SIDNEY, *A Defence of Poetry*[1]

Tyranny consists in the desire to dominate everything regardless of order.

BLAISE PASCAL, *Pensées*[2]

I am condemned to be free.

JEAN-PAUL SARTRE, *Being and Nothingness*[3]

Introduction

Why read the works of Shakespeare and his contemporaries for their political or social meanings? Even if we allow that plays like *Hamlet* or *King Lear* deserve our attention because of the ways they have influenced literature and culture over the centuries, or because they contain powerful and memorable poetry and ideas, surely they have nothing relevant to tell us about matters of power, government, society, and so on? After all, they were written some four centuries ago. They come to us from a world greatly different from our own.

It is the assertion of this book that English Renaissance plays can still engage our interest in matters of fundamental importance. I argue that tragic drama of this period raises and debates (but by no means resolves) a range of questions to do with human freedom. I take the concept of 'freedom' to include the variety of civil liberties that many of us in the twenty-first-century Western world understand as fundamental to our status as citizens: freedom of speech, freedom of movement, freedom of association, and so on – although, at the time of writing, many of these liberties that we have taken for granted appear increasingly under threat.

But, and a bit less straightforwardly, I also take the question of human freedom to include social and economic equality. Poverty and deprivation impinge on freedom because those who suffer them are unable to fulfil their human capacities – are prevented from reaching their potential as freely acting human beings. The English socialist historian R. H. Tawney expressed this idea eloquently in his book *Equality*, first published in 1931. In arguing the case for a civilized social welfare state, Tawney had to counter the arguments of those who insisted that any attempt to make society more equal would imperil liberty – a view, of course, not infrequently encountered today. Tawney's response to this objection was to show that liberty, if it was to be real rather than simply hot air, actually *required* a substantial degree of material equality. Rather than restricting the concept of liberty to 'a minimum of civil and political rights'[1] (such as freedom of expression, association, and so on) he tried to expand our definition of liberty to include economic and social security: in other words, Tawney wanted a society in which real choice of action would not be limited to the well off but available to all. 'A society is free in so far', he wrote, as it 'enable[s] all its members to grow to their full stature'. And where, by contrast, 'the opportunity to lead a life worthy of human beings is needlessly confined to a minority' of the rich, that state of affairs is, said Tawney, better described not as a society based on 'freedom' but on 'privilege' (235). For Tawney, true freedom had a material or economic dimension: people cannot be counted free if they lead lives of such penury that they are unable to reach their full potential – if they have no practical possibility of choosing between different kinds of lives. But if people are to have such choices in life there will have to be some attempt to make social conditions more equitable; and that will involve real constraint on the ability of the wealthy and privileged simply further to enrich and empower themselves. As Tawney wrote, 'Freedom for the strong is oppression for the weak' (228). In short, equality is not the enemy of freedom, but a necessary condition of it; and inequality brings about not freedom for the majority of people but slavery.

Phrased in a very different language, this is an insight not far from that of Aristotle in his *Ethics*. There Aristotle inquired into the conditions necessary for living a fully human life – a life, as he conceived it, of virtue, which meant a full, significant and admirable one. Quite sensibly, Aristotle concluded that such a life required a minimum of wealth, because only with such a sufficiency could one have the leisure to (for instance) participate as a citizen of the *polis*.[2] Absent such wealth one would not be able to achieve one's true human nature as a *zōion politikon*, that is, a 'political animal'. And not to live as a citizen was to fall short of one's human potential (since only gods and animals, Aristotle thought, could flourish outside political structures).[3] But once again it is impossible to take one's calling as a citizen seriously if one is forever living a desperate, hand-to-mouth existence, unable to think of anything else other than physical survival.

The view that I am elaborating here – that freedom properly *includes* equality, and that a life of poverty and deprivation is one of degrading slavery – is, as we shall see, a view we encounter in English Renaissance tragedy. In Shakespeare's *King Lear*, the Earl of Gloucester recounts his first encounter with the crazed beggar 'Poor Tom' (in actuality his disguised son Edgar). Recalling this miserable spectacle, Gloucester muses that 'I'th' last night's storm I such a fellow saw, / Which made me think a man a worm' (4.1.32–3). Gloucester's statement is a vivid reminder of the dehumanizing effects of material deprivation – of how poverty constitutes, among other things, a cruel contraction of human potential: once as deprived as Poor Tom, 'a man' is virtually indistinguishable from 'a worm'.

In what follows I give an overview of tragedy, and its relation to themes of freedom, before discussing particular plays in Part Two. To begin with I discuss the genre of tragedy in quite general terms, its origins in the classical world, the kinds of themes it has taken up, and so on. After that I move to the overall question of tragic freedom – how the genre has traditionally concerned itself with, at once, an idea of something like an existential limit to human freedom, as well as an affirmation of humanity's potential for political and social freedom. Finally, I place these concerns in the historical and cultural context of Renaissance England: what did freedom mean in this period, and how did tragic drama engage this topic?

1

The Tragic Genre

My focus is Renaissance tragedy. But 'tragedy' of course is a much older form of drama, first appearing among the Greeks and associated with the names of Aeschylus, Sophocles and Euripides – though it is arguable that a tragic way of thinking about life is evident before those authors, notably in the *Iliad* of Homer, a war story that tells, among other things, of the death of the Trojan prince Hector. Traditionally, tragedy deals with the fall of great men (and women, though less commonly, because historically it has been rarer for women to hold positions of power). The tradition is sometimes summed up in a Latin phrase: *De Casibus Virorum Illustrium* ('concerning the falls of famous men'). In *The Canterbury Tales*, Chaucer's Monk defines tragedy as 'a certeyn storie, / As olde bookes maken us memorie, / Of hym that stood in greet prosperitee, / And is yfallen out of heigh degree / Into myserie, and endeth wrecchedly'.[1]

This focus on the great does not recommend the genre to a democratic age like ours. So it is worth noting straight away that, while tragedy does indeed generally deal with those of high 'degree', or social rank, it is not always the case that its heroes are kings and aristocrats. *Romeo and Juliet* deals with young people from a well-off, but not a titled or aristocratic, background (though the Capulets and Montagues are among the leading families of Verona). There existed too in Shakespeare's day a sub-genre of 'domestic' or 'bourgeois' tragedy focused on middle-class folk; in Part Two we will consider a key play of this genre, *Arden of Faversham*. So high social rank is not an *indispensable* feature of tragedy, and, as I will attempt to show in these pages, the condition of the common people has been a concern of tragedy since the Greeks. Perhaps the most helpful way to begin thinking about the genre is simply to say that it is concerned with the hundred and one ways in which things go wrong, with failure and catastrophe – which happens to anyone, high or low. Modern tragedy, by which I mean tragedy written roughly since the Romantic period (and here we must include poems, novels, films, television), depicts terrible events happening to so-called 'ordinary' people – Wordsworth's focus on the life of the 'poorest of the poor' qualifies as tragedy in this sense[2] – and 'terrible' here might mean something as outwardly uneventful as disappointed hopes. Frustrated desire is the material of the Russian dramatist Chekhov; and James Joyce's brilliant story 'Clay', about an apparently trivial event in the life of a lower-class woman, is in this sense a tragedy too. Tragedy does not deal with only one type of human being; it has universal application.

One reason for this universality is that tragedy almost always concerns itself with death. Even if the hero of a tragedy does not himself die, death shadows the genre. Sophocles' *Oedipus Rex* ends with the self-blinding of Oedipus (his death must wait for another play); but his wife (and mother) Jocasta does die. *Hamlet* represents the deaths of the hero, his mother Gertrude, his uncle Claudius and Polonius's son Laertes (not a complete tally). Horatio says the play has depicted 'carnal, bloody, and unnatural acts' (5.2.383). This fact – that tragedies deal with violent and extreme events – might seem to contradict the claim above that 'modern' tragedy can deal with relatively low-level misfortunes, such as, for example, an unhappy marriage. (Think of the fate of Isabel Archer, whose marriage to the monstrous Gilbert Osmond is the subject of James's tragic novel *The Portrait of a Lady*.) Tragedy is an imitation of human life; but this means it is also about death, since every life is in one precise and appalling sense headed for disaster.[3] All human life then is material for tragedy because, as Sophocles tells us in *Antigone*, men 'are born to death'.[4] The Chorus in this play praises man as the wonder of the world. He has mastered navigation, agriculture, hunting, language, thought and politics and 'faces no future helpless'; 'There's only death / that he cannot find an escape from' (359–60). When Shakespeare's Lear gives his hand to the Earl of Gloucester, he wipes it first because 'it smells of mortality' (4.6.133). Shakespeare, indeed, seems to have had an especially sensitive grasp of the way in which existence is bounded by death. Macbeth says that 'all our yesterdays have lighted fools / The way to dusty death' (5.5.22–3) – not a day has gone by that has not been the last day for someone. Shakespeare's *Sonnets* are tragic in this sense, because they depict life as death-haunted: every summer is prologue to autumn and winter; every person, no matter how good, beautiful or noble, will one day die: 'Like as the waves make towards the pebbled shore, / So do our minutes hasten to their end' (Sonnet 60). The *Sonnets* depict death as devouring life: even the speaker's beautiful young man 'among the wastes of time must go, / Since sweets and beauties do themselves forsake / And die as fast as they see others grow' (Sonnet 12). Life is always defeated; failure in this sense has always been tragedy's subject.

The question then must be why we bother with the genre. Life is hard enough without wearying ourselves with stories about all the ways (especially that one, ultimate way) in which things go wrong. There are a number of answers to this objection. The novelist Thomas Hardy, for instance, often uses tragedy in order to focus attention on avoidable social evils. The hero of *Jude the Obscure* suffers not because of the human condition but because he lives in a profoundly unequal society that deprives poor people of education; and Hardy's *Tess of the d'Urbervilles* describes a problem that immediately proposes its own solution: an unmarried woman should not be punished because she falls pregnant to a weak and unscrupulous man (though Hardy also plays with the idea that misfortunes such as Tess's are somehow built into the structure of human experience – see the novel's strange closing lines in which the 'President of the Immortals' is invoked to explain Tess's story).[5] Writers like Hardy, then, use tragedy as an appropriately serious genre with which to deal with extreme but, in principle, remediable social problems. As we shall see, this socially critical use of tragedy is a key feature of the works discussed in this book: English Renaissance writers deployed tragedy to highlight and attack tyranny, injustice and inequality.

Another answer to the question of why we should read tragedy is that it shows us the transience of life and, therefore, implicitly urges us to value it. Tragedy is *on the side* of life; its obsession with death flows from a commitment to life. (Would we value life if we lived forever?) This was the conclusion of the philosopher Friedrich Nietzsche. Tragedy, Nietzsche thought, was not pessimistic but on the contrary stimulated one's appetite for existence. The fundamental issue was what sort of art would make us *love* life in spite of suffering, evil and death. Tragedy, Nietzsche argued, revealed how hard and cruel life was, but in such a way that it converted this pain into '*sublime*' or awe-inspiring 'representations', and thus reconciled us to it: in tragedy 'the terrible is tamed by artistic means'.[6] Of course one might object that comic or escapist art could also enhance our appetite for life. But such art, thought Nietzsche, precisely because it was unrealistic, would be less effective as a tonic. Its pleasing illusions might distract us for a while, but, in the end, reality – unjust, illogical, meaningless – would break in upon our dreams. 'Do you know what "the world" is to me?', asked Nietzsche: 'a monster of force, without beginning, without end … self-creating … self-destroying … beyond good and evil, without goal'.[7] True art *seduces* to life – makes us love reality even though we know it is chaotic (knowledge that otherwise might bring us to despair). An art that included as much reality as was compatible with the perception of form and beauty – that inspired while also acknowledging the world as a scene of irrational creation and destruction – would be all the stronger as a cure for life-weariness. Such an art was to be found in Greek tragedy, in which 'passing away appears equally dignified and worthy of reverence as coming into being'.[8] Tragedy made the death and suffering of the hero interesting, alluring and exciting. Rather than simply pretending the painful qualities of life did not exist, tragedy reflected these qualities back under a heightened, life-enhancing glow, the Greek pantheon itself being human life glamorized: 'The Greeks are the artists of *life*; they have their gods in order to be able to live, not in order to alienate themselves from life'.[9] Greek tragedy was a strong illusion because its celebration of life was predicated on unflinching recognition of suffering. 'The only satisfactory theodicy', Nietzsche declared, was that in which the gods 'justify the life of men by living it themselves'.[10] (In Euripides' *Heracles*, Theseus tells us that 'there is no mortal, no god, untouched by fortune's blows, if poets' tales are true'.[11]) For Nietzsche, tragedy made us look at life realistically but also admiringly.

Nietzsche's argument suggests another reason for watching or reading tragedy: it concerns remarkable, indeed magnificent, people. I do not mean remarkable in the sense of 'socially elevated', although, as mentioned, classic tragedy (including that of the Renaissance) is generally speaking concerned with 'important' personages: kings and queens, princes and nobles, dynastic or leading families. I mean rather that tragedy describes people of extraordinary character and charisma. There is something indisputably glamorous and compelling about figures such as Shakespeare's Hamlet or Cleopatra, Webster's Duchess of Malfi, or Marlowe's Tamburlaine. Hamlet defines excellence in at least three walks of life: he has been 'The courtier's, soldier's, scholar's, eye, tongue, sword' (3.1.154). Shakespeare's Antony is a colossus: 'His legs bestrid the ocean; his reared arm / Crested the world' (5.2.81–2). Oedipus is an intellectual prodigy who saves the city of Thebes by solving the riddle of the Sphinx. Some of these characters, we must note, are *great* without being *good*, at least not in the conventional sense of good: Tamburlaine is a world-destroying conqueror merciless towards his victims (he hangs the virgins of one conquered town because their ruler refused to surrender); and Marlowe's Faustus signs a pact with the devil. In Ford's *'Tis Pity She's a Whore*, Annabella and Giovanni practise incest; and Shakespeare's Cleopatra is abused as a 'strumpet' (*Antony and Cleopatra*, 1.1.13).

Nevertheless there is something about all these figures that makes us feel that ordinary rules do not apply: characters like these have a knack of making crime or immorality look beautiful. Enobarbus says Cleopatra is so gorgeous that 'the holy priests / Bless her when she is riggish' – that is, when she is sexually aroused (2.2.249–50). (In *The Tragedy of Mariam*, the lover of the adultress Salome says something similar to her – rather less convincingly, perhaps, although Salome does possess genuine force of character: 'The being yours can make even vices good.'[12]) Antony, wandering drunk about the streets of Alexandria and keeping company 'With knaves that smells of sweat', is 'the abstract', or summary, 'of all faults / That all men follow' (1.4.9–10, 21). Yet his lustre is undiminished. In Webster's *The White Devil*, Vittoria Corombona is an adulteress who conspires in the murder of her husband; her defiance of her accusers in the play's trial scene moves one observer to commend her 'brave spirit' (3.2.142). When she is led off to a 'house of convertites', or institution for reformed prostitutes, she declares that 'My mind shall make it honester to me / Than the Pope's palace' (3.2.295–6): the nobility of her spirit will transform her squalid surrounds into something pure and holy (although it must be admitted that Webster's Protestant audience is likely to have seen a Pope's palace as a rather louche place anyway). Most people feel that Malcolm's thin and bitter description of Macbeth and Lady Macbeth at the end of the play as 'this dead butcher and his fiendlike queen' (5.8.70) is inadequate: they *are* evil, even diabolically, but so much more than that as well. The Shakespeare critic A. C. Bradley, writing at the beginning of the twentieth century, supposed it had something to do with energy: like other memorable tragic heroes (if the word 'hero' isn't too jarring in this context), Macbeth and Lady Macbeth simply seem larger, more vigorous and individual, than anybody else round them.[13]

Tragedy, then, represents radically imperfect human beings who nevertheless impress us as in some sense wonderful. Of course, we can, if we wish, cast a cold eye upon Hamlet and wonder what all the fuss is about. His plan to avenge his father ends with Denmark becoming the possession of a foreign power, and young Fortinbras of Norway (the other prince in the play) knows what he wants and how to get it. Hamlet, instead of advancing the cause of revenge, 'unpack[s] [his] heart with words' (2.2.586); and as for words, those he uses to Ophelia can seem inexcusable. (Like Lear, who also speaks savagely about the opposite sex (see 4.6.118–31), Hamlet has a deep ambivalence about women, to say the least.) Yet notwithstanding all this, Hamlet remains one of the best-loved and most fascinating figures in world literature, partly, no doubt, because he is in many ways his own harshest, most perceptive critic, and also because he is a person not only of extraordinary insight, eloquence and humour but also of profound feeling: perhaps no one in literature has expressed more memorably and richly different aspects of the emotional life of human beings. G. K. Hunter argued that Hamlet actually redefined heroism: in contrast to Fortinbras he is a hero less of 'acting' than of '*being*' – we admire Hamlet not for what he does but for what he thinks and feels.[14]

The point is that there is nothing run-of-the-mill about these figures. Tragic heroes and heroines are not happy, and may not be moral or responsible or effective or prudent – but they are never uninteresting. Tragedy shows us *what human beings can become*, for good or ill. One of the emotions Renaissance literary critics thought tragedy should arouse was (in Latin) *admiratio*: wonder or intense esteem.[15] Lear is a titan – his story fills one with something like awe. And that is another way tragedy makes us love life: we go away from *Hamlet* or

The Duchess of Malfi with a certain pride in our own species: there are no doubt more moral beings to be found in some corner of the universe but surely not many more fascinating. In short, tragic heroes and heroines demonstrate that not everything in life is banal. Not every tragedy describes greatness, of course: *The Revenger's Tragedy* presents characters for whom we feel appalled fascination – but it is fascination. Vindice, the title's avenger, is not admirable but never fails to be amusing and clever. The existentialist philosopher E. M. Cioran believed that it 'is not pity' but 'envy the tragic hero inspires in us'.[16] What he meant was that whereas most of us live rather tepid existences – and are grateful enough for it too – the tragic hero lives life to the full.[17] We may not have the nerve to live like that, but knowing that some people do ennobles existence generally. (Of course, this view depends on the assumption that some *actually existing* people also happen to live heroic, grand and tragic lives: as Hamlet said, art 'hold[s] … the mirror up to nature' (3.2.22). If tragic magnificence occurred solely in books, it is hard to see how the genre could be of value, since it would merely trade in fantasies.) In his poem 'Lapis Lazuli', W. B. Yeats wrote that 'Hamlet and Lear are gay; / Gaiety transfiguring all that dread'.[18] As with the Renaissance literary theorists who claimed that tragedy induces admiration, for Yeats tragedy is inspiring rather than depressing. How wonderful to live as completely and recklessly as Hamlet and Lear! The large intensity of such lives makes one happy.

2

Tragedy: Freedom, Order and Tyranny

So what about tragedy's relation to human freedom? What does this type of storytelling tell us about our capacities for agency, power, fulfilment?

My comments so far may suggest that tragedy is primarily about *lack* of freedom. In its preoccupation with suffering, death, limitation, tragedy appears to describe humanity as *without* agency. A pessimistic recognition of human vulnerability and powerlessness – if only powerlessness before death – is at the heart of the genre. 'Death is an obligation … we all must pay' writes Euripides in *Alcestis*:[1] tragedy addresses those aspects of life over which we can exert little or no control – thus its continual evocation of fate, the gods, fortune, or other arbitrary forces. Despite his authority and preternatural intelligence, Oedipus is helpless before his destiny (killing his father Laius and marrying his mother Jocasta): 'I suffered' these 'calamities', he declares, 'By fate, against my will!';[2] '[C]hance is all in all' Jocasta herself asserts in *Oedipus the King*.[3] In the version of the story by the Roman tragedian and philosopher Seneca, Jocasta tells Oedipus that 'This fault is fate's; no one becomes guilty by fate'.[4] 'Fate has terrible power' proclaims the Chorus in *Antigone* (951).

This basic intuition of *lack of control* underlies the apparently pessimistic outlook of tragedy, which has already been touched on. Tragedy does tell exciting stories about glamorous and charismatic individuals, and this may lead us to agree with Nietzsche that tragedy is, despite appearances, an uplifting genre. But its focus on human powerlessness is troubling. Euripides' Iphigenia tells us that 'All the gods' dealings with us proceed obscurely and no one knows the harm that is to come. Chance leads us on to dark pathways'.[5] Because human life is anxiously insecure, because there abides no safe haven from the vagaries of chance or cruel tricks of fate, because even the happiest state of affairs is hostage to fortune, there is ultimately no happiness at all. This is the message again and again of classical tragedy: '[I]n its very nature fortune, like a crazed man, leaps now in one direction, now in another, and the same man is never fortunate forever,' says Hecuba in Euripides' *Trojan Women*.[6] 'Is anyone in all the world / Safe from unhappiness?' asks Sophocles' Chorus in *Oedipus at Colonus* (1723–4). 'The life of man entire is misery: / he finds no resting place, no haven from calamity' confirms the Nurse of Euripides' *Hippolytus*.[7] 'For of mortals there is no one who is happy.'[8] If happiness is uncertain perhaps it is of some comfort that hardship is too: 'luck ... overturns / the happy or unhappy day by day' (Sophocles, *Antigone*, 1158–9). But knowing that one's current unhappiness may be arbitrarily transformed into an equally insecure and probably temporary happiness is rather bleak consolation. Lack of faith in the ability of human beings to steer their own course through life issues in the profound nihilism of the Chorus in *Oedipus at Colonus*: 'Not to be born surpasses thought and speech. / The second best is to have seen the light / And then to go back quickly whence we came' (1224–6). Such nihilistic attitudes emerge in Shakespeare's Gloucester – 'As flies to wanton boys are we to th' gods; / They kill us for their sport' (*King Lear*, 4.1.36–7) – and also in his Macbeth, who tells us that human life 'is a tale / Told by an idiot, full of sound and fury, / Signifying nothing' (*Macbeth*, 5.5.26–8).

In what follows I will contest this view of tragedy, arguing that the genre grants more room for human agency than this understanding allows for. In doing so I draw upon the thought of the modern philosopher Jean-Paul Sartre, founder of perhaps the most radical philosophy of human freedom ever elaborated. Essentially, I will argue that tragedy shows us people *freely choosing* how to understand, and respond to, the profoundly difficult circumstances they find themselves in. This is a part of my argument that tragedy is committed to freedom, though tragedy also acknowledges that freedom also takes place in a specific, and therefore limiting, context (if it did not, it is hard to see how there could be any choice at all, since there would be nothing to choose between). Needless to say, one does not choose the circumstances in which one finds oneself. The twentieth-century German philosopher Martin Heidegger, an important influence on Sartre, argued that 'thrownness' was an essential feature of the human condition: each human creature is 'thrown', that is, 'brought into [a world] *not* of its own accord' or making, and has to find its own way through that world.[9] The important point for Sartre, however, is that what one makes of such thrownness, how one interprets and acts in regard to one's circumstances, is certainly a matter of choice (Sartre called this basic interpretation of one's circumstances 'the situation').

Tragedy, in other words, shows characters adopting particular stances or orientations towards the conditions in which, willy-nilly, they find themselves: and what we see are how they interpret these conditions, choosing as always within the available options – which may be agonizingly limited – sometimes protesting these conditions or arguing about their meaning, above all *thinking* and *questioning*. *Hamlet*, to take a famous example, shows us a character trying to make sense of the profoundly difficult circumstances in which he finds himself. And, precisely because, like all of us, Hamlet is blessed – and cursed – with human consciousness, he therefore *cannot avoid* taking up a *stance* or *attitude* towards Claudius's usurpation of Denmark's throne, and, in light of that disposition, acting accordingly, either submitting to the new criminal regime (perhaps by pretending to himself that the situation is not really so bad, Claudius has his good points, in any case this is the way of the world, enjoying one's private life is more important than anything else, etc., etc.), or deciding to resist the tyrant, 'tak[ing] arms against a sea of troubles' (3.1.60), as he puts it, and thereby becoming a political actor. And choosing what to do in this context is far from easy, since it necessarily involves Hamlet taking a stand on *the basic kind of person* he wishes to be. As Sartre put it, 'for human reality, to be is to *choose oneself*' (440). This is the emotion Sartre called anguish: the awareness that one is always condemned to choose. Indeed human consciousness is nothing but choice, and therefore anguish: 'we can not overcome anguish', wrote Sartre, 'for we *are* anguish' (43). Put otherwise, freedom is not something we have but what we are: 'Man does not exist *first* in order to be free *subsequently*; there is no difference between the being of man and his *being-free*' (25).

Let us consider a little more closely Gloucester's disturbing statement about 'the gods' and their sadistic treatment of humanity. Nothing of course can detract from the pessimism of this statement – *except that Gloucester is saying it*. In other words, Gloucester's thinking this thought reminds us that humanity is unlike anything else we know in the universe in that it *consciously reflects upon and questions its condition*. Like other characters in the play, and as in tragedies ancient and modern generally, Gloucester attempts to understand why evil and suffering exist. As far as we can tell, no other creature does this. It is as if, by the very act of saying that human beings are the helpless and petty victims of external forces, no more autonomous or significant than 'flies', Gloucester shows us that, in fact, the opposite is true, that human beings are *uniquely* different from everything else round them and absolutely free. The flies that boys 'kill for their sport' do not question or contemplate what is happening to them; only human consciousness turns suffering and evil into an object of reflection, a problem. In doing so, Gloucester attests to human freedom: every other creature simply *is*. It is only human beings who think their existence, turning suffering and evil (for instance) into material for conscious inquiry. Like Heidegger, Sartre holds that humanity (or *consciousness*) is that being for which *'its being is in question'* (lxii). Horses, dogs, trees, clouds, stones, waves, winds, musical notes, yachts and bacteria do not make their or others' existence into a problem for consciousness. But as soon as one acknowledges that human beings, just in so far as they are conscious, do unavoidably stand back from what happens to them and reflect upon it (and again, nothing else in the universe experiences what happens to it in this way), one has granted them freedom, since *one can choose to think about one's condition in any number of ways*. For instance, in response to the evil round him, Gloucester might have said, as Edgar does say to him, that 'Men must endure / Their going hence, even as their coming hither' (5.2.9–10) – might, that is, have taken a different, more stoic, or courageous, or faithful or providential attitude towards his plight. Tragedy, then, is the genre that pre-eminently shows people deliberately and explicitly thinking about some of the harshest problems of life – death, evil, suffering – and choosing among different ways of conceiving these problems. Or, more accurately, it turns these phenomena into problems. In doing so, tragedy depicts free creatures, 'subjects' of their world rather than mere passive unthinking objects inseparable from it.

For Sartre draws the sharpest possible distinction between human consciousness and everything else in the universe. Human consciousness is a kind of nothingness – a 'hole' or gap in being, a 'decompression' within it (74). As he famously puts it, man is 'the being who is his own nothingness and by whom nothingness comes into the world' (45). Everything except the human simply is what it is; is nothing except what it is. It is only man that, for instance, projects himself into the future, imagining or planning what he will be in some future state (as Sartre writes, 'I am always beyond what I am, about-to-come to myself' (192)); again, it is only man who adopts a specific stance towards his own past, deciding what its meaning for him is now. Only the human, then, is not identical with itself, is instead present to itself as a question, a set of goals, a project; only human consciousness, and nothing else, has this fundamentally reflexive quality. As Sartre puts it, 'Man is free because he is not himself but presence to himself. The being which is what it is can not be free. Freedom is precisely the nothingness which *is made-to-be* at the heart of man and which forces human-reality *to make itself* instead of *to be*' (440). This is why Sartre describes human reality as 'nothingness' – because it is in fact a pure 'potentiality' (98), since 'the nature of consciousness simultaneously is to be what it is not and not to be what it is' (70). Thus, for instance, it is only through humanity that a concept of futurity exists (124) – no other thing experiences itself as what it *might* be some time hence. And paradoxically the freedom and choice that *is* consciousness is non-negotiable: consciousness 'condemn[s]' humanity to freedom, Sartre says, because we have no choice but to think our existence. As he puts it, 'no limits to my freedom can be found, except freedom itself ... we are not free to cease being free' (439).

This notion of continual and inescapable self-creation is unmistakably modern (in particular, twentieth-century) in orientation: it is because God does not exist that the human is at once 'unjustifiable' (38) – is the 'unique foundation' of the 'values' it embodies – and 'condemned to be free' (439). Yet analogous attitudes existed in the Christian world of Shakespeare and his contemporaries. In his 'Oration on the Dignity of Man', Giovanni Pico della Mirandola imagined God explaining to his creature Adam the essential freedom of the human soul:

The nature of all other beings is limited and constrained within the bounds of laws prescribed by Us. Thou, constrained by no limits, in accordance with thine own free will, in whose hand We have placed thee, shalt ordain for thyself the limits of thy nature ... We have made thee neither of heaven nor of earth, neither mortal nor immortal, so that with freedom of choice and with honor, as though the maker and molder of thyself, thou mayest fashion thyself in whatever shape thou shalt prefer.[10]

In contrast to all other creatures, human being is for Pico essentially open, undetermined – created by God, but placed in its own hands.

Clearly tragedy does stress limitation – the exposed, mortal dimension of human life. Like the rest of creation, humans are creatures of space and time and vulnerable to fortune – so unless our eyes are one day miraculously opened, and humanity shall be as gods, the genre will persist. It is *because* of death that tragedies are written – but also (and here again the issue of freedom emerges) because humans and only humans reflect on death. Nothing that exists for the human is simply received: it is necessarily taken up into consciousness, and an attitude (explicit or implicit) adopted towards it. Once again, this implies a radical freedom: the human is not simply being, but rather *thought about being*, or being that is present to itself in consciousness; and to think being is unavoidably to *choose* what attitude one will take towards it. As far as we know, dolphins or apes do not wonder, as Hamlet does, what if anything comes after death, that 'undiscovered country from whose bourn / No traveler returns' (3.1.80–1). Only humans ask the *meaning* of death. 'Why should a dog, a horse, a rat have life, / And thou no breath at all?' asks Lear, kneeling before the body of his dead daughter (5.3.312–3). For Lear, the murder of Cordelia is a philosophical scandal, an outrage against the nature and meaning of the cosmos: such horror should not happen to such a person. Here again, though, what matters is that, for Lear, as for any human being, death (like everything else in the world that we run up against) is something we are obliged to take up an attitude towards – *whatever that attitude may be*. Once again, then, the genre underscores humanity's fundamental freedom: for all other creatures death simply is; for humans alone it inevitably has meaning – though *what kind* of meaning is entirely a matter of choice for each individual person.[11]

Tragedy's preoccupation with death has traditionally made it a 'high' or important genre in part because death is, arguably, the most important and mysterious topic there is. But the genre's grave and resolute focus on the destruction of human beings has the effect, too, of according human life a special dignity. Tragedy supports our intuition that there is something peculiarly sombre and momentous about human death, precisely because the life that death destroys is absolutely unique. No person is the same as another, whereas it is harder for us to see animals as absolute individuals. When Keats wrote of the nightingale that 'The voice I hear this passing night was heard / In ancient days by emperor and clown',[12] the implication is that the bird heard now is in some sense identical with that heard centuries previously. By contrast, human beings are not sunk in, wholly identified with, a species identity: each remains a distinct individual locus of consciousness. For the key fact is consciousness. Consciousness individualizes – alienates and separates one from reality and other human beings. Where a bird, or any other non-human thing, simply is, human consciousness is aware that it is – present to itself, to use Sartre's language. Once again, this structurally reflexive nature of human being places a gap between it and everything else in the universe. The destruction of such an individual consciousness is therefore momentous because that consciousness is absolutely unique.

Tragedy does remind us that we are not godlike masters of our destiny. We are born into a scene we never chose and cannot control, the ultimate limit on our autonomy being life-span. Thrust into situations over which it has limited, if any, influence, humanity is 'born unto trouble, as the sparks fly upward' (Job 5.7). Even if we no longer believe, with Kent in *Lear*, that 'It is the stars, / The stars above us, govern our conditions' (4.3.33–4), or with Bosola, in *The Duchess of Malfi*, that 'We are merely the stars' tennis balls, struck and banded / Which way please them' (5.4.56–7), tragedy reminds us of the countless ways in which our agency, or ability to get done what we wish to get done, is subverted by forces outside our will. It is hardly Romeo and Juliet's fault that their families hate each other. Hamlet is not responsible for Claudius having murdered Hamlet's father and married his mother, and Cordelia is not responsible for Lear's decision to divide the kingdom. Nevertheless, each of these characters is required, simply because of the nature of human consciousness, to adopt a stance towards these unwilled facts. And this stance flows out of what Sartre calls 'the unique and original project' that 'constitutes the being' of each person: that basic orientation towards existence that makes of it a 'situation' (39, 489). A situation, for Sartre then, is existence interpreted in light of one's project. His example is that of a cliff that assumes this or that meaning according to a given project (488). Suppose my plan is to get to a destination some distance beyond this crag – in that case the crag turns into a barrier. But if I should be on my way to some other destination, if moreover I think of myself as someone sensitive to natural beauties, if indeed I have chosen to consider beauty one of the most important things in life, the cliff may assume the appearance of an aesthetically pleasing feature of a landscape. Sartre's point is that the world or situation we find ourselves in emerges only in light of our project. As he puts it, 'Human-reality everywhere encounters resistance and obstacles which it has not created, but these resistances and obstacles have meaning only in and through the free choice which human-reality *is*' (489).

It is worth reminding ourselves that Sartre's philosophy of radical choice was inaugurated during a genuinely tragic episode in his country's history, the defeat and occupation of France by the Nazis. Sartre was a prisoner of war, and risked his own life in the Resistance, and so was hardly naïve about the way that history constrains human choice. Nevertheless his point is clear: one does not choose the circumstances into which one is thrown, but the *meaning* of those circumstances is entirely up to oneself. To an unpatriotic and selfish careerist, a foreign tyranny might present itself as an opportunity rather than oppression; and Creon's rule means something entirely

different to the pliant Ismene than it does to the defiant
Antigone. As Sartre puts it, 'our freedom itself creates the
obstacles from which we suffer' (495). Moreover, in order for
there to be a choice there must be a situation, that is, a scene
that, in the light of one's original project, is experienced as
a set of choices: 'I am never free except in situation' (509).
All of one's plans in life, however trivial, will ultimately be
referred back to an *original* project, a basic scale of values, a
commitment to what is important in life. Cordelia's refusal to
flatter her father in the opening scene of *King Lear* reflects an
intuition that such falsity would violate her most basic sense
of herself and, indeed, of the meaning of her own existence.
The situation is very different for Goneril and Regan. In each
case the basic life-project is the decisive determining fact: for
Romeo and Juliet, or Antony and Cleopatra, life itself is love
and passionate desire. A parental injunction forbidding love
will therefore be resisted – and love will oust honour – for, as
Antony says, kissing Cleopatra, 'The nobleness of life / Is to
do thus' (1.1.38–9).

The paradox, however, is that this basic project can appear
as a compulsion, as *lack* of choice: Antigone, we feel, has *no
choice but* to honour her brother by burying him, even against
Creon's orders; Romeo and Juliet, or the Duchess of Malfi and
her servant Antonio, cannot *not* love one another.[13] Come
what may, Cordelia *must* speak the truth: any other consideration is irrelevant in her eyes. We may well ask in what way
such figures are *responsible* for their conduct? 'I am mighty
among men', Euripides' Aphrodite declares (*Hippolytus*, 2);
and Racine's Phaedra says likewise that love is all-powerful –
as imperious a master as death or Fortune herself.[14] Doesn't
desire, like death, simply strike us down? Tragedy seems
to show people acting in certain ways because they must –
because that is who they are. Giovanni and Annabella's love
for each other in *'Tis Pity She's a Whore* is an offence against
nature, but the incest taboo melts away before their desire.
Love is more important to them than any other consideration,
including nature itself. Antony's apparent determination to

leave Cleopatra ('I must from this enchanting queen break off' (1.2.135)) will inevitably collapse because his basic project in life, the life he has chosen, is one of sensual pleasure. Most famously, Hamlet cannot understand why he does not move expeditiously to avenge his father's death. In each case a person is represented as in some sense borne along by a desire that, willy-nilly, has its way with them. This is how it feels and looks; but what tragedy shows us are not automata but human persons who have, deliberately or not, made up their minds about what most matters to them in life – and are willing to sacrifice everything, including sometimes life itself, to that ideal. Once again, consciousness cannot but adopt a stance towards life: must decide (if only implicitly, tacitly, precognitively) what is and is not the goal of existence: love, wealth, honour, truth, loyalty, piety, power, glory, freedom, and so on, infinitely. *Human consciousness must choose, indeed is nothing other than choice*: and what tragedy shows us are people choosing, and living and dying by those choices.

Tragedy brings bad news. The world will never be as we would wish, for it is necessarily limitation. (The concept of an infinite world is incoherent, because an actual, concrete, *specific* world logically entails the exclusion of other possibilities.) Common sense tells us that a wholly just world will see loss, frustration, heartache. The most hopeful and utopian of thinkers are bound to acknowledge unavoidable material and objective constraints on human life. As the Marxist theorist Sebastiano Timpanaro wrote, even a fully emancipated social order will not evade certain 'constant experiences of the human condition' including 'love, the brevity and frailty of human existence, the contrast between the smallness and weakness of man and the infinity of the cosmos … the debility produced by age (with its psychological repercussions), the fear of one's own death and sorrow at the death of others'.[15] Tragedy reminds us of the inevitable hardships of life, of how the world we are born into is never the one we would have elected to live in. But it also shows people choosing what stance they will adopt towards this world and the difficulties and dilemmas it presents, what choices, given the circumstances, they will make according to the ultimate values they live their lives by. This is what Marx meant when he said that 'Men make their own history, but not ... under conditions they have chosen for themselves; rather on terms immediately existing, given and handed down to them'.[16] We do not choose the scene of existence into which we are 'thrown', to use Heidegger's phrase; but simply by living in it as conscious beings we are obliged, day by day, to choose the attitude we adopt to it. In other words we turn mere being into a meaningful 'world' or 'situation', a place understood in light of our fundamental project. In doing so we assert our freedom; and it is this difficult and inevitably conditioned freedom that tragedy concerns itself with.

In what follows I explore the manifold ways in which characters in English Renaissance tragedy choose to assert their freedom. Much of what I will focus on is the powerful yearning for political and social freedom (which, as already suggested, so often encompasses a desire for equality and social justice). Ordinary people living under Elizabeth I or James I were not permitted to participate in the political life of their country. Yet the tragedy of this period constantly takes up questions of freedom, injustice, tyranny and inequality. One of the main assertions of this book is that English Renaissance tragedy intervened in its world. In other words, tragedy in Shakespeare's age was an *oppositional and critical* mode of writing. It set itself against oppression.

It is important, however, to stress that not all of the emancipationist energies of tragedy on the Shakespearean stage were morally or politically admirable. Villains want freedom too; and from his own perspective a tyrant will be merely exercising his own liberty, although this constitutes oppression for those weaker than him (as Tawney put it, 'freedom for the pike is death to the minnows' (164)). We need to recognize that Renaissance tragedy functions as a laboratory for all sorts of new and dangerous thoughts. Poetry, art and the imagination are not easily administered domains – and Renaissance poetic drama is decidedly experimental, open and boundary-breaking. In fact Shakespeare seems to have conceived of poetry itself as a mode of wild freedom: the Poet in *Timon of Athens* says that poetry 'flies / Each bound' (1.1.26–7); and Theseus in *A Midsummer Night's Dream* observes that 'The lunatic, the lover, and the poet / Are of imagination all compact' (5.1.7–8). Likewise Shakespeare's contemporary, Sir Philip Sidney, asserted that the poet,

> disdaining to be tied to any … subjection, lifted up with the vigour of his own invention, doth grow in effect another nature, in making things either better than nature bringeth forth, or, quite anew, forms such as never were in Nature, as the Heroes, Demigods, Cyclops, Chimeras, Furies, and such like: so as he goeth hand in hand with Nature, not enclosed within the narrow warrant of her gifts, but freely ranging only within the zodiac of his own wit.[17]

There is something almost diabolical in Sidney's image of the poet being able to invent anything, however monstrous – of the poet's absolute freedom.

Nevertheless, although the imagination can be diabolical, my basic argument is that characters in these plays so often elect to stand against unjust and corrupt hierarchies, and in doing so assert their own agency. As we have seen, tragedy does deal with unavoidable and absolute problems of human life (mortality, the insecurity of human existence, the vagaries of fortune), though it also shows that human beings always choose how to comport themselves in relation to these perennial problems. But tragedy has also been concerned with problems that are, in part and in principle at least, remediable – political and social matters particularly. This is no accident: tragedy flourished first in a democracy whose citizens (minimally, adult males born to Athenian parents) actively participated in the decision-making processes of the city. In other words, the Athenians accepted that at some level political life could be subject to deliberative control.

Tragedy has always had a public-political dimension. As one medieval theorist put it, 'Differunt *tragedia* et *comedia*, quia *comedia* privatorum hominum continet acta, *tragedia* regum et magnatum'[18] – 'Tragedies and comedies differ because comedy treats of the acts of private men, tragedy those of kings and great ones'. Athenian tragedy, we should remember, was performed as part of a civic festival sponsored by the state. And, like its English counterpart, it is repeatedly concerned with the problem of tyranny.

In fact tragedy has never been exclusively focused on the individual psychology of a hero but has always had a large preoccupation with social and political matters. The early sixth-century philosopher Boethius indicated this political dimension of the genre when he wrote that it depicts 'the overthrow of happy realms by the random strokes of Fortune'.[19] Ancient tragedy frequently contrasts the irrational and selfish will of a tyrant with the laws of the city and cosmos: in other words, *tyranny is seen as a source of disorder*. In Sophocles' *Antigone* the prophet Teiresias rebukes Creon as one of the 'tribe of tyrants' who 'grab at gain' (1056), and Creon's son Haemon tries to remind his father that 'No city is property of a single man' (737). Haemon's suicide in the play, says the Messenger, is the result of Creon's 'crime' of 'reject[ing] good counsel' (1242–3). (For his part, Creon insists instead that 'There is no greater wrong than disobedience' (672); under his rule the common people are cowed into silence (690–1).) The general problem is the arrogance of the man who 'thinks that he alone is wise' (707). So often in Greek tragedy the cosmos (a Greek word meaning 'order' and 'beauty') itself opposes tyranny as unnatural. For Antigone, the conflict is between 'the gods' unwritten and unfailing laws' that 'always live' (455–7) and the laws of men like Creon. For the Chorus in Sophocles' *Oedipus the King*, 'Insolence breeds the tyrant' (874), who sets himself against the 'laws begotten in the clear air of heaven, / whose only father is Olympus; / no mortal nature brought them to birth' (867–9). In Euripides' *Phoenician Women*, Eteocles declares that, 'If it is ever right to do wrong, then for a throne's sake is wrong most right!';[20] tyranny he praises as 'greatest of the gods' (505). Jocasta, however, urges Eteocles to 'honour Equality ... mankind's natural law' (535–7). Atreus asserts the tyrannical principle in Seneca's *Thyestes*: 'This is the greatest value of kingship: that the people are compelled to praise as well as endure their masters' actions'.[21]

Greek tragedies continually draw a distinction between tyranny and democracy. Aeschylus' Queen of Persia asks of the Athenians: 'Who commands them? Who is shepherd of their host?', only to be informed that the Athenians 'are slaves to none, nor are they subject'.[22] In Euripides' *Heracleidae*, Demophon, King of Athens, distinguishes his rule as involving dialogue and compromise: 'As / I'm not a tyrant over savages, / Good government must be both give and take'.[23] Euripides' *Helen* even depicts one of the common folk resisting tyranny: the Egyptian king, Theoclymenus, is intent on killing his sister, who has freed Helen; a Messenger bravely intervenes. 'You should not act as judge in what belongs to me,' snarls Theoclymenus – to which the Messenger replies, 'Yes, if I am in the right'.[24] When Theoclymenus objects petulantly, 'So I am a subject, not the master', the Messenger steadfastly points out that 'You are master – but only to act piously, not wrongfully' (1638). Euripides' *Ion* features a slave who asserts the principle of natural equality: 'Only one thing brings shame to slaves, the name. In all else a slave who is valiant is not at all inferior to free men'.[25] Ion himself contrasts the life of the 'happy commoner' to that of a king, who 'finds his pleasure in friendship of the base and hates men of good character, since he is afraid of being killed' (625–8). Seneca makes the same point in *Hercules on Oeta*: 'golden cups are mixed with blood' while 'the poor man's heart is free of care'.[26] Seneca's Oedipus tells Creon that only those prepared to be 'hated' are capable of rule: 'a throne is safeguarded by fear' (*Oedipus*, 703–4). One of the most interesting of Greek plays devoted to the theme of freedom is Aeschylus' *Prometheus Bound* (one of Marx's favourite pieces of classical literature).

Here Zeus, rather than being the enemy of tyrants, is himself one. Prometheus, who has been the benefactor of mankind and given it the gift of fire, is tormented for having opposed 'sovereign tyranny'.[27] He prophesies, however, the overthrow of Zeus, which shall reveal 'how different are rule and slavery' (929). In all these instances, what are at stake are freedom, justice and the nature of the political and social order.

In his 66th Sonnet, Shakespeare gives us a roll-call of contemporary social abuses:

> Tired with all these, for restful death I cry:
> As, to behold desert a beggar born,
> And needy nothing trimmed in jollity,
> And purest faith unhappily forsworn,
> And gilded honour shamefully misplaced,
> And maiden virtue rudely strumpeted,
> And right perfection wrongfully disgraced,
> And strength by limping sway disabled,
> And art made tongue-tied by authority,
> And folly doctorlike controlling skill,
> And simple truth miscalled simplicity,
> And captive good attending captain ill.
>   Tired with all these, from these would I be gone,
>   Save that, to die, I leave my love alone.

'Tired with all these' – that is, with such ills as 'desert a beggar born', 'needy nothing trimmed in jollity', 'strength by limping sway disabled', 'art made tongue-tied by authority', 'captive good attending captain ill' – the speaker finds himself crying out 'for restful death' (and it is only the prospect of death leaving his 'love alone' that keeps him alive). Each of the abuses itemized in this sonnet are avoidable social ills. It is not written in the heavens that liberty of speech and artistic expression should be forbidden. But the speaker claims they are forbidden when he observes that 'art' is 'tongue-tied by authority' – that is, silenced by state censorship. It is not impossible to build a world in which, on the whole, merit is rewarded, but this is not what happens, Shakespeare observes, in the England of his day, in which meritorious people ('desert') are reduced to beggary, while needy nothings – people lacking in any native worth – jet about as extravagantly attired big shots ('trimmed in jollity'). The sonnet details how inequality prevents certain human potentialities being realized. Naturally talented people ('strength') are rendered impotent ('disabled') by those who have no genuine abilities but who nevertheless happen to be in power ('limping sway'); similarly, good people ('captive good') find themselves at the beck and call of the morally inferior ('captain ill'). In *The Merchant of Venice*, Shakespeare has the Prince of Aragon deliver a heartfelt speech in praise of the principle of merit. It would be over-cautious not to accept that Aragon speaks here for Shakespeare, himself a relatively humble boy from the provinces who rose on the basis of his own amazing talents. 'Let none presume,' says Aragon, 'To wear an undeserved dignity': 'Oh, that estates, degrees, and offices' – that is, social positions and roles –

> Were not derived corruptly, and that clear honor
> Were purchased by the merit of the wearer!
> How many then should cover that stand bare?
> How many be commanded that command? (2.9.39–45)

Aragon's claim is that, in the unlikely event that merit should be rewarded, those who now stand bare-headed, in servile deference to their putative superiors, would be able to keep their hats on their heads ('cover'); and those who currently 'command' would instead 'be commanded'. Everything would be reversed. But this is not, of course, how the world runs – and tragedy is about reality. Indeed the evils that Sonnet 66 describes are the regular subject matter of the tragic drama of Shakespeare's day. Of course, tragedy is not *only* about such abuses. Love stories do not have much to do with injustice or lack of freedom, and English Renaissance tragedy features plenty of them. We must not politicize everything – although, when one comes to think of it, social conditions often do play a significant role even in the fortunes of lovers. Romeo and Juliet cannot openly declare their feelings for each other because the play depicts parents as exercising near-tyrannical power over children. And, if the two leading houses of Verona had got along, we would have had a very different story. Distinctions of social rank, too, enter importantly into a love story such as that of *The Duchess of Malfi*.

Tragedy of this period, I will argue then, *bore witness* – depicted, generally indirectly, the suffering of a world disfigured by tyranny, oppression, injustice, deep inequality and material deprivation – to all the social ills Shakespeare describes in the sonnet, or that he has Hamlet articulate in 'To be, or not to be' (3.1.57). As everybody knows, that speech reflects a debate in Hamlet's mind about whether or not to take his own life. He runs through the reasons that might incline one towards suicide. What is notable, however, is how many of his meditations are taken up with what we would now call 'social criticism' – that is, with an attack on flagrant social injustices. Hamlet calls attention to such matters as the 'oppressor's wrong' and 'proud man's contumely' (that is, the arrogant abuse of ordinary folk by socially powerful people (3.1.72)). He lists, too, other social abuses, such as 'the law's delay' (3.1.73) in correcting crimes, and the 'insolence of office' (3.1.74) – the arrogance of those in official positions of power. Hamlet's thinking here prefigures King Lear's attack on a corrupt legal system that favours the rich over the poor: 'Plate sin with gold,' cries out Lear, 'And the strong lance of justice hurtless breaks; / Arm it in rags, a pygmy's straw does pierce it' (4.6.165–7). It is an old story, one law for the rich, another for the poor, and a common theme in tragedy of the period. In Webster's *The White Devil* the disguised Francisco points out how money and power pervert justice. He compares great men to the indulged birds of a lord: 'You shall see in the country, in harvest-time, pigeons, though they destroy never so much corn, the farmer dare not present the fowling piece [i.e., the shotgun] to them. Why? Because they belong to the lord of the manor, whilst your poor sparrows that belong to the Lord of

heaven, they go to the pot for't' (5.1.126–31). Claudius makes
the same point when he acknowledges how 'In the corrupted
currents of this world / Offense's gilded hand may shove by
justice' (*Hamlet*, 3.3.57–8) and 'the wicked prize itself / Buys
out the law' (59–60): the rich can buy off judges with the very
proceeds of their crimes.

In Shakespeare's late play *Pericles* a Fisherman answers
his companion's question 'how the fishes live in the sea' by
replying that:

> Why, as men do aland: the great ones eat up the little ones.
> I can compare our rich misers to nothing so fitly as to a
> whale: 'a plays and tumbles, driving the poor fry before
> him, and at last devours them all at a mouthful. Such
> whales have I heard on o'th' land, who never leave gaping
> till they swallowed the whole parish, church, steeple, bells,
> and all. (2.1.27–34)

The rich are likened to a ravenous whale driving the small
fish before him and then devouring them by the mouthful.
The speech sums up the competitive, ruthless and unfree
worlds of *King Lear* and *Hamlet* exactly. Another social
abuse Hamlet lists in his soliloquy is 'the spurns / That
patient merit of th'unworthy takes' (3.1.74–5) – the insults
patiently endured by meritorious persons at the hands of
those who are unworthy but nonetheless powerful. Finally
Hamlet mentions back-breaking physical toil – the daily
work of the rural and urban labouring classes – as another
reason why one might look upon death as 'a consummation /
Devoutly to be wished' (3.1.64–5). For, he asks, 'Who would
fardels' – that is, burdens – 'bear, / To grunt and sweat
under a weary life, / But that the dread of something after
death' (3.1.77–9) makes one fear to take one's own life?
The lines summon up a whole world of suffering endured by
the common people of Elizabethan and Jacobean England:
endless and poorly rewarded toil, 'a weary life' of 'grunt[ing]'
and 'sweat[ing]' under burdensome loads. We often think

of 'To be, or not to be' as having a lofty, rather abstractly existential or philosophical focus, and so it does – it concerns, after all, the fundamental question of what happens to us after death, and what attitude we should take towards death. But in another respect the speech is not preoccupied with otherworldy matters at all, but with here-and-now social and political ones: the lack of freedom that one endures living under an oppressor; inequality and injustice; the harsh lives of the poor.[28] And, of course, we might remember that suicide itself was the classical Roman solution to the problem of living under tyranny – as the Earl of Gloucester describes it, taking one's own life was the one reliable way in which to 'beguile the tyrant's rage / And frustrate his proud will' (*King Lear*, 4.6.63–4).[29] In *Agamemnon*, Aeschylus has his Chorus declare its unwillingness to 'drag our lives out long' under the yoke of servility: 'better to be killed. / Death is a softer thing by far than tyranny'.[30] Sartre took this thought one step further when he identified suicide as one of the 'ultimate possibles' that 'must always be present for us' if we can be said to take up a stance in relation to our circumstances (554). Insofar as I choose *not* to kill myself, I am in effect assenting to those circumstances, and must therefore take responsibility for them. In this sense, the possibility of my suicide reminds me of the radical nature of my freedom – I am always free to die rather than do what I do not wish to do.[31] In all of these ways the most famous speech of English drama addresses both contingent (which is to say in principle alterable) facts of human existence (lack of freedom, political and social oppression, etc.) as well as unchanging and absolute problems (mortality itself, and the question of what, if anything, might lie in wait for us after death).

The conjunction of *avoidable and unavoidable* ills in English Renaissance tragedy is neatly illustrated in another of Hamlet's best-known speeches: his confession of melancholy to Rosencrantz and Guildenstern, apparently old friends of Hamlet's but now working as spies for Claudius. 'I have of late,' says Hamlet to them,

– but wherefore I know not – lost all my mirth, forgone all custom of exercises; and indeed it goes so heavily with my disposition that this goodly frame, the earth, seems to me a sterile promontory; this most excellent canopy the air, look you, this brave o'erhanging firmament, this majestical roof fretted with golden fire – why, it appeareth nothing to me but a foul and pestilent congregation of vapours. What a piece of work is a man! How noble in reason, how infinite in faculty, in form and moving how express and admirable, in action how like an angel, in apprehension how like a god! The beauty of the world, the paragon of animals! And yet, to me, what is this quintessence of dust? (2.2.296–309)

Hamlet here speaks to an old theme in tragedy, that of dissolution and futility. Man may well be 'the beauty of the world', 'the paragon', or ideal type, 'of animals', but it is all for naught, because he will eventually return to dust ('Golden lads and girls all must, / As chimney sweepers, come to dust', Shakespeare would later write in *Cymbeline* (4.2.265–6)). But Hamlet's pessimism, his sense of the futility of human life, has here a local and social cause as well as an ultimate, metaphysical one – has as much to do, that is to say, with tyranny as with mortality. He is led to this despairing vision of life only fifty or so lines after declaring to the two court spies that 'Denmark's a prison' (2.2.244). What he is therefore responding to is life in a political and social *prison*; and what presses in upon him is the enormous gap that exists between what man *could* be and what in fact, under such conditions, he actually is. Man is 'infinite' in potential or 'faculty' – he really *could* be almost anything, could have the power and rational self-direction and dignity of an 'angel' or 'god' – if only he was permitted to develop these powers. But instead he is worth no more than inanimate 'dust', is nothing more than a slave and prisoner. Shakespeare seems to have been much preoccupied in *Hamlet* with this theme of a human potential (most obviously, Hamlet's) thwarted by tyranny. Later in the play Hamlet muses on the true ends of a properly human life: 'What is a man', he asks,

> If his chief good and market of his time
> Be but to sleep and feed? A beast, no more.
> Sure he that made us with such large discourse,
> Looking before and after, gave us not
> That capability and godlike reason
> To fust in us unused. (4.4.34–40)

The point here is that Hamlet asserts that the principal 'good' and profit or purpose of human life is the free exercise of rational and discursive powers (consciousness being the faculty that radically marks us off from the animals). Our Maker, he claims, did not give us consciousness – this 'godlike reason' and 'large discourse' (or power of speech) – merely to grow mouldy in us through lack of use. But it takes only a moment to realize that it is precisely under a tyranny that such 'capabilities' as reason and speech fall into decay – because the last thing a tyrant wants, of course, is a populace speaking and reasoning freely. Tyrants prefer their subjects distracted by harmless amusements, sleeping, feeding, sex, and so on. In other words, they prefer to rule passive and unthinking 'beasts' rather than reflective and inquiring human beings. Shakespeare's Caesar is wary of Cassius – Cassius 'thinks too much', and 'such men are dangerous' (1.2.195); Caesar's future assassin 'reads much' and as a result 'looks / Quite through the deeds of men' (1.2.203) rather than accepting them at face value.

So tragedy is concerned with both avoidable and unavoidable problems. Often characters in tragedies are called upon to tell the difference between the two. How much of what ails us is really a matter of 'fate' or 'necessity', and how much is instead our own choice? In *Julius Caesar*, Cassius observes to Brutus that 'Men at sometime' – he means during the Roman Republic – 'were masters of their fates'; and he concludes that 'The fault, dear Brutus, is not in our stars, / But in ourselves, that we are underlings' (1.2.139–41). What Cassius means is that it is not fate, but because people like he and Brutus and other citizens of the Republic have chosen to allow Caesar to become (in effect) a king, that they have become 'underlings' or slaves. In the next scene he proposes that Caesar has been able to assume a position of dictatorship solely because the Roman citizens have permitted it in their willing servility:

> And why should Caesar be a tyrant then?
> Poor man, I know he would not be a wolf
> But that he sees the Romans are but sheep;
> He were no lion, were not Romans hinds. (1.3.103–6)

And he goes on to worry that Brutus, his desired co-conspirator against Caesar, might himself be 'a willing bondman' (1.3.113). Cassius here addresses the whole problem of what Étienne de La Boétie, the great friend of Michel de Montaigne, called 'voluntary servitude'. Tyrants govern because the majority let them: if consent were withdrawn, a tyranny would fall immediately. The real problem lies in our readiness to acquiesce in our own enslavement.[32] Nevertheless, as we will see, tragedy often does show people not, in fact, as servile 'hinds' but as agents who stand up to tyranny.

In the coming pages, we will explore some of the ways in which English Renaissance tragedies engage with a range of avoidable social ills. But in order to do that, we should first consider the ways in which questions of freedom were themselves active in the political and intellectual contexts in which the plays were written.

3

Freedom, Tyranny and Order in the English Renaissance

As I have said, English Renaissance tragedy takes up a range of questions to do with the concept of human freedom. We have seen that tragedy has traditionally concerned itself with both unavoidable ills – questions of fate and mortality – but also with avoidable ones: issues to do with government, tyranny and economic and political injustice. Some of the complexity of the treatment of freedom in these plays can be put down to the complexity of the concept in early modern English society. That society was not 'free' in the sense that we would use the word today – to mean, roughly, freedom to do what you want so long as it does no harm to others.

In order to understand English Renaissance tragedy we have to picture a scene in which, as the historian D. M. Palliser writes, 'power, prestige and economic wealth were distributed very unequally';[1] in which the humane welfare state of Western societies since the end of the Second World War was non-existent; and in which characteristically modern Western ideals, such as equality and freedom of speech, were virtually unknown. Roughly speaking this is the world in which the authors of the works considered in this volume lived and wrote. The basic assumptions of their world were vastly different from ours. Western societies today, for example, take freedom of religion as a self-evident right, which was far from being the case in Shakespeare's age, when England had an officially enforced state religion and religious observance was a civic duty. Non-attendance at church might result in a fine, and Catholic missionaries, bent on converting heretics back to the old religion of Rome, risked torture and a gruesome execution that included hanging, disembowelment and burning. Today all political parties honour (or, at least, pay lip-service to) the ideal of equality, differing only over the means to realize it. In Shakespeare's day the situation was reversed. It was not equality that was idealized but hierarchy, understood as part of the divine architecture of the cosmos. Democracy, called at the time 'levelling', was a dangerous notion, and regarded as contrary to nature, reason and God. A series of state-sponsored 'homilies', or sermons, read out every year in every church in the land, served to remind people of this truth. One such homily, 'An Exhortation Concerning Good Order, and Obedience to Rulers and Magistrates', reads as follows:

> Amighty God hath created and appointed all things in heaven, earth, and waters, in a most excellent and perfect order. In heaven, he hath appointed distinct and several orders and states of archangels and angels. In earth he hath assigned and appointed kings, princes, with other governors under them, in all good and necessary order.

Subjects, therefore, had a godly duty to offer 'obedience, submission, and subjection to the high powers'[2] (the writers are citing Romans 13). However, it might be noted that invoking Christianity, which has a radical core ('the last shall be first, and the first last'; 'Ye cannot serve God and mammon' (Mt. 20.16, 6.24)), was always a double-edged sword. As we will see, tyranny and the selfish rule of the rich was conceived of as *ungodly*.

Nor was freedom of speech in any way an official social ideal (though, interestingly, English men and women seem to have prided themselves on not living under the kind of *absolute* tyranny they attributed to, for instance, the Russians: Webster's Duchess of Malfi protests indignantly at the idea that, 'like to a slave-born Russian', she must 'Account it praise to suffer tyranny' (3.5.77–8)). As the courtier and intellectual Francis Bacon wrote, Elizabeth,

> (not liking to make windows into men's hearts and secret thoughts, except the abundance of them did overflow into overt and express acts and affirmations,) tempered her law so, as it restraineth only manifest disobedience in impugning and impeaching advisedly and maliciously her Majesty's supreme power.[3]

As the old adage had it, thought was free[4] – no one would bother you overmuch if you entertained heretical ideas, just so long as you kept them to yourself. Likewise, after the death of Elizabeth, James insisted he had never wished to constrain 'the politic government of the bodies and minds of all [his] subjects to [his] private opinions', and that his 'mind was ever ... free from persecution, or thralling of [his] subjects in matters of conscience'.[5] But the notion that one might have the right to convert one's fellows to Roman Catholic beliefs or, perhaps, even to atheism would have struck contemporaries as preposterous. Writers were not infrequently imprisoned for offending against orthodoxy or touching on sensitive matters of state. In 1599 the bishops ordered satires to be burnt. London Bridge (along which theatre-goers might proceed to visit a performance in the afternoon at the theatres on the southern bank of the Thames) featured the heads of traitors stuck up on spikes.[6] A writer unhappy with the Elizabethan or Jacobean court would, of course, have been foolhardy to write a play dealing with this theme directly and openly, or to refer unflatteringly to the reigning monarch or his or her immediate predecessor. Direct representations of contemporary persons of great power are rare in English Renaissance drama; when they do appear, they tend towards the hagiographic, as when, in Shakespeare's late play *Henry VIII* (probably a collaborative effort with John Fletcher), the baby Elizabeth is eulogized as a future queen: Elizabeth will be a 'pattern' (or model) 'to all princes' (5.5.23).

A device of playwrights reluctant to be 'tongue-tied by authority' was to set their plays in far-off lands or distant times. Of the plays under discussion in Part Two of this book, only the early Elizabethan tragedy *Gorboduc*, Shakespeare's *King Lear* and Marlowe's *Edward II* are set in England, and all three take place in the historical past; all the others have Mediterranean, European or Near Eastern settings (*Arden of Faversham* is an exception, but its focus is domestic). This ruse allowed dramatists to raise in a covert way questions about freedom, inequality and injustice. A particularly self-reflexive episode in *Hamlet* illustrates the point: seeking to find out whether his uncle Claudius is guilty of murdering his father, Hamlet stages a play about the murder of a duke. 'The play's the thing,' exults Hamlet, 'Wherein I'll catch the conscience of the King' (2.2.605–6) – Claudius's reaction to the performance will indicate his guilt or innocence.[7] The play works like a charm. 'Have you heard the argument? Is there no offense in't?' Claudius inquires edgily as he watches (3.2.230–1). Soon enough he orders a halt to the performance: 'Give me some light. Away!' (3.2.267). The cessation of *The Mousetrap* (the title of the play Hamlet commissions) opens a small window onto the repression of speech and art in the period we are concerned with. Hamlet's retort to Claudius's question about whether there is any 'offense' in the play is characteristically clever: 'No offense i'th' world' he insists: ''Tis a knavish piece of work, but what of that? Your Majesty, and we that have free souls, it touches us not' (3.2.232–3, 238–40). 'What's to worry about?' Hamlet in effect asks Claudius. 'We know *you* would never commit murder, or play the tyrant, for your soul is as free from sin as ours. So since this episode in the play can't allude to you, it can't offend you.'

Another tactic was to place dissenting views in the mouths of obvious villains or cultural outsiders (in which case the dramatist can have his cake and eat it too: the offending doctrine is disseminated while he himself remains free of any taint of unorthodoxy). As the brutalized, and brutal, Bosola puts it in *The Duchess of Malfi*, 'Sometimes the devil doth preach' (1.1.293): occasionally even a wicked person like himself can be a vehicle for the truth. One of the most remarkable features of English Renaissance tragedy is its interest in such truth-talking outsiders – figures who don't fit in, who provide a jaundiced perspective on the established order, who threaten to defy or overturn it (for good or bad reasons), who are motivated by some kind of resentment, who are individualistic rebels of one kind or another. Such figures can be villainous or heroic or somewhere in between: in one sense or other (and to confine ourselves only to the plays considered here) Hamlet, the Duchess of Malfi, Bosola, Edmund, Tamburlaine, Vindice (in *The Revenger's Tragedy*), Giovanni and Annabella (in *'Tis Pity She's A Whore*), Iago, all fit this pattern. Each of these figures is distinct from the others, but each also stands outside his or her world and acts against its norms. And such figures can have a 'truth-function' within the play, expressing unacknowledged realities of one kind or another.

When Hamlet claims 'Denmark's a prison', or when the Duchess of Malfi declares 'This is a prison!' (4.2.11), each protests against a world that denies people fundamental liberties. One of the most exciting elements of the plays considered here is their interest in characters who choose to defy tyranny. Part of the Duchess's heroism consists in a breath-taking refusal to submit to the brutal bullying of her brothers: 'I am chained to endure all your tyranny,' she declares (4.2.60). A similar defiance can be seen in Gloucester's extraordinary refusal to bend to the will of Goneril, Regan and Cornwall in the blinding scene of *King Lear*. He admits he sent Lear to Dover because he 'would not see [Regan's] cruel nails / Pluck out his poor old eyes' (3.7.59–60). And when the

Duchess declares, in ringing tones, 'I am Duchess of Malfi still' (4.2.138), we have another instance of courageous defiance of tyranny.

If early modern English society was not 'free' in the sense in which we would use that word today, ideas about freedom were nevertheless at the heart of political discourse in the period. An intriguing feature of Renaissance tragedy is the frequency with which words like 'traitor' and 'tyrant' appear. The difficulty is in knowing precisely how the writer is using them: one man's traitor is another's freedom-fighter. In *King Lear*, for instance, are the old Earl of Gloucester, Kent and Cordelia 'traitors', as Cornwall, Regan and Goneril believe them to be, or are they, on the contrary, loyal followers of a legitimate king?[8] Audiences watching the play in London in the early years of the seventeenth century would have had to choose which side they thought legitimate, and whether rebellion or armed invasion of England by Cordelia and her husband, the King of France, was justified. Plays in the period take a complex view of issues of government and freedom. Many draw on a tradition of thought, going back to Plato, that sees the tyrant as fundamentally *unfree*, since genuine liberty amounts to rational self-restraint. The tyrant by contrast is enslaved to unreasoning appetites. He is the least happy, or free, man, argued Plato, because completely at the mercy of his own unbridled passions: 'There's nothing, no taboo, no murder, however terrible, from which [the tyrant] will shrink' in order to gratify his inordinate and compulsive drives; 'His passion tyrannizes over him'.[9] Macduff's statement that 'Boundless intemperance' in human nature 'is a tyranny' expresses the same idea (*Macbeth*, 4.3.67–8). In *Lear*, the savage Earl of Cornwall is a case-study of the type. He admits that his mutilation and torture of Gloucester will lack 'the form' – that is, the official proceedings – 'of justice', nevertheless 'our power / Shall do a court'sy to our wrath, which men / May blame, but not control' (3.7.26–8). This classical understanding of the tyrant is a Renaissance commonplace. 'Rational' or 'true liberty', thought Milton,

> always with right reason dwells
> Twinned, and from her hath no dividual being:
> Reason in man obscured, or not obeyed,
> Immediately inordinate desires
> And upstart passions catch the government
> From reason, and to servitude reduce
> Man till then free.[10]

Even King James agreed that the distinction between tyrant and king turned upon this question of self-government: a tyrant is 'prey to his passions and inordinate appetites'.[11] This was the understanding, too, of the mid-sixteenth-century compendium *The Mirror for Magistrates*, a popular collection of 'tragic' tales of the sorry ends of various worthies that was intended to serve as both instruction and warning to those holding positions of power. The title of the work turns on a double-meaning of the word 'mirror', as at once a reflection or imitation of reality (these are true stories of the fall of important persons) and an instruction as to how reality ought to be (the relating of the stories is intended to serve a monitory function: don't do this!). This is the same sense Hamlet has in mind when he speaks of drama as holding a 'mirror up to nature': the 'purpose of playing' is to 'show virtue her feature, scorn her own image, and the very age and body of the time his form and pressure' (3.2.20, 22–4). Dedicating *The Mirror* 'To the nobility, and all other in office', William Baldwin, editor of the 1559 version, cited Plato on the appropriate 'government of a common weal'.[12] Baldwin summarized Plato as saying that 'Well is that realm governed in which the ambitious desire not to bear office' (63). High office and judicial authority are 'not gainful spoils for the greedy to hunt for, but painful toils for the heedy to be charged with' (63):

> For if the officers be good, the people can not be ill. Thus the goodness or badness of any realm lieth in the goodness or badness of the rulers. And therefore not without great cause do the holy Apostles so earnestly charge us to pray

for the magistrates: For indeed the wealth and quiet of every common weal, the disorder also and miseries of the same, come specially through them. (64)

Among the 'tragedies', or instances of misrule, described in *The Mirror* is that of Robert Tresilian, Chief Justice of England from 1381 to 1387 during the reign of Richard II, who, 'for our Prince's pleasure corrupt with meed and awe / wittingly and wretchedly did wrest [that is, pervert] the sense of law' (73), and Richard II himself, a king who 'transcend[ed] the limits of his law, / Not reigning but raging by youthful insolence' (78). What is especially interesting about this passage from *The Mirror* is how clearly it identifies disorder with tyranny: a king who, with the conniving of a corrupt justice, goes beyond the law, does not 'reign' but 'rage'; and whether a kingdom is to be orderly or chaotic, peaceful or conflict-ridden, is ultimately up to the rulers, for it is they who are responsible for the state (Richard, of course, was overthrown in a coup d'état by Henry Bolingbroke). *The Mirror* understands that good government has as its end the good of the 'commonweal' – literally, the common wealth – not merely the interests of the monarch, the land-owning aristocracy, or the well-to-do generally. As we will see, this commonwealth ideal is central to English Renaissance tragedy.

The drama of the period often depicts just or otherwise good kings as models of moderation and self-government, and tyrants as the slaves of Milton's 'upstart' or unruly 'passions'. At the opening of *The Duchess of Malfi*, the intellectual Antonio praises the French king's household. The king imposes upon 'both state and people ... / ... a fixed order' (1.1.5–6). But 'order' here, we need to understand, does *not* mean absolute rule. The king has banished from the court 'flatt'ring sycophants', hearkening instead to virtuous advisers:

And what is't makes this blessed government
But a most provident council, who dare freely

Inform him the corruption of the times?
Though some o'th'court hold it presumption
To instruct princes what they ought to do,
It is a noble duty to inform them
What they ought to foresee. (1.1.8, 16–22)

A king, then, should heed advice, be instructed by a 'council' permitted to speak 'freely' about the corruption in his realm. Indeed, Antonio's praise of the French king's court is close to a defence of the parliamentary principle. *King Lear*, on the other hand, begins with a monarch taking the catastrophically wilful decision to divide his kingdom. He spurns the counsel of the Earl of Kent, who urges him to 'Reserve [his] state' (1.1.150) – that is, to retain his royal authority, instead of transferring it to Cornwall and Albany – and instead insists upon his own absolute power: 'The bow is bent and drawn. Make from the shaft' (1.1.143). Lear will do as he pleases. The question Shakespeare's audience had to decide, then, was this: is Lear acting as a monarch of the kind wished for by the authors of *The Mirror for Magistrates*, or is he, instead, guilty of lawlessness and even impiety? Kent challenges Lear's conviction that it is only Lear who can tell Lear what to do: 'Think'st thou that duty shall have dread to speak / When power to flattery bows? / To plainness honor's bound / When majesty falls to folly' (1.1.147–50). Kent sees it as his duty to tell the king plainly and directly that he is doing 'evil' (1.1.169). In doing so he rejects Lear's claim to absolute authority. And when banished from the kingdom, he declares, magnificently, that 'Freedom lives hence and banishment is here' (1.1.184) – which smuggles in the idea that living under a king *ought* to be a state of freedom rather than slavery. The whole opening of *Lear* is a thrilling depiction of the conflict between the principle of absolute power and the right of subjects, such as Kent, to restrain it. And, we should note, Kent assumes he has a *right* to 'freedom': to continue to live under Lear's reign would amount to 'banishment' from his natural and proper state of liberty. One thinks of Cassius's plain statement of the principle in *Julius Caesar*: 'I was born free' (1.2.97).

James I asserted that kings were 'God's Lieutenants upon earth'.[13] Lear thinks of himself in similarly lofty terms. He is wonderfully grandiloquent: 'Come not between the dragon and his wrath', he warns Kent (1.1.122). But extravagant claims for the prerogatives of monarchs were not universally shared. Indeed, religious strife – the 'hot ardent zeal' that 'would set whole realms on fire' (*Timon of Athens*, 3.3.34–5) – inevitably encouraged the questioning of princely authority. How could one obey a ruler who might lead one to eternal damnation? In 1570, Pope Pius V pronounced Queen Elizabeth a heretic, and his successor decreed that whoever assassinated her would be doing God's work.[14] In the Netherlands the Protestant subjects of the Spanish Catholic monarch Philip II had waged a long armed rebellion against their ruler. Writing in the wake of the English Civil War, Milton pictured the second race of men who grew up after the Flood as living in a state of 'fair equality', an harmonious state of affairs until Nimrod, 'Of proud ambitious heart', aspired to become king. In other words, for Milton the first king was himself a rebel against God's law of 'equality' – and notwithstanding Nimrod's brazenly accusing of 'rebellion' all those who resisted his grab for power. For Milton, as for other dissident seventeenth-century Englishmen, the true rebels were kings, not those trying to constrain monarchical power.[15] Again, one man's order (monarchy) is another's anarchy (tyranny). A great part of Hamlet's objection to the reign of Claudius stems from his conviction that Denmark is misgoverned by a man whose appetites – for power, sex, drink – are uncontrolled (see the discussion about the king's drunkenness at 1.4.7–38: Claudius fits the standard characterization of the tyrant as the man helpless before his own drives). The free and freedom-loving man, by contrast, masters his desires. Hamlet describes his friend Horatio in just such terms: 'Dost thou hear?' he asks,

Since my dear soul was mistress of her choice
And could of men distinguish her election,

Sh' hath sealed thee for herself, for thou hast been
As one, in suffering all, that suffers nothing,
A man that Fortune's buffets and rewards
Hast ta'en with equal thanks; and blest are those
Whose blood and judgment are so well commeddled
That they are not a pipe for Fortune's finger
To sound what stop she please. Give me that man
That is not passion's slave, and I will wear him
In my heart's core, ay, in my heart of heart,
As I do thee. (3.2.61–73)

What this passage gives us is an image of freedom – but a particular kind of freedom, one distinguished from the heedless satisfaction of desires. Horatio is not the sort of man to sing what Hamlet elsewhere calls 'the / Tune of the time' (5.2.188–9) – to adopt, slavishly, the currently dominant outlook. A figure of supreme self-control, whose passions ('blood') are tempered by reason ('judgment'), he is not a pipe for Fortune to play on, passive material for anyone to shape and manipulate. Horatio neither fears Fortune's 'buffets' nor craves her 'rewards' – and, consequently, neither fears the oppressions, nor desires the blandishments, of tyrants like Claudius. What Horatio at bottom values in life (what Sartre would call his 'original project') liberates him from any concern with what people like Claudius can do to him.

At the heart of this passage from *Hamlet*, and at the heart of a lot of works of this period, is an idea of order. Horatio has an ordered soul and is as a result free. Here is a key feature of the concept of freedom in the early modern period: it was often seen to inhere in states of order (thus subjects living in ordered political states were deemed to be free, while those living in disordered ones were supposed to lack freedom). The whole concept of order – the order of the cosmos, as well as social and political order – has been a key topic for discussion of Renaissance tragedy. In a famous book, E. M. W. Tillyard wrote that 'The conception of world order was for the Elizabethans a principal matter'.[16] It was second nature for Christians of this period to think of the cosmos as an expression of the divine government of creation (in *The Merchant of Venice*, Shakespeare depicts the heavens as imbued with 'sweet harmony', each 'orb' or heavenly body 'choiring' the other (5.1.57, 60, 62)). Thinkers in the period often understood harmony in the political, social and familial spheres to reflect a divine or cosmic unity. Just as God ordered the cosmos, so a king ordered his realm, and a husband and father his wife and children. In his *True Law of Free Monarchies* (1598), James I wrote that 'By the law of nature the king becomes the natural father to all his lieges at his coronation'; like a father he should 'care for the nourishing, education, and virtuous government' of his subjects, administering 'chastisement' when necessary.[17] The fundamental principle of subordination and obedience applied in nature, the family, government. There is no question that English Renaissance tragedy spoke directly to this major theme of English and European culture of this period, that is, the theme of an orderly, harmonious and good society. Monarchs, nobles and churchmen everywhere, and across the Protestant–Catholic divide, championed the ideal of order and identified themselves with it.

Yet harmony and stability can hardly provide material for the 'carnal, bloody, and unnatural acts' (*Hamlet*, 5.2.383) tragedy depicts. The corpse-strewn end of a play like *King Lear* demonstrates that order has entirely collapsed. As Thomas Heywood wrote, citing an ancient authority, 'tragedies begin in calms and end in tempest'.[18] Nevertheless, the view that tragedy is concerned above all with order leaves open the question of the *attitude* of the plays to the breakdown of harmony. For, notwithstanding Hamlet's praise of Horatio as a figure of order in the speech quoted above, it is not clear that tragedies straightforwardly mourn collapses of the apparently orderly nature of things. Of course, in one sense they do – the needless destruction of Lear, Cordelia, Gloucester, the Fool is meant to be appalling. But that does not quite capture our emotions at the end. Paradoxical as it sounds, we may find ourselves thinking that there is something necessary, right, even welcome about what happens in that play. Despite our conviction that Lear in no sense 'deserves' his fate, it is possible to feel that the dreadful train of events set in motion by the play was somehow needed – that in some strange manner we only dimly apprehend the world is better for these events. We may, for instance, come to believe that the world of *King Lear* was in fact not all that harmonious, or orderly, to begin with.

Here we find ourselves encountering again the idea that tyranny, although it presents itself as order, is actually a kind of *disorder* – a violation of a higher divine or natural order. As it turns out there was not a little disorder in Lear's reign – the opening scene, in which he self-indulgently proposes to divide up his kingdom, is an instance. To adapt Marcellus's words in *Hamlet* (1.4.90), perhaps something originally was 'rotten in the state' of Lear's Britain? Lear himself suggests as much. Forced to take shelter in what Cordelia later calls a 'hovel', suitable only for 'swine and rogues forlorn' – that is, for wretched vagabonds (4.7.40) – the king exclaims he has 'ta'en / Too little care of this!' (3.4.32–3) – paid too little attention to the homeless people of his kingdom, to 'Poor naked wretches', whose 'houseless heads and unfed sides', and 'looped and windowed raggedness' (3.4.28, 30–1), render them helpless against 'pitiless storm[s]' such as the one Lear himself now endures (3.4.29). It is at this very moment that he encounters the supposed beggar 'Poor Tom', who embodies the material deprivation Lear has been deploring. The social criticism implicit in this moment is not affected by our knowledge that Tom is an impersonation. After all, the reason Edgar's disguise works is that it allows him to go incognito: there are thousands of *real* Toms, people whom 'penury' has reduced to the level of 'beast[s]' (2.3.8–9), wandering hopelessly across Lear's kingdom.

What we learn, then, is that prior to the conflict between Lear and his daughters, the kingdom was at least in one respect a place of moral *dis*order, because full of human beings enduring the most squalid deprivation. To put this in different terms, Lear comes to see extreme economic inequality, and mass economic misery, as disorder. As he goes on to say in the speech just quoted:

> Take physic, pomp;
> Expose thyself to feel what wretches feel,
> That thou mayst shake the superflux to them
> And show the heavens more just. (3.4.33–6)

This is a remarkable statement, its message bracing today. Lear is calling for a radical redistribution of wealth. He addresses 'pomp', the rich or elite political class, as if it was morally sick. The rich must take medical treatment ('physic'), and the cure consists in submitting themselves to the regime Jesus prescribed the Rich Man: they must give away their wealth to the poor, or at least that part constituting the 'superflux', the bit they do not need.[19] Only through this sacrifice will the rich demonstrate that the heavens are just – that there actually is good order in the universe. And, just in case we failed to grasp this point, Shakespeare has Gloucester express precisely the same idea a little further on. He gives his purse to Tom in reward for the beggar's agreeing to take him to Dover Cliffs. As he does so he reflects on this action as a salutary image of the redistribution of wealth. 'Heavens,' Gloucester declares, 'deal so still!',

> Let the superfluous and lust-dieted man,
> That slaves your ordinance, that will not see
> Because he does not feel, feel your pow'r quickly!
> So distribution should undo excess
> And each man have enough. (4.1.65–70)

What Gloucester highlights is a profound disorder within Britain. The man who lives in luxury, corruptly indulging his lust for wealth and pleasure, has enslaved divine law. The ruling elite has not noticed the suffering all around it – has not noticed it because it does not (yet) feel such suffering itself. And Gloucester ends as Lear did, with the conviction that the only way to fix this state of affairs is for the rich to give their wealth to the poor, so that 'each man [will] have enough'.[20]

These two speeches of Lear and Gloucester are unambiguous: the realm ruled over by Lear has been unjust. So in fact the play does *not* describe a trajectory from harmony and order to division and chaos. There was plenty of chaos and division around beforehand – it was just that the well-to-do blinded themselves to it. Once again we return to our intuition that, while it would make no sense to think of what happens to Lear, Gloucester, Cordelia and so on as right (it is too appalling for that), we do feel there was something very wrong in the world of the play from the beginning, so that its tragic outcome was in a way inevitable. Lear's Britain was poorly governed. And while we mourn the deaths of such figures as Cordelia, we may find ourselves *not* mourning the passing of the particular *non*-order the play so violently abolishes. 'Order' has proven to be chaos. Moreover, we may feel that King Lear's painful recognition of this fact is itself a gain – coming at terrible cost but an advance on ignorance. Perhaps we may even hope *some* good may come from this new awareness – perhaps Edgar will prove a better king?

Hierarchical order was in other spheres no less subject to argument. Take the notion, commonly expressed in the period, that women are properly subordinated to men. Shakespeare has Luciana expound this idea eloquently in *The Comedy of Errors*: 'The beasts, the fishes, and the winged fowls / Are their males' subjects and at their controls' (2.1.18–19). It stands to reason that 'Man, more divine' than these imperfect creatures, will be 'masters to their females, and their lords' (2.1.20, 24). But Shakespeare also has Adriana express in this scene precisely the opposite opinion: 'Why should,' Adriana asks, men's 'liberty than ours be more?' (2.1.10). Even if we grant that the ideal of female subordination was, broadly speaking, accepted by sixteenth- and seventeenth-century English men and women, there remains the problem of what that would mean *in practice*, in particular circumstances. It cannot have followed that women were simply slaves: what if one was commanded by one's husband to do something self-evidently wicked? The analogy in the political sphere is obvious. What if the monarch required one to do something (such as change one's religion) that might imperil one's soul? Did he rule lawfully? Or was he a heretic to be resisted? Going by the subordination theory of order, Emilia, in *Othello*, ought to have obeyed Iago in everything – but it is obvious the play requires us to wish that she had *not* yielded to her husband's demand to give him the handkerchief that he later uses to convince Othello that Desdemona has been unfaithful. Iago's attempt to kill Emilia in the final scene is evidence of his unworthiness to rule her. He embodies disordered rule, and Emilia is his moral superior. Obedience to such a devil would be a perversion of the notion of 'order'. The general rule (women should obey their husbands) is not of much help when it gets down to cases. And drama, of course, is all about cases – particular men and women in particular circumstances.[21]

The point is, then, that we can agree that English Renaissance tragedy very often has at its heart an ideal of 'order' without our knowing precisely in advance what the exact nature of that ideal is. We need to read the texts attuned to nuance. If one thing is certain about the genre it is that the masterworks comprising it are pre-eminently complex and multivocal, debates not dissertations. And yet one feature common to many of them, I think, is that they do not hesitate to advance oppositional and dissident views on numerous standard or orthodox ideological positions in the period.

4

The Rhetoric of Disenchantment

Yet if it is true that English Renaissance tragedies engaged with an idea of human freedom as consisting in order and rational self-government, it is also the case that the writers of these works were alive to another strain in early modern intellectual life, one that served persistently, if sometimes covertly, to debunk the whole notion of an orderly, hierarchical cosmos. One common attitude we find in the plays is a new worldliness or cynicism, which may indeed have helped to desacralize monarchy. Perhaps this demystifying effect was in part an outcome of the emergence of what we might think of as a new technology for the realistic representation of human life. During the sixteenth and seventeenth centuries English poets and dramatists became progressively better at representing how people actually think, talk, act, feel. Shakespeare alludes to this new imitative power of literature and art in his allusion to the painter Julio Romano in his late tragicomedy *The Winter's Tale*. Julio, we are told, 'had he himself eternity and could put breath into his work, would beguile Nature of her custom, so perfectly he is her ape' (5.2.98–101): it is only lack of time, and of the power to instil living breath into his creations, that prevents Julio from stealing nature's trade of creating human beings, so completely is he her imitator. It seems likely this new power of imitation, or mimesis, had the effect of naturalizing – rendering all-too-human – elite power. Under the gaze of artists such as Shakespeare and Webster – with their extraordinary power to create utterly life-like human beings – kings, queens and princes ceased to be the unearthly symbolic figures of royal propaganda and became instead actual men and women – 'with', to adapt Old Hamlet's words about himself, 'all [their] imperfections on [their] head[s]' (1.5.80).[1] Lear is undoubtedly a great character – but also finally, as he himself admits, 'a very foolish fond old man' (4.7.61). When kings, princes and great nobles come to be represented not as ideal types but particularized flesh-and-blood individuals, their charisma is potentially compromised. We find this disenchanting effect in Shakespeare's English history play *Richard II*. Richard's spectacular fall from power, and the rise of his opponent Henry Bolingbroke, eventually reveals his true merely human nature. 'Cover your heads' he tells his followers (it was a mark of a respect to take off one's hat), 'and mock not flesh and blood / With solemn reverence':

> Throw away respect,
> Tradition, form, and ceremonious duty,
> For you have but mistook me all this while.
> I live with bread like you, feel want,
> Taste grief, need friends. Subjected thus,
> How can you say to me I am a king? (3.2.171–7)

Of course, Richard's sense of the ultimate meaninglessness of social distinctions has an ancient history. It is central to Christianity, with its conviction that at the end of time 'the last shall be first, and the first last' (Mt. 20.16). But the tragic drama of the English Renaissance may in its own way have contributed to this demythologizing perspective. What was a technical advance in the means of representation (greater depth of characterization – we can understand what it is actually like to be Richard) allowed for a profound ideological transformation too: an audience can be reminded that kings are, once stripped of their ceremonial glory, no better than any commoner. Lear puts this vividly in the moment he encounters the naked beggar Tom. 'Is man no more than this?' he asks. 'Consider him well,' he urges Kent and the Fool: 'Thou ow'st', he tells Tom,

> the worm no silk, the beast no hide, the sheep no wool, the cat no perfume. Ha! Here's three on's are sophisticated; thou art the thing itself. Unaccommodated man is no more but such a poor, bare, forked animal as thou art. (3.4.101–7)

Like Richard in the passage just quoted, Lear underscores the creaturely vulnerability and neediness of all human beings, not excluding kings and nobles. Monarchs and aristocrats are not quasi-divine beings whose right to lord it over others is decreed by heaven. Stripped of the trappings of civilization, such as clothing, any man is merely a poor naked two-legged animal. Renaissance tragedy reveals 'the thing itself', the imperfect creature behind the magnificent appearance. Thus the improved mimetic quality of Renaissance theatre (by comparison with the more symbolic or allegorical drama of the Middle Ages) seems essentially democratizing. Part of the moral and political lesson of plays like *King Lear* or *Richard II* is that, as Montaigne put it,

> when we come to consider a peasant or a monarch, a nobleman or a commoner, a statesman or a private citizen, a rich man or a poor man, we find ... an immense disparity between men who ... differ only by their breeches ... [When] you see actors in plays imitating ... dukes or emperors, only to return suddenly to their original natural position of wretched valets and drudges: so too with that Emperor whose pomp in public dazzles you ... – draw back the bed-curtains and look at him: he is but a commonplace man, baser perhaps than the least of his subjects.[2]

It is only social convention (such as the clothes they wear) that creates the impression that people of different rank belong to different species. This egalitarian outlook is a major feature of English Renaissance tragedy, and one reason for stressing its avant-garde and critical character. Disguised as the Moorish soldier Mulinassar, Duke Francisco of Florence gives expression to this sentiment in Webster's *The White Devil*. 'I shall never flatter' the Duke Bracciano, he avers:

> I have studied man too much to do that. What difference is between the Duke and I? No more than between two bricks; all made of one clay. Only 't may be one is placed on the top of a turret, the other in the bottom of a well by mere chance. If I were placed as high as the Duke, I should stick as fast, make as fair a show, and bear out weather equally. (5.1.105–11)

Such egalitarian sentiments fly in the face of the official rhetoric of blood and breeding, and look forward to democratic assumptions.

Of course this need not imply that the playwrights themselves were hell-raising radical egalitarians – though it is surely significant that the writers considered here came from the middle ranks of society: Shakespeare the son of a well-to-do glover and leather worker, Webster of a wheelwright, Middleton of a bricklayer, Marlowe of a shoemaker. Ford, the younger son of Devon gentry, is something of an exception to the list, but none came from the apex of the social pyramid. Middleton, we know, wrote a speech welcoming James's accession to the throne of England, and Shakespeare and Webster enjoyed close connections at court as members of The King's Men. When James negotiated a peace treaty with Spain in 1604, the Spanish ambassador was 'waited upon by Shakespeare as groom of the chamber' (Chambers, 1.24). Still, it is possible for ambitious men, with every practical and material motive to please the powerful, to use their writing indirectly to express their disgust at elite depredations and privilege (and in the knowledge, too, that such a perspective would find a ready audience in the theatres – one of the reasons for the vogue for history plays, for example, on Shakespeare's stage must have been the desire of audiences to engage with political questions). It is also possible that men quite conservative in their religious and other opinions might find themselves entertaining avant-garde ideas in their plays – partly because such ideas made for exciting theatre, partly because the dialogical nature of drama encourages debate, and finally because audiences themselves developed an appetite for unconventional perspectives on life.

Montaigne's naturalistic perspective on social rank is well captured in *The Malcontent*, a tragicomedy by John Marston in which the character Malevole says that 'there goes but a pair of shears betwixt an emperor and the son of a bagpiper—only the dyeing, dressing, pressing, glossing makes the difference' (4.5.117–20). Social rank is a matter of appearance only. Or, as Montaigne put it:

> The souls of Emperors and of cobblers are cast in the same mould. We consider the importance of the actions of Princes and their weight and then persuade ourselves that they are produced by causes equally weighty, equally important. In that we deceive ourselves. They are tossed to and fro by the same principles as we are. The reasons that make us take issue with a neighbour lead Princes to start a war; the same reason which makes us flog a lackey makes kings lay waste a province. (531)

This naturalist or 'realist' critique of the mystifications surrounding social authority and privilege is of the essence of English Renaissance tragedy.[3] Bosola, 'The only court gall' (1.1.23) – that is, supreme satirist of court life – expresses the same thought pungently in *The Duchess of Malfi*:

> Search the heads of the greatest rivers in the world, you shall find them but bubbles of water. Some would think the souls of princes were brought forth by some more weighty cause than those of meaner persons. They are

> deceived. There's the same hand to them; the like passions
> sway them. The same reason that makes a vicar go to law
> for a tithe-pig and undo his neighbours makes them spoil
> a whole province and batter down goodly cities with the
> cannon. (2.1.100–8)

Thus, the greatest rivers have the humblest origins; likewise,
princes and ordinary ('meaner') folk are cut from the same
cloth, created alike; identical emotions influence both. A
country vicar going to court to claim the tithe owed him
is no different from a great king invading and despoiling a
country.[4]

To sum up: the disenchanting, demystifying effect of
English Renaissance tragedy was the outcome of its focus on
the human reality of privilege. It presented its audiences with
actual men and women rather than gods in human shape and
implicitly asked why such imperfect beings should lord it over
others. There is a strong vein of passionate indignation at the
glaring fact of unjust hierarchy. '[P]laces in the court,' Bosola
tells us, 'are but like beds in the hospital, where this man's
head lies at that man's foot, and so lower and lower' (*The
Duchess of Malfi*, 1.1.66–8). The image would have spoken
mordantly to the soldiers in the audience, who knew what
hospitals were, but anyone could grasp from it the hateful fact
of inequality itself.

A chief element, then, of English Renaissance tragedy is its
probing, sceptical, interrogative outlook. One gets the sense
of writers trying out all sorts of fascinating new opinions. In
this regard the theatres seem to have catered for an unruly
youth culture, bored by the opinions of its forebears: think
of Hamlet's disdain for 'tedious old fools!' (2.2.219) such as
the insufferably pompous Polonius. The sceptical outlook is
connected to a critique of authority, in part the consequence
of the period's widespread and intense confessional conflicts.
For John Donne, as for other Renaissance English men and
women, life was a frequently tortured search for certain belief
and true religion. 'Satire 3' pictures this search. 'Seek true

religion,' Donne writes, and immediately asks: 'O where? ... / On a huge hill, / Cragged, and steep, Truth stands, and he that will / Reach her, about must, and about must go'.[5] But the quest that Donne describes might lead to discouragement. Perhaps truth could never be found? The intense critique of Catholic orthodoxy by Protestant thinkers, and the equally ferocious attack on Protestant doctrines by Catholic polemicists, may well have led many to say, with Mercutio in *Romeo and Juliet*, 'A plague o' both your houses!' (3.1.98–9). Montaigne worried about the effects on ordinary people of the bloody conflict in France between supporters of the old religion (Roman Catholicism) and new (Protestantism). He predicted ordinary folk who became Protestants might thence become atheists:

> Once you have put into their hands the foolhardiness of despising and criticizing opinions which they used to hold in the highest awe (such as those which concern their salvation), and once you have thrown into the balance of doubt and uncertainty any articles of their religion, they soon cast all the rest of their beliefs into similar uncertainty. They had no more authority for them, no more foundation, than for those you have just undermined; and so, as though it were the yoke of a tyrant, they shake off all those other concepts which had been impressed upon them by the authority of Law and the awesomeness of ancient custom ... They then take it upon themselves to accept nothing on which they have not pronounced their own approval, subjecting it to their individual assent. (490)

Shakespeare and the other writers discussed here were living through a time of intellectual emancipation. Hallowed religious doctrines and institutions had been violently overthrown. What prevented this process from continuing? Why stop at the critique of Catholicism? Why not criticize Christianity itself?

English Renaissance tragedy reflects, and contributes to, the intellectual turmoil of its age. The genre depicts characters holding the most unorthodox and dangerous opinions. Much of the *frisson* of the genre involves saying the unsayable, including blasphemy and atheism. Part of the thrill of the plays lay in hearing what exotic non-Christians, such as Marlowe's Barabas and Ithamore (in *The Jew of Malta*) or Shakespeare's Aaron the Moor (in *Titus Andronicus*), had to say about God and believers, including Christians. 'Yet, for I know thou art religious' says Aaron to Lucius (*Titus Andronicus*, 5.1.74) – as if being 'religious' were somehow a foible or mere personal choice. Aaron compares religious belief to the 'bauble' (or fool's stick) that an 'idiot' holds to be his 'god' (5.1.79). Because Aaron wants Lucius to hold to the bargain he aims to strike with him, he urges the Roman to 'vow / By that same god, what god soe'er it be / That thou adorest and hast in reverence' (5.1.81–3). Again, religious belief here appears contingent: 'what god soever it be that you happen to believe in and I do not' is what Aaron says. Barabas and Ithamore both hate Christians (with, it must be admitted, good cause); 'setting Christian villages on fire' (*The Jew of Malta*, 2.3.204) is a specialty of Ithamore's.

Marlowe relished depicting other faiths because it enabled him to get away with blasphemy. Having a villainous Jew assault Christianity gratified his own wildly iconoclastic instincts. In Part Two of *Tamburlaine*, the hero burns 'the Turkish Alcoran' (that is, the Koran) 'And all the heaps of superstitious books / Found in the temples of that Mahomet / Whom I have thought a god' (5.1.171–4). As the fire is lit, Tamburlaine declares 'In vain, I see, men worship Mahomet': Tamburlaine has killed 'millions of Turks' and slain 'all [Mahomet's] priests' but yet 'live[s] untouched by Mahomet' (*2 Tamb.*, 5.1.177–80). A little further on and Tamburlaine may appear to sound like a right-thinking intolerant Christian. He braves Mahomet, defying him to 'work a miracle' and stop him carrying out this sacrilege: 'Thou art not worthy to be worshipped / That suffers flames of fire to burn the writ / Wherein the sum of thy religion rests' (*2 Tamb.*, 5.1.187–9). Since Mahomet is powerless to stop Tamburlaine's impious act, Tamburlaine advises his soldiers to 'Seek out another godhead to adore, / The God that sits in heaven, if any god, / For he is God alone, and none but he' (2 *Tamb.*, 5.1.198–200). Yet just a minute or so later and Tamburlaine complains he is 'distempered suddenly' (2 *Tamb.*, 5.1.216) – the abrupt onset of illness marking the beginning of his decline and subsequent death. The whole episode is curious. At one level Tamburlaine is being punished for blasphemy, so orthodoxy is upheld. But that would mean that the play is somehow endorsing Islam – since Tamburlaine would, in that case, be divinely punished for blaspheming against the Muslim religion. On top of that we have the extraordinary sight of a man burning Holy Scriptures (an audience cannot but have compared the Koran to the Bible). A thrill must have run through the theatre during this spectacle. And when Tamburlaine urges his soldiers to 'seek out another godhead' he does not sound like a Christian at all: 'if any god', indeed, suggests that one might choose *not* to worship 'The God that sits in heaven' – and, anyway, this God is at no point identified as the God of the Christians. In the Scripture-burning scene, Marlowe is truly playing with fire: the scene sets going all sorts of mental possibilities for members of the audience. And because religion is, inevitably in the sixteenth century, a state matter (on the basis that, as the maxim went, *cuius regio, eius religio*, the religion of the prince is the religion of the land), when a play depicts characters who are in some sense against God (such as Aaron, or Marlowe's Faustus, Barabas or Tamburlaine) this has an inescapable social and political meaning. To be against God is to be against the cosmic hierarchy, and to be against that means one is against hierarchy in other spheres: against kings, against nobles. As we have seen, in the sixteenth and seventeenth centuries God is to man as king is to subject as husband is to wife as father is to children. No God, no king.

As we shall see, one of the most daring aspects of English Renaissance tragedy was this subtle trick of putting Christianity in its place – of hinting that Christianity is just one religious option among many. This was a form of cultural-religious relativism that revealed that what most English men and women took to be absolutely true was in fact an historical phenomenon confined to a particular time and place. The historicizing perspective can come about via incidental features of the plays. When Orcanes, King of Natolia, makes a treaty with Sigismond, King of Hungary, in Part Two of *Tamburlaine*, he asks him to 'swear in sight of heaven and by *thy Christ*' (1.1.132, my emphasis). Marlowe sets up an intriguing symmetry in the way the leaders speak about their faiths:

SIGISMOND
By Him that made the world and saved my soul,
The son of God and issue of a maid,
Sweet Jesus Christ, I solemnly protest
And vow to keep this peace inviolable.

ORCANES
By sacred Mahomet, the friend of God,
Whose holy Alcoran remains with us,
Whose glorious body, when he left the world,
Closed in a coffin, mounted up the air
And hung on stately Mecca's temple roof,
I swear to keep this truce inviolable. (1.1.133–42)

It must have been shocking – but also exciting – for Marlowe's audience to hear a Muslim speak so slightingly and casually about 'thy Christ': there were parts of the world where belief in Christ was unknown. Orcanes's oath and Sigismond's are virtually identical in form – perhaps relativizing both religions, suggesting to some, at least, that there was little to choose between them. When Barabas the Jew refers to 'these swine-eating Christians' (*The Jew of Malta*, 2.3.7), or when Cosroe, brother of the King of Persia, refers to 'the Christians' (*1 Tamb.*, 2.5.42), Christianity is likewise put into relation with other faiths and viewed from outside. Of course the potentially destabilizing effects of such moments can be contained. Who cares what pagans and heretics say? And Barabas is an out-and-out villain (though the greedy and treacherous Christians of the play are hardly models of conduct either). But the important point is the distancing perspective an audience gets on Christianity. Momentarily it is presented as a belief system that for some is outlandish or disgusting.

English Renaissance tragedy, then, frequently indulges in what we might think of as a 'rhetoric of disenchantment' – a way of describing the world that has no truck with religion or the supernatural. Gloucester's assertion that the expulsion of Cordelia, and other calamities, is connected to eclipses and the like is roundly mocked by the modernizer Edmund as the world's 'foppery' (*King Lear*, 1.2.121). Edmund will have none of this attempt to blame the planets for our crimes: 'I should have been that I am' – that is, 'lecherous' – 'had the maidenliest star in the firmament twinkled on my bastard-izing' (134–6). He is a voluptuary because that is the person he wants to be – it is his own free determination, not the stars or some other metaphysical force, that has made him who he is. Edmund revels in his villainy – and takes full responsibility for it. Ferdinand expresses a similar contempt for superstitious accounts of human behaviour in *The Duchess of Malfi*. When Bosola speculates that the Duchess's affair may be the result of 'sorcery', he retorts that 'The witchcraft lies in her rank blood' (3.1.64, 78) – that is, in her own lustful will. At the same time, in both the Duchess's and Edmund's case there is an important ambiguity: to what extent is the passionate will to pursue a particular end *itself a kind of compulsion*? Shakespeare's notorious Sonnet 135 addresses this problem in the context of sex. The poem plays upon radically different meanings of the word 'Will': agency, lust, the male and female sexual organs, the poet's own name. The suggestion is of, at once, aggressive purposiveness and the *unwilled* or involuntary desire of sex organs. Characters in tragedy also regularly exemplify this profound ambiguity in the concept of will: do they choose or are they compelled to act as they do?

English Renaissance tragedy frequently allows for a kind of contempt for the supernatural, the dramatic conflicts of the plays often involving a violent split between traditionalists and modernists. *King Lear*, for instance, depicts a cultural revolution, as men and women suddenly discover that there are no laws in nature to restrain their wills. One can do anything; there is absolutely nothing in the heavens obliging me to do this or that. Indeed law turns out for some, such as Edmund, to be a human contrivance. It is true that such sentiments are condemned, but they stick in the memory nonetheless: often the devil has the best tunes. It may be going too far to describe the naturalistic perspective of much English Renaissance tragedy as 'scientific', but the genre does display an interest in the ways in which humanity might be free of Providence or divine guidance. Bosola's idea that 'We are merely the stars' tennis balls, struck and banded / Which way please them' is interestingly muddied. There is little room here for divine Providence, though there remains also some notion of astrological influence (but with the emphasis on chance – a rally in tennis is not an orderly event). Tragedy shows a growing interest in the concept of force. A character like Edmund thrives, if only briefly, because of natural faculties, energy and intelligence among them ('Let me, if not by birth, have lands by wit' (*King Lear*, 1.2.187)). Tamburlaine's rise is an effect of his audacity and strength of will. Renaissance tragedies so often tell their stories without meaningful reference to divine schemas and with much more emphasis on the absolute choice of the protagonists.

Writers of tragedy in the Renaissance could also make use of ancient irreligious philosophical tendencies, such as materialism, naturalism, scepticism and relativism, to challenge the idea of divine government. Atheism is not a necessary, though it is a possible, consequence of scepticism (the doctrine that human reason is fallible) – after all, if we can be certain of nothing it follows that rationalistic critiques of religious belief are themselves vulnerable to doubt. Montaigne was a Catholic whose scepticism taught him to be wary of the philosophers' arrogant claims to knowledge. Nevertheless, scepticism can also be a step on the path to materialism and unbelief. When Webster's Flamineo dies, he seems to have no faith in an afterlife (good or bad) but rather to think, in atomistic or proto-scientific terms, of death as mere dissolution: 'Whether I resolve to fire, earth, water, air, / Or all the elements by scruples, I know not / Nor greatly care' (*The White Devil*, 5.6.115–17). A kind of 'naturalism' in the period tends towards the view that nature and culture are opposed: it is mere timid moral convention that forbids certain practices; nature, or reality, does permit them, indeed permits anything. We can choose. And of course cultural relativism – the view that practices and institutions are relative to particular peoples and nations and that there are no universal moral laws – was given a boost by encounters with non-Christian cultures in the age of exploration, and could itself lead to a critical view of established customs.

Marlowe in particular was associated with such heterodox opinions. Reputed to be an atheist, some of his alleged opinions were recorded by a government spy named Richard Baines in 'A note containing the opinion of one Christopher Marlowe concerning his damnable judgment of religion, and scorn of God's word'. According to Baines, Marlowe claimed that the common understanding that the world was 6,000 years old was false ('the Indians and many authors of antiquity have assuredly written of above 16 thousand years agone whereas Adam is proved to have lived within 6 thousand years'); that Moses was a mere 'juggler' or trickster and that the mathematician and inventor Thomas Harriot could do 'more than he'; and that 'the first beginning of religion was only to keep men in awe', that is, that the real function of religion was to terrify men into obedience to established rulers.[6] As Flamineo puts it in *The White Devil*, 'Religion – oh, how it is commeddled with policy! The first bloodshed in the world happened about religion' (3.3.37–9). Francisco says something similar: 'Divinity, wrested by some factious blood, / Draws swords, swells battles, and o'erthrows all good' (4.1.93–4).

Relativistic attitudes surface in Montaigne. 'Any object,' he wrote, 'can be seen in various lights and from various points of view: it is chiefly that which gives birth to variety of opinion: one nation sees one facet, and stops there; another sees another' (655). One might compare Hamlet's assertion that 'there is nothing either good or bad but thinking makes it so' (2.2.250–1). Montaigne exemplifies the intellectual openness of the period, in which, as Donne famously said, the new philosophy had 'call[ed] all in doubt'.[7] English tragedy reflects this conviction that fundamental matters of belief were in play. The Greek sceptics, who emphasized the total unreliability of human reason, fascinated Montaigne; the writings of Sextus Empiricus had a particular impact. (Sextus prompted Montaigne to such thoughts as 'There is a plague on Man: his opinion that he knows something' and 'No reason but has its contrary' (543, 694).) Like others, Montaigne was intrigued by different cultures, both ancient and contemporary (for example in the Americas). The result again was a cultural relativism:

[T]he same authority which Numa gave to his laws by citing the patronage of the goddess Egeria was given to him by Zoroaster, the lawgiver of the Bactrians and the Persians, in the name of his god Oromasis; by Trismegistus, the lawgiver of the Egyptians, in the name of Mercury; by Zamolxis, the lawgiver of the Scythians, in the name of Vesta; by Charondas, the lawgiver of the Chalcidians, in the name of Saturn; by Minos, the lawgiver of the people of Candy, in the name of Jupiter; by Lycurgus, the lawgiver of Sparta, in the name of Apollo; and by Draco and Solon, lawgivers of the Athenians, in the name of Minerva. And all polities have a god at their head, truly so in the case of the one drawn up by Moses for the people of Judaea on leaving Egypt; the rest, falsely so. (716)

The passage in fact begs the question as to why we should accept Moses' claim for the divine origin of his laws but not Numa's, Zoroaster's, Trismegistus's, and so on; intellectuals of Marlowe's stripe took the next obvious (and impious) step in the argument. Montaigne is one of the period's great critics of ethnocentrism, the vice of accepting uncritically the values and outlook of your own *ethnos* or nation. It is, Montaigne writes, 'a common failing not only of the mob but of virtually all men to set their sights within the limitations of the customs into which they were born' (331). Montaigne stands for a speculative freedom unconstrained by the opinions of one's countrymen. He emphasizes the diversity of ideals of beauty, such as discoverers of new lands had reported:

> [I]f [what is beautiful] had been prescribed by Nature, we would all hold common views about it [but instead] [w]e give human beauty any form we fancy ... For a painter in the Indies beauty is black and sunburnt, with thick swollen lips and broad flat noses; there, they load the cartilage between the nostrils with great rings of gold, so that it hangs right down to the lips ... In Peru, big ears are beautiful: they stretch them as far as they can, artificially ... Elsewhere there are whole nations who carefully blacken their teeth and loathe seeing white ones. Elsewhere they dye them red ... The women of Mexico count low foreheads as a sign of beauty. (537–8)

Assaults on received wisdom like this one find their way into tragedy. Take Edmund's famous address to Nature: 'Thou, Nature, art my goddess; to thy law / My services are bound' (*Lear*, 1.2.1–2). Edmund is a villain, to be sure, but the speech brims over with intellectual energy and excitement as he derides the convention that children born out of wedlock should be disadvantaged in comparison with legitimate offspring.[8] Edmund follows Nature – not culture, morality, human law, or, as he puts it, 'the plague of custom' (1.2.3). Why should he permit the 'curiosity of nations' (1.2.4) – the arbitrary rules of each nation surrounding inheritance – to disadvantage him because he happened to be born on the wrong side of the bed? The thrill of the speech lies in the flouting of a whole ancient system of law and convention in the name of a new freedom of thought. The mockery of 'legitimate' ('Fine word, "legitimate"!' (1.2.18)), a word Edmund repeats five times in this speech, makes the point: legitimacy is just a word – there is *nothing* in nature that decrees legitimate children should be preferable to bastards. But why stop there? How many other social fetters might we liberate ourselves from if we followed 'Nature'?

'Nature', indeed, is one of the most frequently used words in *King Lear*. But its meaning is ambiguous: when Lear calls on nature to punish Goneril for her cruel treatment of him ('Hear Nature, hear! Dear goddess, hear!' (1.4.274)) he is appealing to a different sort of nature from that Edmund pledges allegiance to. Lear's nature sides with the convention that, for example, children should obey their parents. But the play shows us what it is like to live through a cultural revolution, when old certitudes evaporate. Characters begin to think all sorts of new, strangely liberating thoughts. The Ten Commandments tell us we should honour our parents. Tudor and Stuart English men and women took this rule seriously: theirs was a profoundly gerontocratic society.[9] It was taken for granted that the old ruled the young (though of course children defying their parents for love is a topic of both Shakespearean comedy and tragedy). *Lear* however shows us not obedience to but abuse of a parent – the king's kneeling to his daughter in Act Two, Scene Four would have been a shocking sight to a seventeenth-century audience. And the play shows people starting to question this conventional reverence for the elderly. Why should seniority have everything its own way? Does nature indeed support the prerogative of age – perhaps it would be *more natural* if the strong governed the weak? Edmund writes a letter (passing it off as Edgar's) arguing this position:

This policy and reverence of age makes the world bitter to the best of our times, keeps our fortunes from us till our oldness cannot relish them. I begin to find an idle and fond bondage in the oppression of aged tyranny, who sways not as it hath power but as it is suffered. (1.2.47–52)

The 'policy' or law that holds that the strong and youthful should give way to the feeble and elderly is ridiculous. Might is Right. What is the point of waiting years for a parent to die so we can finally come into our inheritance? (We won't be able to 'relish' it then anyway because by that far-off stage we ourselves will be old.) Why not follow nature? If only the old Earl of Gloucester could be hurried on his way his sons might be able to make good use of his wealth. But this will require bold and ruthless action.

This 'Might is Right' thinking is associated forever with the name of Niccolò Machiavelli, the Florentine philosopher who became a byword for evil during the English Renaissance. Machiavelli's *Prince* urges rulers to simulate piety but do whatever it takes to acquire and hold onto power. Morality and Christianity are (like laws surrounding inheritance) a 'curiosity of nations' and 'plague of custom'; rulers should instead follow nature. Machiavelli makes an appearance in the Prologue to *The Jew of Malta*: 'I count religion but a childish toy,' he says, 'And hold there is no sin but ignorance'. Legitimate rule is a fiction; all states are founded on an original criminal seizure of power:

> Many will talk of title to a crown;
> What right had Caesar to the empery?
> Might first made kings, and laws were then most sure
> When, like the Draco's, they were writ in blood.
>   (Prologue, 14–21)

Again, nature has everything to do with force and power, nothing to do with law or morality ('right'); indeed the so-called 'laws' are themselves strongest when most severe, like those of the Athenian legislator Draco. To have this sort of sentiment publicly propounded to all and sundry in the theatre, in a world in which it was routinely claimed that kings ruled as the anointed of God, that the state and laws were the expression of revealed truth, must have been startling. Theatre here has become an instrument of intellectual liberation.

English Renaissance tragedy, then, shared with some of the most advanced intellectuals of the day a desire to strip away veils, to penetrate to 'the thing itself', to demystify matters (such as kingship and law) often shrouded in supernatural fog. The genre highlights free-thinking intellectuals – Hamlet of course, but also Marlowe's Doctor Faustus, who 'The fruitful plot of scholarism graced' (A-Text, Prologue, line 16),[10] or the incestuous Giovanni in *'Tis Pity She's A Whore*; even the thuggish Bosola is a 'speculative' and 'fantastical', that is, eccentric, 'scholar' (*The Duchess of Malfi*, 3.3.47, 41). Intellectuals feature heavily because tragedy has a truth-telling and emancipatory function: their target is what William Blake would later call 'mind-forged manacles'.[11] When Montaigne tells us the laws are often unjust, he is doing the sort of thing tragedy often does. The

> laws remain respected not because they are just but because they are laws. That is the mystical basis of their authority. They have no other ... Laws are often made by fools, and even more often by men who fail in equity because they hate equality ... No person commits crimes more grossly, widely or regularly than do our laws. (1216)[12]

Montaigne's point is that, like the 'willing bond[men]' of *Julius Caesar*, we have a stupid tendency to worship power; we honour power not because it is worthy of respect but because it is power. We assume people hold office because of some wondrous ability, intelligence or merit when actually they have power because they have it. Montaigne is describing our capacity for self-delusion, and the powerful role fantasy, imagination and the passions play in human life. Appearances bamboozle us. Pascal highlighted this weakness in his *Pensées*: 'Imagination,' he observes there, 'decides everything.' We are awed by magistrates not because they embody 'true justice' but because of their 'red robes, the ermine in which they swaddle themselves like furry cats, the law-courts where they sit in judgment, the fleurs de lys, all this august panoply'. All this theatrical paraphernalia augments the air of 'mystery' surrounding judges. We revere their costumes not their virtue.[13] Lear pursues a like-minded critique of the system of so-called justice when he rails against an utterly corrupt and hypocritical judiciary. He enjoins Gloucester to 'See how yond justice rails upon yond simple thief. Hark in thine ear: change places and, handy-dandy, which is the justice, which is the thief?' (4.6.151–4). Jesus' dictum, 'Judge not, that ye be not judged' (Mt. 7.1), is in the background. As Lear says, 'The usurer hangs the cozener' (4.6.163): the big-time crook, the money-lender charging an extortionist rate on his loans, hangs the small-time cheat. Or as the proverb had it, 'The great thieves hang the little ones.'[14] Lear asks Gloucester whether he has ever seen 'a farmer's dog bark at a beggar', and then 'the creature' (that is, the beggar) 'run from the cur'? If Gloucester has witnessed that wretched scene, he has viewed 'the great image of authority: a dog's obeyed in office' (4.6.154–9). This is Montaigne's and Pascal's point: we obey people not because they are intrinsically better than us, but because they have the whip-hand. (Do bankers, hedge-fund managers and modern executives merit their multi-million-dollar bonuses? Or is it rather that they have the power to have themselves paid at that level?) You could stick a dog in the boss's chair, Lear claims, and people would still suck up to him. Lear's point is profoundly demoralizing. Power is corrupt but we obey it anyway. Nevertheless, knowing this to be the case is the first step towards changing a shabby reality – so the overall effect of these speeches is mentally liberating and invigorating rather than depressing. Once again, theatre here is expanding the range of what spectators can think.

5

Going to the Theatre in Shakespeare's London

So far we have been considering some of the ways English Renaissance tragedies take up questions to do with power, tyranny, lack of freedom, equality and injustice. I have suggested tragedy is on freedom's side. But the question still remains, why theatre? What was it about this particular institution that encouraged writers to address such questions?

Perhaps the first thing to notice is that the English Renaissance stage fused profoundly different worlds. Writers for the stage were by and large trained in the elite literary traditions flowing from the poetry, drama and prose works of ancient Greece and Rome. Dramatists were the self-conscious inheritors of an illustrious tradition of eloquence rehabilitated in the libraries, schools, universities and courts of Renaissance Europe. The theatres themselves, however, are frequently represented as rather notorious places. Moral critics of the Elizabethan and Jacobean eras associated plays with debauchery and condemned the theatres as places of sexual promiscuity, in which prostitutes picked up customers and lovers made assignations. It is easy to dismiss such commentary as puritanical hysteria, but a reading of the plays themselves suggests the stage's opponents had it broadly right. The theatre really was a site of intellectual, moral and psychological freedom. For example, one of the most prominent features of English Renaissance tragedy was its frank depiction of sexual desire.[1] Take this exchange between the villain Ithamore, Barabas's sidekick in *The Jew of Malta*, and the courtesan Bellamira after they kiss:

BELLAMIRA
Come my dear love, let's in and sleep together.

ITHAMORE
O, that ten thousand nights were put in one, that we
    might sleep seven years together afore we wake!

BELLAMIRA
Come, amorous wag, first banquet and then sleep.
    (4.2.131–4)

These are wicked characters (Marlowe knew how to depict them) ostensibly held up for the audience's disapprobation. But the important point is that such lines put into public circulation worldly and sensuous attitudes towards life rather than ascetically religious ones. A similar moment occurs in *The Revenger's Tragedy*. Facing execution, the rapist Junior jauntily declares, 'My fault was sweet sport, which the world approves; / I die for that which every woman loves' (3.4.78–9). The remark is throwaway, the sort of thing a villain would say. Yet it also makes available to an audience a way of seeing at odds with moral orthodoxy. (Junior, we should add, is a hard case; he cannot even be bothered to pray at his own death – though as far as Ambitioso is concerned that stubbornness merely shows him 'a gentleman' (3.6.45), a comment that conveys something of the insouciantly wicked flavour of the court in this play.)

Audiences got from the theatre a glimpse of lifestyles that had little to do with the standard official scheme of sin, salvation, heaven, hell, or even morality itself. Certainly the moral critics found enough to dislike in the theatres, the volume and ferocity of their attacks on these popular institutions being remarkable. The playhouses were 'seminaries of impiety',[2] 'schools of vice' (Chambers, 4.197). They were 'markets of bawdry', in which prostitutes plied their trade (4.218) – 'a general market of bawdry' where 'every knave and his quean' (that is, prostitute) 'are there first acquainted' (4.203–4). Plays taught the 'filthy lusts of wicked whoredom' and 'how to disobey and rebel against princes' (4.199). Was it any wonder that, with crowds flocking to such disgraceful spectacles, God regularly punished Londoners with the plague? A sermon of 1577 had it that 'the cause of plagues is sin ... and the cause of sin are plays: therefore the cause of plagues are plays' (4.197). Because plays appealed to the emotions of their audiences, they undermined, the pamphlet writer Stephen Gosson claimed in 1582, rational self-control: 'tragedies and comedies stir up affections, and affections are naturally planted in that part of the mind that is common to us with brute beasts' (4.217). Tragedies weakened character, Gosson said: 'The beholding of troubles and miserable slaughters that are in tragedies, drive us to immoderate sorrow, heaviness, womanish weeping and mourning, whereby we become lovers of dumps [i.e., depression], and lamentation, both enemies to fortitude' (4.215). Playhouses competed with churches: 'Will not a filthy play,' asked a preacher, 'with the blast of a trumpet, sooner call thither a thousand, than an hour's tolling of a bell, bring to the sermon a hundred?' (4.199). 'More have recourse to playing houses, than to praying houses,' lamented a pamphleteer of 1615 (4.254). In 1615, Lord Coke wrote to the Corporation of Coventry requiring the city 'to suffer no common players whatsoever to play within your city for that it would tend to the hindrance of devotion, and drawing of the artificers and common people from their labour' (1.338, note 3). Crowds generally were eyed askance by officialdom, since there was always the possibility of a disturbance; and whatever the nature of the plays theatre crowds were watching they were certainly *not* listening to the sermon of a government-appointed minister. (The suspicion that crowds might spread plague was another reason for city authorities to dislike playhouses.) All of this consternation might well have led to a permanent ban on playing had it not been for Elizabeth's and James's own interest in seeing that the theatres flourished – these establishments were homes to those professional and highly-skilled troupes that entertained the court (the players could never have made a living performing solely for royalty). Nevertheless, the enemies of the theatres were not wrong to feel that the playhouse constituted in some sense a rival institution to both state and church.

Far from being elite, then, as the scholarship of classically-minded Renaissance humanist intellectuals necessarily was, the theatres themselves were prominent sites of an uproarious mass entertainment industry. Other entertainments provided in or near the theatres included tumbling or acrobatic feats; bear- and bull-baiting; displays of fencing; clowning, singing and dancing. One of the earliest built-for-purpose playhouses in London, known simply as The Theatre, was founded by the carpenter and impresario James Burbage in 1576; Shakespeare's theatre, the Globe, opened in 1599. They depended for their survival on entertaining ordinary folk. (Exactly in what proportions the common people attended the theatres has been a matter of scholarly debate, but that the theatres were attended by non-elite spectators is not in dispute.) At the same time the most important companies were directly linked to the court. Shakespeare's, the Lord Chamberlain's Men, eventually became, with the accession in 1603 of James I, The King's Men; along with the Queen's and the Prince's acting companies, Shakespeare and his fellow actors were each awarded four and a half yards of red cloth to make a uniform for themselves for James's coronation procession (Chambers, 1.312). The consequence of this mixing of social strata is that performance of an English Renaissance tragedy was a hybrid, cross-cultural affair, the merging of the elite literary culture of contemporary and ancient Europe with the barely literate world of ordinary people. And the collision in the theatre of high and low social worlds engendered a fundamentally *critical* outlook on economic, social and political matters. As we will see, social rank or degree (what we today call class) is a *fundamental* preoccupation of many of the plays discussed here: a theatre that was itself a socially mixed affair is likely to have found such a topic irresistible. And we should not forget that the players themselves occupied a rather uncertain or ambivalent status: if lucky, they might be servants of great lords, or even the monarch, yet many of their brethren were associated by the civic authorities with the riff-raff. In 1572 'An Act for the Punishment of Vagabonds' targeted 'rogues, vagabonds, and sturdy beggars' along with 'fencers, bearwards [i.e., bear-keepers], common players, ... minstrels, jugglers, pedlars, tinkers' (Chambers, 4.269–70). Such 'rogues', if they contravened the relevant laws, could be severely punished: 'grievously whipped, and burnt through the gristle of the right ear with a hot iron' for instance (ibid.). An Act of 1598 stipulates that vagabonds or common players 'taken begging, vagrant wandering or misordering themselves' should 'be stripped naked from the middle upwards and ... openly whipped until his or her body be bloody' (Chambers, 4.324). This was a long way from the experience of men like Shakespeare, Richard Burbage or Edward Alleyn, who became wealthy from the theatre. But it is a reminder that many notables thought society would be better off without their type: 'the players of plays ... and tumblers and such like', wrote the Lord Mayor of London in 1580, 'are a very super-fluous sort of men' (Chambers, 4.279).

In the remainder of this section I want to explore what I see as perhaps the primary challenge theatre-going in Elizabethan and Jacobean England posed to the established order. This challenge lay simply in the plays' encouraging ordinary people to think about matters that in the normal course of life they had no business concerning themselves with. What I mean is that the best examples of English Renaissance tragedy do not simply entertain their audiences, but also invite them to think. The plays considered in this book are chock-full of debate, topical comment and reflection, and regularly tackle weighty philosophical, moral and political ideas. The theatre, then, was an arena in which *ordinary folk were addressed as thinkers*, as people and indeed citizens rather than beasts of burden. Tragedies in the period have of course more than their fair share of sensationalistic and entertaining spectacle; this was showbiz after all. But they are also linguistically self-conscious and intellectually ambitious *poetic* dramas that make a deliberate appeal to the ear and mind. In so addressing the *cognitive* faculties of playgoers, Renaissance tragedies constructed their audiences as composed of deliberative beings – not (to quote Hamlet) as 'beast[s]' that lack 'discourse of reason' (1.2.150), that is slaves devoted merely to animalistic appetites (sleeping, feeding, etc.), but rather as *free persons* capable of thought and judgement. The theatres were laboratories for intellectual, literary and imaginative experimentation – places of freedom.

Perhaps the primary way in which dramatists fostered an engaged, critical perspective in their audience was via the use of sophisticated and complex arts of language and rhetoric. The most important fact about the origins of English Renaissance tragedy is that highly educated poets – trained at Oxford or Cambridge, or (as in Shakespeare's case) at well-run grammar schools – began to write for the public stages.[3] Without good writing there could be no significant drama; without a rigorous education in rhetoric and style there could have been no good writers. Tragedy in this period is nothing if not rhetorical; writers for the stage strive to use words in powerful, innovative, musical, attractive, memorable ways. Shakespeare's friend and rival dramatist Ben Jonson spoke of 'Marlowe's mighty line': Marlowe was understood to be doing something radically fresh and exciting with language on the Elizabethan stage.[4] The Prologue to the first part of *Tamburlaine* singles out the 'high astounding terms' of the play's hero; and the printer's epistle ('To the Gentleman Readers') praises Marlowe's 'eloquence'.[5] Characters in many of the plays considered here evince a pronounced language-consciousness. When Vindice, in *The Revenger's Tragedy*, launches into a tirade against lust, Hippolito observes 'You flow well, brother' (2.2.143); Lussurioso praises the disguised

Vindice as 'A fellow of discourse, well mingled' (2.2.7). Marlowe's characters comment on each other's eloquence: 'Not Hermes, prolocutor to the gods, / Could use persuasions more pathetical' (that is, emotionally moving), observes the Persian commander Theridamas of Tamburlaine (*1 Tamb.*, 1.2.210–11); and 'You see, my lord,' he says later to Cosroe, brother of the Persian king, 'what working words [Tamburlaine] hath' (*1 Tamb.*, 2.3.25). It is in part Tamburlaine's extraordinarily 'working' or persuasive way with language that forces Theridamas to abandon the Persians to become one of his followers ('Won with thy words', he owns to Tamburlaine (*1 Tamb.*, 1.2.228)). Likewise Othello explains that Desdemona fell in love with him in part through listening to his tales of his marvellous adventures, 'moving accidents by flood and field' (1.3.137) – and the whole speech (beginning 'Her father loved me, oft invited me, / Still questioned me the story of my life' (1.3.130–1)) is itself an instance of the potent rhetoric that captivated Desdemona. Othello insists his speech is the only 'witchcraft I have used' in wooing Desdemona (1.3.171) – but this language is indeed 'witchcraft'. 'Rude am I in my speech' he modestly declares to the Venetian Senators (1.3.83), but the account of his courting of Desdemona is anything but the 'round unvarnished tale' (1.3.92) he says it was. In the fiction he is a simple soldier apparently unversed in the arts of language; on stage he is one of the most eloquent speakers ever.

If the characters of Renaissance tragedy are themselves aware of the power of language this is because language-consciousness was a feature of the world in which Shakespeare and his peers grew up. As noted, all the writers discussed in this book were the beneficiaries of an ambitious school system focused on correct language and style. Renaissance schools trained boys in eloquence and argument, setting them to study key classical authors (for example Virgil and Ovid) as models of sound Latin style. Budding dramatists found in such texts material for stories as well as standards of eloquence. Although Shakespeare did not attend university, his education in classical authors and texts, almost certainly at the King Edward VI Grammar School in Stratford, would have been intensive. Nothing is more characteristic of the Renaissance than the enormous importance placed on the ability to use language artfully and effectively. And this was, of course, a culture devoted to one book in particular, the Bible, with Protestantism, the version of Christianity established in England by Henry VIII and his successors in their break with the Church of Rome, placing signal importance on close and thoughtful scrutiny of that text in particular. Renaissance England was a bookish, word-conscious age.

One of the features of the literary training of authors such as Shakespeare was an emphasis on disputation. Students were expected to be able to argue any case effectively. One might be required to prosecute one side of the question 'Whether Day or Night is the More Excellent' – and then affirm exactly the opposite position.[6] (A poeticized example of this ability to take either side of a debate is Milton's pair of poems arguing respectively for and against melancholy: 'Il Penseroso' and 'L'Allegro'.) No other body of literature is as addicted to and excited by the contest of ideas as English Renaissance drama. Again and again we see characters engaged in arguments that touch upon some of the most sensitive topics of the age, though, as we have seen, writers had to be careful not to stray too recklessly into religion and politics.[7] But the evidence of the texts themselves indicates that audiences hungered for material that, even if indirectly, addressed such issues, and dramatists were bound to sate this appetite. One could do worse than think of the drama of this period, and especially tragedy (conventionally a genre addressing high and weighty topics), as a series of *arguments*, quarrels over some of the most enduring issues of human life, not least freedom and justice.

Thought and eloquence, then, were central to the theatre of Shakespeare and his contemporaries. (Renaissance dramatists were gloriously ignorant of the credo of modern writing-instructors that one must never use two words where one will do.)[8] Where we value plainness, economy, reality and directness, they preferred decoration, fantasy, flamboyance. This is not to say that Renaissance writers of tragedy disdained simplicity entirely. Othello's 'But yet the pity of it, Iago! Oh, Iago, the pity of it, Iago!' (4.1.198–9) could not be more naked; and the poignancy of Desdemona's 'I hope you will not kill me' depends upon its plainness (5.2.37). But these unaccommodated words derive their power from their contrast with the rhetorically intricate utterances surrounding them. Renaissance drama was part of a language-aware culture; the emphasis of the Renaissance playhouse is ultimately more on speech than spectacle (indeed speech there *is* spectacle; dramatists are forever painting vivid word-pictures). This tells us something else about the social meaning of literary art in this period: that writing for the stage (or page) was often a deliberate display of rhetorical virtuosity. Writers were exhibiting a flair for language, a skill they thought bankable. (It is, for example, almost certain that Shakespeare's writing of two ornate mythological poems in the early 1590s was part of a campaign to make himself attractive – and, perhaps, employable – to the powerful and rich Earl of Southampton, to whom the poems are dedicated.) Potentially at least, eloquence in this period was social power, a route to greater freedom.

To sum up, the plays considered in this book all make an appeal *to the mind*; their commitment to analysis and debate takes them beyond mere entertainment, and this notwithstanding their containing plenty of humour and straightforward amusement. Indeed a good part of the pleasure they offer audiences is *cognitive* – the nimbleness and knottiness of language, the precision of ideas. This is a theatre of language and – since we think in words – a theatre of thought. Following the dynamic shifts of thought in tragedy from this period is almost never easy, and one can be sure that the less educated members of the audience would frequently have found the language of the plays difficult. But this is, to repeat, itself a crucial fact about English Renaissance tragedy:

it treats its audience, however humble, as capable of thought – interested in following arguments about fundamental issues of life, not least moral and political ones. The plays ask their audiences to decide between characters and make judgements on them; we are very often required to decide whose side we are on. In this sense the genre might be thought of as addressing its audience in proto-democratic terms, as a deliberative assembly rather than unthinking herd – a remarkable achievement in a society that, generally speaking, took it for granted that ordinary folk had no business doing anything other than obeying their betters.

Other aspects of the theatres conduced to the formation of a critical, intelligent, socially probing drama. The mimetic capacities of English Renaissance theatres were limited. Of course poetry and rhetoric can summon up another world, explore the complexities of character. But even the language of a Shakespeare or Marlowe must have struggled to make spectators forget that they were in a theatre, watching a performance – certainly in the open air theatres such as the Globe, in which actors would have had to compete with the distractions attendant upon playing in daylight, when all members of an audience can see each other. The theatres were not rich in scenery, props or other means of illusion-making: Shakespeare apologizes for his 'unworthy scaffold' (or stage) in the Prologue to *Henry V*. (Costuming was probably a different matter: on 'the lavish use of apparel' in the theatre, see Chambers, 1.372.) In such circumstances it must have been difficult for spectators to give themselves over wholly and mindlessly to the fiction; they probably preserved a certain freedom of thought in relation to it. Stars such as Burbage (Hamlet, Lear, Othello) or Alleyn (Faustus, Tamburlaine) would have been familiar to many members of the audience, once again, perhaps, qualifying the extent to which spectators could lose themselves in a fantasy world. One was watching not just Hamlet, but Burbage-as-Hamlet, just as one had already seen his Richard III and would later see his Lear. Such a theatre, in which one is never completely swept away by the spectacle, has the merit of permitting an audience to *think* about what it is watching.

Probably the open-air theatres required a rather exaggerated, rhetorical style of performance. The plays themselves provide evidence for this claim. When Desdemona says to Othello 'you're fatal then / When your eyes roll so' (5.2.39–40), and, later, 'why gnaw you so your nether lip? / Some bloody passion shakes your very frame' (5.2.45–6), she presumably refers to actions visible on stage. Similarly, when Ophelia describes Hamlet's behaviour –

He took me by the wrist and held me hard.
Then goes he to the length of all his arm,
And, with his other hand thus o'er his brow
He falls to such perusal of my face
As 'a would draw it. Long stayed he so. (2.1.89–93)

– she also summons up highly formalized stage business. Again, Hamlet's allusion to the sort of player who 'tear[s] a passion to tatters' and 'out-Herods Herod' (3.2.9–10, 14) – who overdoes everything, in the manner of the old stereotyped part of the ranting stage tyrant – is no doubt a description of an all-too-well-known type of over-the-top acting.[9] Perhaps playgoers found some of this excessively rhetorical mode of acting funny, just as we would today.[10] Perhaps too, again, it afforded audience members a certain detachment from what they were watching.

All these conditions of performance seem likely to have engendered among regular theatregoers a degree of critical distance on dramatic fictions. 'Realism' is a word usefully applied to English Renaissance tragedy, as long as we do not intend by it the realism of modern films and novels. Tragedy in Shakespeare's day was far from being a documentary, slice-of-life sort of genre: for one thing it not uncommonly breaks the frame of illusion by addressing its audience directly. When Hamlet refers to the sky as 'this majestical roof fretted' (or adorned) 'with golden fire' (2.2.302–3) he reminds the audience of the ceiling (with heavens painted on it) that extended over the Globe's stage. English Renaissance tragedy is, nevertheless, 'realist' if we mean by that term an interest in *criticism*, or comparing reality with conventional, official or normal attitudes.[11] In other words, tragedy in this period encourages a thoughtful detachment in its audience. Hence perhaps the genre's fondness for topical jokes not very seamlessly integrated into the action. When the Venetian Iago says he learned a drinking song in England, 'where indeed they are most potent in potting' (that is, skilful in drinking, 2.3.72–3), one must suppose the line got a cheer from the audience. Perhaps Iago hammed it up, addressing or teasing the audience directly. The continuation of the joke suggests he probably did: 'Your Dane, your German, and your swag-bellied Hollander … are nothing to your English' (2.3.73–5). It is an instance of how tragedy in this period frequently cracks open the fictional illusion to allow for different, and not necessarily harmonized, attitudes: this is a genre capacious enough to include all manner of miscellaneous materials. Again, it is a mode of writing that seems intended to foster a mentally lively, alert responsiveness.

None of this rules out the possibility of intense emotional identification with the characters and events on stage. Hamlet himself tells us of how an actor could enter so completely into a role he could be moved to tears: 'What's Hecuba to him, or he to Hecuba, / That he should weep for her?' (2.2.559–60). Nevertheless, conditions of performance in the period seem to have invited, at least sporadically, a peculiarly conscious and self-aware attitude on the part of the audience. And part of this effect may have been to permit the audience to grasp something of the essentially theatrical nature of public or political life – to understand that, as we saw above with reference to Montaigne, the difference between king and pauper is all in the performance. Caesar is no greater man than Casca, but the 'foolery' of his being offered the 'crown' before the 'rabblement', just as if he were in a 'theater', makes him seem (to the uncritical) a wholly superior kind of being (*Julius Caesar*, 1.2.236, 221, 244, 261).

The mix of genres in the tragic drama of the period must also have contributed to this mentally independent attitude on the part of the audience. English Renaissance tragedy seldom allows us to view any phenomenon from one angle alone; it is multi-perspectival. Hardly any of the tragedies discussed in this book, for instance, are without some admixture of comedy, especially *Hamlet*, which one critic has well described as 'the world's most sheerly entertaining tragedy, the cleverest, perhaps even the funniest'.[12] Samuel Johnson praised *Hamlet* for its 'variety':

> The incidents are so numerous, that the argument of the play would make a long tale. The scenes are inter-changeably diversified with merriment and solemnity; with merriment that includes judicious and instructive observations, and solemnity, not strained by poetical violence above the natural sentiments of man. New characters appear from time to time in continual succession, exhibiting various forms of life and particular modes of conversation. The pretended madness of Hamlet causes much mirth, the mournful distraction of Ophelia fills the heart with tenderness, and every personage produces the effect intended, from the apparition that in the first act chills the blood with horror, to the fop in the last, that exposes affectation to just contempt.[13]

In *Hamlet*, Polonius gives a notoriously pedantic account of the types of drama the visiting players can perform, which moves from established, relatively coherent genres such as 'tragedy' to highly mixed ones such as 'tragical-comical-historical-pastoral', all the way to 'poem unlimited', the sort of play with no generic boundaries at all (2.2.396–400). But in fact much drama in the period, even tragedy, falls into the 'unlimited' category. The classically-minded Sir Philip Sidney deplored the way dramatists 'mingl[ed] kings and clowns'.

Comic and tragic matter, he insisted, should be kept separate; instead, the players 'thrust in the clown by head and shoulders, to play a part in majestical matters, with neither decency nor discretion'.[14] The generic variety Johnson pointed to is, again, the sort of feature we might expect of a fundamentally intelligent type of theatre, since it requires spectators and performers continually to switch between different attitudes and mindsets. Spectators are invited to compare and choose between one type of experience or scale of values and another – precisely the activity of a free person.

English Renaissance tragedy, then, stimulates thought. Perhaps this seems a rather unexciting conclusion: after all, we take it for granted that serious art makes one think. But, as we have seen, in Elizabethan or Jacobean times it was by no means supposed to be a normal, let alone welcome, state of affairs that ordinary folk should reflect upon such important matters of state, philosophy or religion as tragedy routinely invites us to do. The duty of the common people was not to reason why but to obey. From the establishment's point of view, the idea of unlettered folk speculating about higher matters of belief, for example, would have seemed preposterous, dangerously so. But, as we shall see, this is exactly what Renaissance tragedies do – ask their audiences to make up their minds about indisputably important matters, to choose between different worldviews, and, indeed, often to sit in judgement on their betters.

We need only look to depictions of the theatre in the plays themselves to deduce that playwrights seem to have been aware of the critical potential of their medium. Thomas Kyd's *The Spanish Tragedy* represents the genre as a weapon of justice in a quite literal sense: it is during his staging at court of 'the tragedy / Of Soliman the Turkish Emperor' that Hieronimo is able to take bloody vengeance on his powerful enemies at the court of Spain.[15] We have already seen that Hamlet stages *The Mousetrap* in the Danish court in order to trick Claudius into betraying his guilt: 'The play's the thing / Wherein I'll catch the conscience of the King' (2.2.605–6). Theatre for Hamlet has a truth-telling function (it holds a 'mirror up to nature'). Accordingly he shows the greatest respect to the actors when they appear at Elsinore: 'Good my lord,' Hamlet addresses the snobbish court heavyweight Polonius, 'will you see the players well bestowed? Do you hear, let them be well used, for they are the abstract and brief chronicles of the time' (2.2.522–4). Tragedy has a weighty, politically serious purpose; it is not escapist entertainment. It provides an 'abstract' or concise and readily understandable account (suitable, indeed, for an unscholarly audience) of the reality of the times. The notion of 'the time' suggests a broad political and social content: the real topic of the genre, however indirectly this is broached, is always 'the time' or world of the playgoers themselves. The point connects up with Hamlet's assertion, in his advice to the players, that the 'purpose of playing' is to show 'the very age and body of the time his form and pressure'. Once again, it is 'the time' that matters: tragedy has largeness of aim. It is not concerned merely with private matters but with the state of whole kingdoms and commonwealths.

This educative purpose of tragedy necessitates a commitment to truth. Tragedy exposes to public gaze the sins of the rulers, refusing to 'skin and film' (cover over) 'the ulcerous place' (*Hamlet*, 3.4.154). As a result it often features courageous truth-tellers. Towards the end of *Othello*, Desdemona's maid Emilia realizes her husband Iago's role in her mistress's death. Iago brutally tells her to 'hold [her] peace' and 'get … home' (5.2.226, 230). But Emilia defies him, she 'will speak as liberal as the north' (227) – as freely as the north wind blows. It is a heady moment of rebellion – of free and open speech – against her husband's domestic tyranny. Kent too is a robust truth-teller who, when disguised as the common man Caius, is mocked by Cornwall for his supposed insolence in 'speak[ing] truth': Kent 'cannot flatter, he', Cornwall jeers (*King Lear*, 2.2.100, 99). Kent admits to Cornwall that he indeed relished beating the greasy servant Oswald because he knew such types all too well: servants who, instead of telling their masters the truth, prefer instead to 'smooth' or flatter 'every passion / That in the natures

of their lords rebel' (76–7). The episode is thrilling because
Kent is willing to tell it as it is: 'Sir,' he says to Cornwall, '"tis
my occupation to be plain: / I have seen better faces in my time
/ Than stands on any shoulder that I see / Before me at this
instant' (93–6). *Lear* describes a world in which it is difficult to
tell the truth ('Truth's a dog must to kennel' says the Fool: 'He
must be whipped out, when the Lady Brach may stand by th'
fire and stink' (1.4.109–11): the powerful can speak, but no one
else). Kent, though, does speak out.

Tragedy did not need openly to invite spectators to draw a
link between what happened on stage and the state of affairs
outside the playhouse. In *The Duchess of Malfi*, Antonio
describes the Duke's court as a sewer of corruption. The Duke
is of 'A most perverse and turbulent nature' (1.1.169), his
brother the cardinal an acknowledged Machiavel – a master
at deploying 'flatterers', 'intelligencers' (spies), and numerous
other 'political monsters' (1.1.162–3). Antonio's friend Delio
observes that the Duke uses the law as a 'spider' uses 'a foul
black cobweb' – that is, 'makes it ... a prison / To entangle' his
enemies (1.1.178, 179–80). Tragedy no doubt helped in the
formation – and circulation among a broad non-elite audience
– of new and oppositional attitudes, all under the screen of
an ancient and hallowed genre. As Sir John Harington wrote
in 1591, tragedy 'represent[ed] only the cruel and lawless
proceedings of princes, moving' in the audience 'nothing but
pity or detestation' (Chambers, 4.237–8).[16] Tragedy was not
socially netural: explicitly or implicitly, it took a stand against
the delinquencies of a ruling elite.

Tragedy, then, in this period frequently entertains the kind
of thought that Angelo, in *Measure for Measure*, describes
as 'lawless and incertain' (3.1.128): oppositional, heterodox,
free, dangerous. It was not simply a mode of diversion;
scandalous and unhallowed speculation was part of its appeal.
The energy of these plays lies in the ideas that challenge the
received wisdom of their authors' world. The simplest, but
also the truest, thing to say about the tragic drama of the
period is that it is intellectually alive: writers rehearse critical

and avant-garde modes of thinking. We have seen that this doesn't require us to believe that dramatists were willing openly to endorse subversive or heterodox opinions. That would have been a risky strategy indeed. But, again and again, we do find such opinions aired in the texts.

In the readings that follow, I explore in detail some of the main ways tragedy in this period addresses key issues of freedom, equality and justice. I do not attempt extensive and complete interpretations of each text but instead pursue my chosen theme (and acknowledge that this entails neglecting many other matters of interest). Each of the plays discussed are complex works, repaying many readings; and a book might be written about each. And, of course, there are countless such interpretations already in existence. However, there is also reason to wonder whether providing a full-scale, unified 'interpretation' of each of these works is quite the right way to go about things. We touch here upon the question of the unity of English Renaissance plays. There is a long history of assuming that art works of any value ought to display coherence – develop a single unified vision of reality, not display contradiction. But it is debatable whether this criterion of excellence can be applied here. The works treated in this book raise so many different points of view, are so committed to exploring a range of ways of looking at the world, and do so many different things along the way, that demanding coherence of them risks approaching them in precisely the wrong spirit. Instead, I will attend to just some of the perspectives that receive airing in the plays – perspectives that suggest a commitment to freedom in a variety of guises.

PART TWO

Pursuing Freedom in English Renaissance Tragedy

Tragedy ... plots the urge of the individual to assert his freedom against the restrictions imposed by the community, against power as it is embodied in the existing social system.

G. K. HUNTER, *English Drama 1586–1642: The Age of Shakespeare*[1]

Oh, happy they that never saw the court, / Nor ever knew great men but by report!

Vittoria, in *The White Devil* (5.6.262–3)

6

Gorboduc

An early instance of the political focus of English Renaissance tragedy is *Gorboduc*, a collaborative effort by Thomas Norton and Thomas Sackville first performed at Christmas in 1561, and, later, at the court of Elizabeth. The beginning of the play (which like Shakespeare's *Lear* is set in ancient Britain) finds Gorboduc 'dividing his land to his two sons', Ferrex and Porrex, a decision leading to civil war. The play engages with the notion of disordered government explored in Part One of this book, advising us that 'a state knit in unity doth continue strong against all force, but being divided is easily destroyed' (see the explanation of the 'dumb show' preceding Act One).[1]

Like Lear, Gorboduc acts 'Against all law and right' (28) – absolutely, and with no respect for good counsel. The play depicts an irresponsible, self-indulgent ruling elite with little concern for the security and stability of the kingdom: 'lords, and trusted rulers under kings' who 'To please the present fancy of the prince / With wrong transpose the course of governance' (59–61). Gorboduc himself seeks 'greater ease' rather than the burdens of office (126). One of the play's bad counsellors, Philander, supports the king's proposal to divide the realm, asserting that smaller domains will enable the 'wronged poor' to have readier access to ' justice' (239). But in fact the poor will be *less* secure under the arrangements Gorboduc proposes, which, it would have been recognized by the audience, are bound to issue in conflict. It is significant, nonetheless, that Philander feels the need to invoke 'justice' as a projected benefit of Gorboduc's plan: publicly at least it is accepted that rightful government is founded on justice and must not deteriorate into a mere 'conspiracy of the rich' against the poor, as Thomas More described government.[2] Commonwealth ideals shine through every page of *Gorboduc*.

The worthy counsellor Eubulus speaks out against Gorboduc's scheme. He worries for 'the safety' of the king's 'commonweal' (324), prudently pointing out that 'Within one land, one single rule is best' (328). Eubulus is mindful of the 'desire of sovereignty' (335) in human nature – what we, following Nietzsche, might call will-to-power. As the Chorus subsequently points out, 'Lust of kingdom' tramples on 'sacred faith', 'rule of reason', and 'kindly love' (951–3). Divided government will trigger 'disdain' and 'envy' between the brothers (362, 363); *Gorboduc*, like later tragedies, is much preoccupied with the outcomes of political factionalism (in *The Duchess of Malfi* the soldier Pescara comments that 'These factions amongst great men' cause 'all the country / About them' to go 'to wrack for't' (3.3.37–40) – exactly what happens in *Hamlet* and *Lear*).[3] The central problem is that addressed so often in English Renaissance tragedy: the catastrophic effects of lawless aristocratic 'ambition' and 'usurping pride' (387, 389). Gorboduc rejects Eubulus's reasoned advice, declaring that 'in one self purpose do I still abide' (411). The combination on the king's part of innocent naivety and absolutism (*'one self'*) is disastrous. Nevertheless, it is noteworthy that Gorboduc also condemns 'oppressing of the rightful cause' (426), thus acknowledging the responsibility monarchs have to punish 'wrongs done to the poor' (427).

The dumb-show before Act Two delineates the difference between good and bad political counsel. The good sort is 'plain and open', the bad full of 'pleasant words' – poison in a golden cup. Ferrex's parasite Hermon advises his patron that the law does not apply to kings: 'Murders and violent thefts' may be 'crimes' in 'private men', but, when monarchs perform them, they are 'deck'd with glorious name / Of noble conquests' (616–17). The play, however, understands that Ferrex and Porrex violate 'those bounds which Law of Nature sets' (1069), what Gorboduc calls 'the law of kind' (1075).

The play raises the spectre of popular rebellion against unnatural tyranny: 'Shall subjects dare with force / To work revenge upon their prince's fact?' (1365–6). It does not support rebellion, but certainly sees it as the inevitable result of misgovernment by corrupt and selfish elites. The Queen has slain her son, and in turn been killed by the people: 'Shall yet the subject seek to take the sword, / Arise against his lord, and slay his King?' (1368–9). Rebellion is inexcusable: 'subjects must obey as they are bound' (1398); the 'common people's minds' are 'giddy' (1419). Eubulus condemns popular rebellion at length (1518ff.) and the insurrection is bloodily crushed (1567–70). But the cause of all of this mayhem, the play has made clear, is ruling-class self-seeking and criminality. Eubulus wishes that on the death of Gorboduc a parliament had been held to appoint an heir and thus re-establish obedience in the people (1781–8). But all that is now too late: elite misconduct has brought the kingdom to ruin.

The 'fall' of Gorboduc is a 'mirror ... to princes all' (462, 461). 'Mirror' here conveys the sense not only of 'reflection', or imitation, of reality, but also of 'lesson', as in the title of Baldwin's *Mirror for Magistrates* (discussed in Part One). The word suggests the way that tragic drama in the period both revealed reality but also aimed to change it for the better: *Gorboduc* fulfils Hamlet's definition of the drama as 'hold[ing] the mirror up to nature', showing the 'age and body of the time its form and pressure'.

7

Tamburlaine, Parts One and Two

In Part One we noticed how tragedies of the period debunked or demystified power. Like other plays of Marlowe, discussed below, both parts of *Tamburlaine* are obsessed with the overturning of hierarchies – social, cosmic, ethical. The hero is an uproarious, anarchic figure. Emerging from a country backwater, the 'Scythian shepherd' turns social and political hierarchies upside down, becoming in short time a 'great ... conqueror' and 'mighty ... monarch'.[1] For the Greeks, the Scythians were beyond the pale of civilization – so Tamburlaine is a geographical as well as social outsider. As we have seen, Marlowe's England was anything but a democracy. People were used to being told what to believe, especially from the pulpit. By contrast, Marlowe's Prologue invites its audience to 'applaud [Tamburlaine's] fortunes *as you please*' (*1 Tamb.*, 8, my emphasis). Make up your own mind, Marlowe says in effect. But could one 'applaud' Tamburlaine's wild career without taking a critical view of social hierarchy *outside* the playhouse as well?

The court of Persia abuses Tamburlaine as a 'sturdy Scythian thief' (*1 Tamb.*, 1.1.36) and leader of 'barbarous arms' (1.1.42); the Egyptian Sultan reviles him as 'A sturdy felon', 'base-bred thief' (*1 Tamb.*, 4.3.12), 'base, usurping vagabond' (4.3.21) leading an 'inglorious crew' (4.3.67), a 'peasant ignorant / Of lawful arms or martial discipline' (4.1.64–5). He 'came up of nothing' (2 *Tamb.*, 3.1.74) and is 'shepherd's issue' (3.5.77). Yet lineage is of no account to Tamburlaine: 'I am a lord,' he declares, 'for so my deeds shall prove, / And yet a shepherd by my parentage' (1 *Tamb.*, 1.2.34–5). The story's opening sees him trade a shepherd's garments for a suit of 'complete armor' (1 *Tamb.*, 1.2.42): 'Lie here, ye weeds that I disdain to wear!' (1.2.41). (We might compare Aaron, another lowly cultural outsider on the make, in *Titus Andronicus*: 'Away with slavish weeds and servile thoughts! / I will be bright, and shine in pearl and gold' (2.1.18–19)). To the daughter of the Egyptian ruler, Zenocrate (whom Tamburlaine later marries), the shepherd-warrior is a 'mean', or lower-class, man (1 *Tamb.*, 1.2.8). It must have been a strange moment in the theatre to watch this plebeian transform himself into a military and political commander. His follower Techelles prophesies that Tamburlaine will have 'kings kneeling at his feet' (1 *Tamb.*, 1.2.55). (Usumcasane boasts similarly that 'kings shall crouch unto our conquering swords' (1 *Tamb.*, 1.2.220), and Tamburlaine also vaunts, at the conclusion to Part One, that 'Emperors and kings lie breathless at my feet' (5.1.468).) When Tamburlaine crowns his victorious commanders Kings of Fez, Moroccus and Argier, he claims that they 'Deserve' their 'titles'

> By valour and by magnanimity.
> Your births shall be no blemish to your fame,
> For virtue is the fount whence honour springs,
> And they are worthy she investeth kings. (1 *Tamb.*,
>   4.4.130–33)

(Later, he asserts that 'virtue solely is the sum of glory, / And fashions men with true nobility' (1 *Tamb.*, 5.1.189–90).) Chief among the play's several daring stage-pictures is Tamburlaine's self-coronation with the Persian crown (1 *Tamb.*, 2.7). To this day, coronation rituals derive their power from the notion that the new monarch receives his or her authority from another legitimate power (in particular, the Church). In Marlowe's play, Tamburlaine claims kingship on the basis of his own selfhood. Such an idea would have had a bracing effect on people for whom the principle of deference to superiors was second nature.

Much of the zest of the *Tamburlaine* plays derives from their unbridled mockery of the elite – and no doubt this accounted for their popularity as well. Unearned magnificence and pomp are ongoing targets. The 'most great and puissant monarch of the earth' (*1 Tamb.*, 3.1.41), Bajazeth, Emperor of Turkey, is a monstrously vain and ridiculous figure, one set up to fall. 'All flesh quakes at your magnificence' flatters Argier: 'True, Argier,' concurs Bajazeth complacently, 'and tremble at my looks' (*1 Tamb.*, 3.1.48–9). Bajazeth cannot contain his shock at 'the presumption' of Tamburlaine, 'this Scythian slave' (*1 Tamb.*, 3.3.68), who addresses him as an equal; as the Emperor observes to the as yet undefeated kings of Fez, Morocco and Argier, 'He calls me Bajazeth, whom you call lord!' (3.3.67). The play takes sadistic pleasure in humiliating the great. The crown of Zabina, Bajazeth's wife, is handed over to Zenocrate: 'Injurious villains, thieves, runagates' (or vagabonds) rails Zabina, 'How dare you thus abuse my majesty?' (*1 Tamb.*, 3.3.225–6). But the *Tamburlaine* plays are all about abusing majesty. Bajazeth is made Tamburlaine's 'footstool' (*1 Tamb.*, 4.2.1ff.), and, in a reversal of his own earlier terms of opprobrium, mocked as 'Base villain, vassal, slave to Tamburlaine' (4.2.19) and hauled about in a cage; elsewhere he is addressed as 'Sirrah', a mode of address used for inferiors (*1 Tamb.*, 4.4.36). Zabina is mocked as Zenocrate's 'handmaid's slave' (*1 Tamb.*, 4.2.69). The torment of Bajazeth and Zabina is intricate, extended and cartoonishly exaggerated: at some dark level the audience is invited to participate in it. When the Emperor and Empress commit suicide by dashing their brains out against Bajazeth's cage, the savagery and sensationalism of the episode hints at the intensity of the social resentments being channelled. A more sedate version of the abuse of royalty occurs in the depiction of the witless, cowardly, ineffectual king of Persia (Mycetes) who tries to hide his crown on the field of battle because 'kings are clouts' (that is, targets) 'that every man shoots at' (*1 Tamb.*, 2.4.8). The audience is encouraged to feel contempt for this poltroon – a figure indeed of 'absurd pomp', to use Hamlet's phrase (3.2.59).

Tamburlaine asserts he 'love[s] to live at liberty' (*1 Tamb.*, 1.2.26): in fact he acknowledges *no* social or natural limits to his ability to choose his life, and in political terms presents as a kind of freedom fighter. The Persian commander Ceneus says Tamburlaine dared 'with shepherds and a little spoil', and 'in disdain of wrong and tyranny', to 'Defend his freedom 'gainst a monarchy' (*1 Tamb.*, 2.1.54–6). His army constitutes a kind of alternative society based on comradeship, a band of brothers rather than a hierarchy: 'These are my friends,' he declares of his commanders, 'in whom I more rejoice / Than doth the king of Persia in his crown' (*1 Tamb.*, 1.2.241–2). Theridamas comments on the 'amity' between him and his fellow soldiers Techelles and Usumcasane (*1 Tamb.*, 2.3.32): they are 'loving followers' rather than subordinates (*1 Tamb.*, 5.1.521). On the other hand, Bajazeth and the establishment repeatedly accuse him of tyranny (see, for example, *1 Tamb.*, 4.4.106, 2.7.41), charges that have some truth yet ring hollow: it is Tamburlaine's rise from the bottom of the social pyramid that captures our imagination and which would have thrilled humble folk watching his career in the theatre. Even his carni-valesque violence is likely to have been felt as cleansing. (One thinks of the violent retribution prophets like Isaiah call down upon unjust greedy rulers: the 'princes are rebellious, and companions of thieves', unconcerned with 'the cause of the widow', but 'the loftiness of man shall be bowed down, and the haughtiness of men shall be made low' (Isa. 1.23, 2.17).) The torment of Bajazeth in particular may well have fed into socially undistinguished spectators' fantasies of revenge upon the great and powerful. Tamburlaine is no democrat, yet, like his later reincarnation, Napoleon Bonaparte, his war is against 'golden palaces' (*2 Tamb.*, 4.1.193) rather than the ordinary folk. Kings are 'dogs' (2 *Tamb.*, 4.1.181) and draw his chariot (2 *Tamb.*, 4.3).

Tamburlaine's campaign against kings, emperors and sultans is mirrored by his ambition to 'march against the powers of heaven' and carry out a 'slaughter of the gods' (2 *Tamb.*, 5.3.48, 50). He sets his face against all hierarchies, including religious ones. In Part One, we noted his burning of the (Islamic) Scriptures. Elsewhere he indulges in vaultingly deicidal rhetoric. His 'looks ... menace heaven and dare the gods' (1 *Tamb.*, 1.2.157), according to one witness; another says he 'opposeth him against the gods' (1 *Tamb.*, 2.6.39). Tamburlaine boasts that Jove himself, 'viewing me in arms, looks pale and wan, / Fearing my power should pull him from his throne' (1 *Tamb.*, 5.1.451–2). The important thing about such rhetoric is that it is of a piece with that unleashed against social hierarchy. When Tamburlaine attacks God he attacks kings, and vice-versa, since kings derived their sovereignty from the divine (we have already noted that Tamburlaine is his own authority in this regard). In this sense religious blasphemy and political opposition are indistinguishable.

Like other Marlowe plays, *Tamburlaine* is profoundly atheistic. Zabina acknowledges that 'no Mahomet, no God' can help her or Bajazeth (1 *Tamb.*, 5.1.239) and Techelles owns Mahomet cannot curb Tamburlaine's willingness to use torture (1 *Tamb.*, 4.4.55). The play suggests a radically material and worldly perspective on life rather than a God-centered one. 'To be a king,' says Usumcasane, 'is half to be a god', to which Theridamas retorts: 'A god is not so glorious as a king. / I think the pleasure they enjoy in heaven / Cannot compare with kingly joys in earth' (1 *Tamb.*, 2.5.56–9). For Tamburlaine – as, one must suspect, for Marlowe – there could be no higher meaning, pleasure or good than 'The sweet fruition of an earthly crown' (1 *Tamb.*, 2.7.29). Tamburlaine's ideal is one of absolute autonomy. It is not just power that excites him – it is the world itself, and the pleasure and delight it affords. The emphasis on a purely *earthly* bliss suggests a play astoundingly outside its own time and place.

As noted in Part One, there is something jarringly relativizing about allusions to 'Christians' in these plays, as if that group should be just another sect or *ethnos*. When Orcanes, King of Natolia, remarks 'if there be a Christ, as Christians say' (*2 Tamb.*, 2.2.39), a formulation repeated a few lines later (2.2.64), the phrase startles because it raises the possibility of there *not* being a Christ – and 'Christians' here appear as a group that would simply be expected to affirm the existence of their god. In any case they are a seedy lot in *Tamburlaine* Part Two, their perfidy on display when they break the oaths sworn with Orcanes. Sigismond is shocked at Frederick's suggestion that they should take advantage of the peace treaty to surprise their opponent (who has 'dismissed the greatest part / Of all his army' (*2 Tamb.*, 2.1.16–17)). Such an action, he points out, would be an act of 'treachery' (2.1.31), since they have made an oath 'calling Christ for record of our truths' (2.1.30). But Christians, Baldwin argues, are not bound to honour oaths with 'infidels' (2.1.33). The whole conversation reeks of hypocrisy. Orcanes is revolted by the Christians' lack of honour: 'Have I not here the articles of peace / And solemn covenants we have both confirmed, / He by his Christ and I by Mahomet?' (*2 Tamb.*, 2.2.30–2). When Orcanes triumphs over the Christians he wants to thank Christ, since the Christian defeat is clear evidence of divine intervention: 'God has thundered vengeance from on high' (*2 Tamb.*, 2.3.2) and Orcanes had appealed to Christ prior to the battle ('On Christ still let us cry. / If there be Christ, we shall have victory' (2.2.63–4)). But a cooler assessment of what has happened is offered by Gazellus: ''Tis but the fortune of the wars, my lord', so often falsely represented as the outcome of 'a miracle' (2.3.31–2).

Yet if *Tamburlaine* is invested in the lurid representation of violent assaults upon the ruling classes, and in the blasphemous rejection of Christian doctrine, it also – and perhaps unexpectedly – persistently targets the classical ethic of martial glory and honour. Tamburlaine's ne'er-do-well son Calyphas is a dissenter in his father's camp, playing a role not unlike that of Shakespeare's Thersites, who dismisses the Trojan War as 'war for a placket' (*Troilus and Cressida*, 2.3.19), a 'placket' being a slit in a skirt and therefore metaphor for the female sexual organ. After a long, technical and rather tedious speech by Tamburlaine about the 'rudiments of war' (*2 Tamb.*, 3.2.54), Calyphas observes reasonably enough that 'this is dangerous to be done. / We may be slain or wounded ere we learn' (3.2.93–4); and when the indignant Tamburlaine cuts his own arm to show his son 'A wound is nothing' (*2 Tamb.*, 3.2.115), Calyphas finds it 'a pitiful sight' (3.2.130–1). Later, dozing contentedly in his tent, he scorns his brothers' urging him to join them in the battle: 'Away, ye fools! My father needs not me' (4.1.15) – Tamburlaine being more than capable of looking after himself. 'I take no pleasure to be murderous,' Calyphas admits: he prefers to 'quench [his] thirst' with 'wine' rather than 'blood' (4.1.29–30). When his bellicose brothers insist he accompany them to the battlefield to acquire a warrior's renown, he replies, 'Take you the honour. I will take my ease' (4.1.49), soon proposing a round of cards (4.1.61). Like Thersites in *Troilus*, Calyphas disputes the dominant militaristic value system. The radicalism of such a perspective should be obvious: warfare was the traditional vocation of noblemen in medieval and Renaissance Europe. When Tamburlaine encourages his sons to be 'a scourge and terror to the world', Calyphas suggests he might be left out of that unpleasant business: 'But while my brothers follow arms, my lord, / Let me accompany my gracious mother'. His brothers, he points out, 'are enough to conquer all the world' (*2 Tamb.*, 1.3.63, 65–7). Where Tamburlaine insists his sons must, to be worthy of their father, 'wade up to the chin in blood' (1.3.84), Calyphas charmingly and humanely prefers pleasure to glory. Calyphas's civility doesn't stop his father stabbing him to death as an 'effeminate brat' (4.1.161). No matter: what has been aired is a wholly different way of living from the courtly-monarchical culture of perpetual war.

We may suppose that some spectators in Marlowe's England (perhaps even veterans of the anti-Spanish conflict in the Netherlands) found themselves drawn to Calyphas's dislike of war rather than to Tamburlaine's glorification of it.

8

Doctor Faustus

Like *Tamburlaine*, *Faustus* is a Marlovian social fantasy. Its hero is a scholar – 'base of stock' like the Scythian shepherd (B-Text, Prologue, 11) – who rises to social eminence not by 'proud audacious deeds' or military conquests (B-Text, Prologue, 5) but through wit and magic. Magic is presented in the Prologue to the play as surpassing all the more pedestrian university sciences Faustus has mastered: logic, medicine, law, divinity. Faustus's story suggests how intellectuals (what the Epilogue calls 'forward wits' (7)) might, by intelligence and personal talent, triumph over social disadvantage.

As with *Tamburlaine*, a measure of gleeful revenge accompanies the rise of the lowly hero. When Faustus appears as an entertainer at the court of Charles V, the knight Benvolio sneers 'He looks as like a conjuror as the pope to a coster-monger' (B-Text, 4.1.72–3); the jibe earns Benvolio a set of horns on his head, with the result that 'every servile groom jests' at him (B-Text, 4.2.5). After Benvolio has been suffi-ciently humiliated, Faustus dismisses him with the order 'And hereafter, sir, look you speak well of scholars' (B-Text, 4.1.159); Benvolio is aghast Faustus should 'thus abuse a gentleman' (A-Text, 4.1.75). The joke of the episode with the Emperor and Benvolio is that Faustus is a kind of dramatist bringing the fabled dead back to life. The Emperor longs to see Alexander the Great and his 'beauteous paramour' (A-Text, 4.1.35): Faustus admits he can't present to the Emperor 'the true substantial bodies of those two deceased princes' since they are 'long since ... consumed to dust' (A-Text, 4.1.44–5). What he can do is supply life-like images – 'such spirits as can lively resemble Alexander and his paramour' (A-Text, 4.1.48–9). They will appear 'in that manner that they best lived in, in their most flourishing estate' (A-Text, 4.1.49–50). The whole show, then, is a miracle of art, the technical mastery of imitation, which has almost always been regarded as a defining criterion of the aesthetic (art holds up the mirror to nature). For Faustus the representation he will summon up before the Emperor is an achievement of the 'art and power of [his] spirit' (A-Text, 4.1.41), again suggesting the vocation of dramatist or poet. When the Emperor tries to embrace Alexander and his paramour, Faustus calls an end to the performance: 'My gracious lord, you do forget yourself. / These are but shadows, not substantial' (B-Text, 4.1.102–3). 'Shadows' was occasionally used for performers: at the end of *A Midsummer Night's Dream*, Puck speaks for all the actors: 'If we shadows have offended' (5.1.418).

The Faustus story (it existed in previous versions) was tailor-made for Marlowe, presenting an opportunity to give public expression to all sorts of extreme and outlandish opinions. When Faustus declares 'hell's a fable' (A-Text, 2.1.127), or says that the notion that 'after this life there is any pain' is one of many religious 'old wives' tales' (135), one can easily imagine the shiver such sentiments would have elicited among Marlowe's audience (similarly when Faustus brazenly confesses to being 'wanton and lascivious' (A-Text, 2.1.140–1), or when the devil Mephistopheles dismisses marriage as 'but a ceremonial toy' (A-Text, 2.1.149)). When at his death Faustus cries out that 'All beasts are happy, for, when they die, / Their souls are soon dissolved in elements; / But mine must live still to be plagued in hell' (B-Text, 5.2.172–4), we have a typical instance of Marlowe having it both ways. On the one hand the spectre of damnation is raised: only man faces an afterlife. Simultaneously, however, a purely material perspective on existence is toyed with – what if man was no different from the animals? Faustus's dedication to a life of 'pleasure and ... dalliance' (B-Text, 3.1.61) implicitly suggests the soul is not something to be bothered about: what *is* real is the here and now. It must have been possible for spectators to pick and choose here: to be intrigued by the materialism of these lines and be bored by the restatement of the all-too-familiar official theology (Faustus being whisked off to eternal punishment in hell). And it must have been exciting simply to hear such things *said*, notwithstanding their condemnation (for we are never allowed to forget that Faustus is making a very large mistake). The obtrusive moral framework sees Faustus packed off to hell, though to the untheologically-minded spectator it is not clear why he deserves such punishment. He does not commit any alarming crimes with his new-found power, and his escapades are mostly of the order of pranks and showing-off – little that is really blood-curdling. The Epilogue dutifully draws the moral –

> Regard [Faustus's] hellish fall,
> Whose fiendful fortune may exhort the wise
> Only to wonder at unlawful things,
> Whose deepness doth entice such forward wits
> To practise more than heavenly power permits. (A-Text,
>   Epilogue, 4–8)

– but is inadequate to the fun and humanity of the play itself, in which the essential harmlessness, excitement and spiritedness of Faustus's 'hellish' career are what impresses. There is nothing fiendish in serving up 'a dish of ripe grapes' in 'the dead time of the winter' (A-Text, 4.2.9–11), after all, or putting on an invisibility cloak and playing tricks on the Pope and a group of friars (A-Text, 3.1). Perhaps what is truly unacceptable is that Faustus, like Tamburlaine, articulates an unapologetically worldly, amoral view of life (though not, understandably, when facing an eternity in hell at the end of the play). A thorough-going sensualist, he asserts (referring to himself in the third person) that 'This word "damnation" terrifies not him, / For he confounds hell in Elysium. / His ghost be with the old philosophers!' (A-Text, 1.3.59–61). Elysium, the classical paradise, is not distinguished from the 'hell' of the Christians. He is content to go there, where he imagines himself conversing pleasantly with Plato and Aristotle – which, once again, does not sound especially wicked.

Faustus is the mouthpiece of what he calls 'strange philosophy' (A-Text, 1.1.88). He does not mean the logic and metaphysics taught in the universities, which he dismisses as 'odious and obscure' (1.1.108), but the 'lawless and incertain thought' we noted in Part One – unhallowed, adventuring thought. Magic stands outside the received order of knowledge. It is, for Faustus, a creative and anti-institutional pursuit unconstrained by academic structures and traditions, and stands for a new, more original and zestful, way of thinking and being. One of the oddest aspects of the play is its repeatedly making clear to Faustus exactly what is in store for him should he not desist from rebellion against God. Even Mephistopheles admits the devils' true 'torment' consists in their being deprived of 'the face of God' and 'eternal joys of heaven' (A-Text, 1.3.78, 79). In a simple yet profound line, Mephistopheles confesses that 'this is hell, nor am I out of it' (A-Text, 1.3.77). In other words, for the damned, hell is not a location but a mode of existence: they can be anywhere, but that 'anywhere' is always, unbearably, the same place. The point is made again a little later: 'Hell hath no limits,' observes Mephistopheles, adding, 'where we [that is, the devils] are is hell' (A-Text, 2.1.121–2). It is difficult to understand why Faustus, apparently so clever, fails to understand that trading twenty-four years of diversion for an infinity of torment is a poor bargain. For all his noted intelligence he seems remarkably dense in these interviews with Mephistopheles. But perhaps, in another sense, he *does* grasp what is at stake. Faustus articulates that view that holds that the highest good is earthly experience, and that the hope that there could be something other and better than worldly sensuous life is illusory and incoherent (and it is true that visions of heaven often do lack the richness, substantiality and sheer variety of human life – as the negation of the only life we know, heaven can look remarkably like death). Mephistopheles gives expression to this sentiment when he asks Faustus, who is beginning to fear he may have made a bad bargain, 'Think'st thou heaven is such a glorious thing?' and goes on to answer his own question: 'I tell thee, 'tis not half so fair as thou / Or any man that breathes on earth' (A-Text, 2.3.5–7). This is not unlike Theridamas's assertion that 'the pleasure they enjoy in heaven / Cannot compare with kingly joys in earth' (*1 Tamb.*, 2.5.58–9). When Mephistopheles says he is 'now in hell', Faustus cockily misconstrues the devil's meaning: 'How? Now in hell? Nay, an this be hell, I'll willingly be damned here. What? Walking, disputing, etc.?' (A-Text, 2.1.138–9). Faustus wants to live 'in all voluptuousness' (A-Text, 1.3.93) – to taste life to the full. If you do in fact suspect that life on earth really is the only existence worth having, then the deal that Faustus strikes with the Devil may not look so irrational. When Faustus kisses Helen of Troy he exclaims, 'Sweet Helen, make me immortal with a kiss,' and later: 'Here will I dwell, for heaven be in these lips, / And all is dross that is not Helena' (A-Text, 5.1.92, 95–6). One feels this is not mere poeticizing, that Faustus truly believes that the only immortality we humans are capable of is that which we sometimes feel we achieve in moments of sensual bliss on earth – an extraordinarily radical position for his era, as, perhaps, for ours.

A key moment in the play is Mephistopheles' refusal to answer Faustus's query as to 'who made the world' (A-Text, 2.3.65). This is the one thing Faustus must *not* think about. To do so would be to realize that his natural role is to obey and glorify his Creator. (Compare the personification of the sin of Pride who 'disdain[s] to have any parents' (B-Text, 2.3.108).) Faustus instead consciously and freely chooses to live for himself. Because much of our own culture can be described as human- rather than God-centred, Faustus thus appears, for all his pre-modern infatuation with magic, as a peculiarly modern kind of hero. As well as instructing Faustus never to think about how the world came into being, Mephistopheles is anxious that Faustus not consider how he might be saved. Lucifer insists 'Christ cannot save thy soul, for he is just' (A-Text, 2.3.83). This is a lie: God is omnipotent and just as well as merciful. There may be nothing Faustus can actually *do* to engineer his own salvation, but for the reformers it was a grievous sin to doubt the divine's ability to impart Grace to any sinner. (As the Second Scholar says, 'mercy is infinite' (B-Text, 5.2.42).) And yet for all that, Faustus remains curiously innocent, without any real hardness of heart.

Faustus chooses 'four-and-twenty years of liberty' over everything else (B-Text, 3.1.60) and, for about two hours during a performance on the Renaissance stage, he must have presented an exhilarating instance of absolute freedom. There is something charming even in his obtuseness: he may not have understood and inwardly digested well-known theological axioms of his time, but sometimes one has to be a bit stupid in order to live freely. (Too often 'wisdom' means playing by the rules.) He is frequently blustering, grandiose and naïve, and he does nothing very important with his wondrous new arts. But in the end what we like about him is simply his astounding audacity and originality. Whatever else he is, Faustus is memorably himself. The other characters are background by comparison.

9

The Jew of Malta

Part of the appeal of many of the plays discussed in this book resides in their representation of a certain anarchic, amoral energy, for example in Shakespeare's Aaron the Moor, whose radically anti-Christian thinking we noted in Part One. It is not just that Aaron stands for a different kind of order to that represented by Christianity, rather that he stands for no order at all. Towards the end of *Titus Andronicus*, Shakespeare gives Aaron a speech that, for swaggering evil, outdoes anything in the oeuvre. Lucius asks him whether he regrets his 'heinous deeds'. 'Ay, that I had not done a thousand more,' replies Aaron, and goes on to 'curse the day' in which he did not undertake 'some notorious ill',

As kill a man, or else devise his death,
Ravish a maid, or plot the way to do it,
Accuse some innocent and forswear myself,
Set deadly enmity between two friends,
Make poor men's cattle break their necks,
Set fire on barns and haystacks in the night
And bid the owners quench them with their tears.
Oft have I digged up dead men from their graves
And set them upright at their dear friends' door,
Even when their sorrows almost was forgot,
And on their skins, as on the bark of trees,
Have with my knife carved in Roman letters,

'Let not your sorrow die, though I am dead'.
    (5.1.123–40)

Aaron's violence has no discernible 'oppositional' or 'critical' character, yet part of the thrill of the play lies in watching him, like Shakespeare's Richard III or the bastard Edmund in *King Lear*, cut a swathe through the established social hierarchy to place himself at the centre of political power (he becomes the lover of Tamora, wife of the Roman Emperor Saturninus). As noted earlier, putting such sentiments into the mouths of maniacal villains enabled playwrights to have their cake and eat it too: the offending thought can be at once aired and disowned. Shakespeare evidently enjoyed making Aaron. The baroque and wild nastiness of his crimes at times collapses into comedy: monomania of Aaron's sort has a hint of absurdity about it.

To that extent Aaron is reminiscent of Marlowe's Barabas (the Jew of Malta) and his comrade Ithamore. 'As for myself,' breezily declares Barabas in conversation with Ithamore, 'I walk abroad a-nights / And kill sick people groaning under walls' (2.3.175–6); he 'poison[s] wells' (2.3.177) too, lends out money at extortionate rates such that many of his clients go mad or hang themselves (2.3.191–9), and has been known to 'Pin … upon [a dead debtor's] breast a long great scroll / How I with interest tormented him' (2.3.198–9). Ithamore's own japes include cutting the throats of travellers in inns and crippling pilgrims to the Holy Land (2.3.206–13). All of this mayhem is largely unmotivated, festive in its uselessness. Perhaps such sensationalism helped channel resentments against an identifiable evil Other; people unhappy with their lot (and there can have been no shortage of those in a society so drastically unequal as that of Elizabethan England) want to be able to blame someone for their woes. Villainous outsiders like Barabas possibly served the same psychic function as Catholics, Spaniards, witches, Turks, immigrant craftsmen (who were suspected of taking English jobs) and other supposed or real malefactors. At the same time these riotous villains may well have expressed the barely acknowledged rage and frustration of members of the audience. There was surely something cathartic about watching characters as free, wicked and flamboyantly outspoken as these in a society in which the main 'moral' duty for most people was silent unquestioning obedience. Barabas, Aaron and Ithamore are extravagantly hostile to the principle of deference. (Like that of Faustus or Tamburlaine, Ithamore's 'birth' is 'but mean' (2.3.166).)

The Jew of Malta demonstrates in any case that Barabas's 'betters' (in this case the Christians) are frauds. This is what we might expect anyhow from the opening speech of Machiavel (another Renaissance villain who speaks the truth), in which elite authority is exposed as cynically ruthless craft. When towards the end of the play the Turks conquer Christian Malta through Barabas's treachery, the Jew advises him that, since 'by wrong' the Turk gained his current 'authority', he will now have to secure it 'by firm policy' – that is, ruthless guile (5.2.35–6). Barabas's next step is to betray the Turks for a Christian bribe. 'Authority' here is stripped of its divine mystique and emerges as nothing more than a high-level criminal enterprise – as Barabas confides to the audience, his plan is to double-cross the Turks: 'is not this / A kingly kind of trade, to purchase towns / By treachery and sell 'em by deceit?' (5.5.46–8). The view of politics is like Swift's in *Gulliver's Travels*: so-called statesmen are impelled by 'violent desire of wealth, power, and titles'.[1] Of course, Barabas is in turn betrayed by the Christians once the Turks are dealt with. Betrayal is the norm in this world.

'I can see no fruits in all their faith,' observes Barabas of the Christians, 'But malice, falsehood, and excessive pride / Which methinks fits not their profession [i.e., the professing of their religion]' (1.1.114–16). When the Christians have to pay tribute to the Emperor of Turkey they determine to rob Barabas and the Jews of half their fortune. When Barabas protests ('Is theft the ground of your religion?' (1.2.96)), his punishment is to lose everything. Ferneze, the Governor of Malta, has the gall to sermonize Barabas on the virtue of patience and the sin of 'covetousness':

> If thou rely upon thy righteousness,
> Be patient, and thy riches will increase.
> Excess of wealth is cause of covetousness,
> And covetousness, O, 'tis a monstrous sin. (1.2.122–5)

As Barabas points out to this glozing phony, this is nothing but a flagrant case of 'Bring[ing] ... scripture to confirm [the Governor's] wrongs' (111). The total effect of the passage is to discredit religion, which appears as a mere tool of statecraft, as Machiavelli thought it often had to be. (Shakespeare does something very similar in Act Three, Scene Seven of *Richard III*, when the tyrant Richard appears before the citizens of London prayer book in hand and flanked by two clergymen: this is, as Shakespeare makes clear, a blatant piece of political theatre.) The Christians' 'Grave Governor' (1.2.129) is a whited sepulchre, like those of the religious establishment whom Christ denounced, who were 'beautiful outward' but inside 'full of dead men's bones' and 'uncleanness' (Mt. 23.27). Justice is a sham. 'Content thee, Barabas' Ferneze says, 'thou hast naught but right' (that is, justice), to which Barabas replies, trenchantly: 'Your extreme right does me exceeding wrong' (1.2.153–4). As Barabas says, the 'profession' or faith of Christians is 'policy' or statecraft rather than 'simplicity' (1.2.161–2). An Elizabethan audience watching this episode could perhaps have viewed it as concerning people in a far-off country, but might also be expected to have drawn the general moral that what those in power *do* (wherever they are) is often a long way off from what they *say*. Barabas is an obvious villain and, since his wealth exceeds 'all the wealth in Malta' (1.2.135), we need not feel heartbroken at his fate at the hands of the Christians, but there is something thrilling about his taking vengeance on these moralizing frauds: the other Jews ('base slaves' according to Barabas (1.2.215)) accept their fate, but Barabas fights. Throughout the play we see the 'hateful Christians' (1.2.341) just as he sees them, and are invited to enjoy his determination to 'smile when the Christians moan' (2.3.173) – another instance of that capacity of Renaissance tragedy to see the Christians' religion in an exterior, analytical way. Barabas's incongruously virtuous daughter Abigail (who later converts to Christianity) agrees that the Christians have 'manifestly wronged' them (1.2.276): 'religion / Hides many mischiefs from suspicion' notes Barabas (1.2.282–3). Anyhow, as far as Barabas is concerned the Christians were originally a mere heretical sect ('poor villains') that had come to dominate the Jews by a contingent fact of history (the crushing of the Jewish revolt of 66–70 AD by the Roman Emperors Titus and Vespasian (2.3.7–10)). Historicizing Christianity in this way – seeing it as an effect of historical circumstance rather than part of the Divine Plan – is central to Marlowe's atheistical strategy. Barabas suggests (at least to those 'rare-witted gentlemen, / Scholars, ... learned and liberal' (3.1.7–8))[2] a way of seeing Christianity as bounded by time and place rather than as coming from outside history. There is also, however, straight-out abuse of Christian practice. When Barabas poisons a whole convent of nuns, the ringing of bells for them cheers him immensely: for once these don't sound 'like tinkers' pans' (4.1.3). Marlowe excels at such debunking redescriptions. Of course he can draw on a long tradition of anti-clerical, and, especially, anti-Catholic, invective. Surely 'the nuns [have] fine sport with the friars now and then?' asks Ithamore saucily of Abigail (3.3.32–3), the sort of joke bound to go down well with a Protestant audience. But, as with Faustus's teasing of the Pope, there is the possibility of such anti-Catholic rhetoric blurring into the anti-religious (it is relevant here that the Church of England was itself thought by many to be insufficiently purified of Roman Catholic practices and governance). The point is that the material dramatists deploy can have multiple effects – can confirm orthodoxy ('that's what papists are like') as well as foster more free-wheeling modes of thought ('that's what Christians are like').

The other perspective well to the fore in *The Jew of Malta* is a militant worldliness. When Barabas is being ground down by the Christians he explicitly rejects suicide: life is too precious. 'No,' he vows, 'I will live, nor loathe I this my life' (1.2.267). Rather than hanging himself out of despair, he chooses resistance: 'I'll rouse my senses and awake myself' (1.2.270). Barabas's determination to love life no matter what is characteristic: the mission of revenge never weighs down his jaunty demeanour. We are invited to admire the artistry and invention of his crimes: 'was there ever seen such villainy, / So neatly plotted and so well performed?' wonders Ithamore at the killing of Ferneze's son Lodowick and the latter's friend Mathias (3.3.1–2); he thinks it all 'the bravest policy' – that is, the finest cunning (3.3.12). For all Barabas's cynicism, his fundamental commitment is to the vivid pleasures of this world. When Barabas declares he 'will rouse his senses and awake himself' he means he will use all the intelligence and alertness at his disposal to achieve his goal. At the same time the statement can be taken as a kind of Marlovian credo: Marlowe really is committed to the rousing of the senses, to a vivid, awake, intense engagement with the world. Abigail's decision to take Christian orders dismays Mathias: 'Fair Abigail,' he remarks to himself in disbelief, 'Become a nun?' (1.2.367–8). The prospect is appalling: 'she were fitter for a tale of love / Than to be tired out with orisons; / And better would she far become a bed, / Embraced in a friendly lover's arms, / Than rise at midnight to a solemn mass' (1.2.370–4). It would be a mistake to treat this episode in an overly histor- ically-aware fashion, for example as a piece of anti-Catholic sentiment, though it is true the Protestant reformers opposed clerical celibacy. The import of these lines goes much further than that now remote and historically regional struggle: what they amount to is a manifesto in favour of the senses and the earth. (A less exalted version of this sentiment occurs when Abigail dies: Friar Barnardine's response to her affirmation that she 'die[s] a Christian' is the flip comment 'Ay, and a virgin, too; that grieves me most' (3.6.40–1) – the joke is partly a comment on Christian hypocrisy but also articulates Marlowe's own commitment to worldly pleasure.) Marlovian libertinism comes through not least in the occasional use of obscenity, for instance in the drunken Ithamore's song to the prostitute Bellamira: 'Let music rumble, / Whilst I in thy incony lap do tumble' (4.4.27–8). ('Incony' means rare or delicate, but there is also a pun on 'cunny', the female genitalia – the same pun Hamlet makes when he asks Ophelia if she thought he 'meant country matters' (3.2.114) when he asked her permission to lie his head in her lap.) *The Jew of Malta* concludes in the most orthodox fashion. The Christians regain Malta from the Turkish forces and Barabas falls into the cauldron he had designed for the Turks. Ferneze thanks heaven: 'let due praise be given / Neither to fate nor fortune, but to heaven' (5.5.122–3). It is difficult to take this resolution seriously. The play is completely devoid of a trace of divine influence; Ferneze is a mere politician, and Marlowe's drama radically, utterly secular.

10

Edward II

English Renaissance tragedies routinely depicted acts of extreme violence: the gouging out of Gloucester's eyes in *King Lear*, the suicides of Bajazeth and Zabina in *Tamburlaine*. The end of Marlowe's play about the downfall of the English king Edward II (who reigned from 1307–27) finds the titular hero confined to a dungeon at the behest of his own lords and barons, who resent the favour the king has shown his base-born friend and lover Gaveston. Edward's powerlessness is complete: his tormentors wash his face with sewer water before murdering him by inserting a red-hot poker into his anus (condign punishment, apparently, for a homosexual). Aside from satisfying audience lust for sadistic spectacle, what was the point of such horrors?

It is certainly true that such episodes gratified an appetite for cruelty; we should not forget the playhouses were located near venues that saw bears and dogs tortured and killed for sport. Nevertheless, the bloodthirstiness of tragedy in this period seems connected to a broader, more general violence. If the official view emphasized social order, tragedy drew attention to the cruelty upon which this putative order was based. As noted in Part One of this book, the period was one of grievous inequality and suffering. Tragedy, simply by the fact of its extremity, arguably gave this suffering 'a local habitation and a name' (*A Midsummer Night's Dream*, 5.1.17). State violence was a central part of the society in which the genre emerged: recall Lear's comparison of 'authority' to a farmer's cur chasing off a beggar.

In *Edward II* this netherworld of material deprivation emerges momentarily in the appearance of 'three Poor Men' at the beginning of the play. They offer their services to Gaveston, who has been recalled to England by his lover Edward. (Of course Marlowe never explicitly says that Edward and Gaveston are lovers, but there is no doubt we are to assume it.) Gaveston treats the Poor Men with contempt. He doesn't need servants but artists and performers able to divert the king. The episode reminds us that the life of a soldier in this period was quite likely to end with an agonizing death in a disease-ridden hospital: like the other two, the Third Poor Man, who has 'served against the Scot' (1.1.33), begs for 'service' (1.1.25), but Gaveston denies the request, airily remarking, 'Why, there are hospitals for such as you,' before dismissing him without a thought: 'I have no war, and therefore, sir, begone' (1.1.34–5). The spurned veteran heartily curses the king's favourite (1.1.36–7). Thus the play gives us right at the beginning a glimpse of the condition of the poor in Marlowe's England – people whose fate worries neither Gaveston nor Edward. As Gaveston remarks, 'As for the multitude, that are but sparks / Raked up in embers of their poverty, / *Tanti* [i.e., So much for them!]' (1.1.20–2).

The appalling conclusion to the play reduces Edward to a Poor Man himself – indeed to the exact position of the beggarly 'Poor Tom' in *Lear*, helpless and covered in filth. (Both *Lear* and *Edward II* show us kings stripped bare.) There is a touch of sadism in these moments when greatness and pomp are reduced to beggarly desperation. It was only in the playhouse that common folk could witness such a spectacle: everything else in the culture attempted to persuade them that their betters were of a different order of nature, that kings (for instance) were quasi-divine beings. Tragedy exposes the fictive nature of this view. The torment of the fifth Act of *Edward II* is drawn out, Mortimer instructing his followers to 'Speak curstly' to Edward and 'amplify his grief with bitter words' (5.2.63, 65). One can see how this spectacle might have fed a desire to see the great brought low and revealed as no better than the rest of us. It is humanly improbable that ordinary people did not at some level resent those who lived in extravagant luxury above them. It would have been gratifying to see that, when all was said and done, kings were no better than they. As Edward says, 'But what are kings when regiment is gone, / But perfect shadows in a sunshine day?' (5.1.26–7). The sentiment is common in tragedy of the period: there is something fantastical about the whole hierarchical system, about kingly status and social distinctions generally. The truth of nature is played off against the empty shadows of art and social convention. When Lear strips off his fine clothes as 'lendings', he is gripped by a viewpoint similar to that of Edward in his prison cell. As 'unaccommodated man' (*King Lear*, 3.4.101–7), Edward is no different from the Poor Men dismissed by Gaveston. The extremity of the play – the indignities to which Edward is subjected – is part of its truthtelling: a king is just a man. Tragedy shows the reality beneath the mystifications of 'regiment'. Hence the humiliating ending, the drinking from 'puddle water' (5.3.30), the ghastly death.

Truth-telling in *Edward II* goes further still. The play is about a king's self-indulgence and the cruelty and deceit of nobles. The most artful example of aristocratic guile is Mortimer's 'unpointed' (unpunctuated) letter: he sends a note that, because of its slippery punctuation, can be read either as commanding Edward's death or as sparing him (5.4.6–20). The ambiguity will enable him to deny he had any role in the crime, in which Edward's queen connives (5.2.45). Mortimer and the Queen are thus shown as Machiavellian 'dissemble[rs]' (5.2.74; also 86). Warwick's 'wit and policy' (2.5.95) is blatant falsehood (he promises his friend the Earl of Pembroke that he will allow the captured Gaveston to visit Edward for one last time but treacherously kidnaps the favourite on the way and kills him (see 3.1.1ff.)). No audience could fail to notice the political class's ruthlessness, irresponsibility and violence. As so often in English Renaissance tragedy, however, it is unwise to look for a totally coherent perspective. Profoundly unattractive as are the earls (and Mortimer is himself an aspiring tyrant), it does not follow that the play is 'pro-Gaveston' – at least not uniformly. He is, as we have seen, contemptuous of the people, in this regard a typical corrupt favourite. Mortimer tells us that Gaveston 'riot[s] it with the treasure of the realm'. While 'soldiers mutiny for want of pay' (1.4.405–6), Gaveston 'wears a lord's revenue on his back' (1.4.407); and while England's 'garrisons are beaten out of France', the 'lame and poor lie groaning at the gates' (2.2.161–2). Gaveston and Edward appear here as selfish, cruel and heartless, the enemies of the commons.

The play presents two court factions: on the one hand, a decadent ruling clique bent on pleasure, sex and fantasy; on the other, a group of nobles brutally obsessed with power. While the latter comes off poorly in comparison with Edward (who is at least sensitive, passionate and intelligent), the nobles nonetheless have a point: the king's selfishness imperils the realm. 'A plague o' both your houses' (*Romeo and Juliet*, 3.1.98–9) is perhaps the natural response. Late sixteenth-century spectators did not have to look far afield, or into the distant past, to understand the dangers posed by a weak king. Across the Channel, whole countries were engulfed by bloody disputes between Catholics and Protestants; and, of course, many were aware of England's own history of a divided kingdom as a result of the Lancastrian–Yorkist rivalry of the fifteenth century, if only from Shakespeare's history plays on the topic. The French king has 'seized Normandy' (3.2.64), taking advantage of Edward's neglect of politics to invade English possessions in France. The Queen claims that 'Care of my country' (4.6.65) has forced her to wage war against her husband (but also conducts an affair with Mortimer). Edward is accused of ransacking the treasury to sate his appetite for entertainments. 'Flatterers' make havoc with 'England's wealth' (4.4.26–7). Mortimer tells us that 'idle triumphs, masques, lascivious shows, / And prodigal gifts bestowed on Gaveston / Have drawn [the] treasure dry and made [the king] weak' (2.2.156–8). Now 'The murmuring commons' have started to resent the king's depredations (2.2.159). (As often in English Renaissance tragedy, here too the populace is awarded a political role.) The problem is that the opposition to Edward's neglectful reign is itself corrupt, Mortimer being a sleek unscrupulous Machiavel. On seizing total power he boasts, in the manner of any tyrant, 'I do what I will' (5.4.51), and introduces a reign of terror: 'Feared am I more than loved. Let me be feared, / And when I frown, make all the court look pale' (5.4.52–3).

We likely leave *Edward II* with a general antipathy towards elite power politics. Oddly, though, the voice for that perspective is that of the king himself, who is essentially unconcerned with power. The loss of Normandy is a 'trifle' (2.2.10). He chooses to live for love, and remains true to that commitment no matter what. (In a way he stands for the anti-political hedonistic ethic of Shakespeare's Antony and Cleopatra.) Edward ascends to an otherworldly philosophic contempt for politics in his final moments, when he learns to 'despise this transitory pomp' (5.1.108). 'But what is he,' he asks, 'whom rule and empery / Have not in life or death made miserable?' (4.7.14–15). He throws his lot in with 'Plato and … Aristotle' and the 'life contemplative' rather than political power (4.7.19–20). A similar moment occurs in *Lear* when the old defeated king sees through the absurd game of 'who's in, who's out' (5.3.15). 'Empery' and misery go hand in hand.

Edward is a deeply ambivalent figure. His irresponsibility would have alarmed audiences aware of the calamities ensuing upon the reigns of weak kings – as we have seen in Part One, tyranny was often conceived of in this period as disordered rule. Yet his championing of love and pleasure is liberating. He lives authentically, by his own sense of what ultimately matters. Certainly the nobles' brutality is repellent: would that 'some base slave', says Mortimer, might 'greet his lordship' – that is, and sarcastically, Gaveston – 'with a poniard' (or dagger: 1.4.265–6). A burning issue of the play is constitutional-political. 'Is this the duty that you owe your king?' demands

Edward's brother, Edmund, Earl of Kent, of the fractious nobles
(1.4.22). 'We know our duties,' retorts Warwick, 'Let [the king]
know his peers' (1.4.23). Authority itself is at stake. 'Unnatural
wars,' laments the Queen, 'where subjects brave their king'
(3.2.86). (Compare Edmund's prayer to God to 'punish this
unnatural revolt!' (4.6.9).) Edward will not brook encroachment
on his royal authority: 'Rebels,' he asks, 'will they appoint
their sovereign / His sports, his pleasures, and his company?'
(3.2.174–5). At the same time, however, Edward himself is
represented as a 'Tyrant' (3.4.21) and 'Unnatural king' (4.1.8)
– and seems such when he says he would rather see 'England's
civil towns huge heaps of stones / And plows to go about our
palace gates' than to be 'braved' by the rebels (3.3.30–2) – an
'unnatural resolution', according to Warwick (3.3.33). The point
is that in all of this debate about the legitimacy of Edward's
rule an audience is introduced to political matters of the highest
importance. There is a continuous preoccupation with the nature
of legitimate rule, with competing rights and prerogatives ('the
barons' right' versus 'King Edward's right' (3.3.35–6)), and with
what a ruler of England lawfully can and cannot do. Words such
as 'traitor' and 'rebel' are used everywhere and by both sides.
When Spencer Senior is taken off to be executed as a rebel, he
replies: '"Rebel" is he that fights against his prince; / So fought
not they that fought in Edward's right' (4.6.71–2). Nonetheless
confusion reigns as to who is, and is not, a 'traitor':

EDWARD
Lay hands on that traitor Mortimer!

MORTIMER
Lay hands on that traitor Gaveston! (1.4.20–1)

After crossing over to the side of Mortimer and the earls, the
Queen describes the king as 'Misgoverned' (4.4.9). Marlowe's
play invites ordinary folk in the playhouse to reflect upon the
duties of subjects in such circumstances – something they were
never called upon to do elsewhere.

Edward's world, like Antony and Cleopatra's, is one of imagination and poetry: sexuality is ideal and intellectual rather than mere lust. In Act One, Scene One, the language of Gaveston's love for Edward is heightened and intensely erotic. Edward declares himself, in a letter full of 'amorous lines' (1.1.6), Gaveston's 'dearest friend' (1.1.2). So long as Gaveston can 'upon [Edward's] bosom … die' ('die' here means swoon, but the word can also suggest 'experience sexual climax') he is content (1.1.14): what cares he if 'with the world' he is continually 'at enmity' (1.1.15)? The world, and its ways of ranking humanity, is a matter of indifference to Edward and Gaveston. As such, they resemble the lovers in Donne's 'The Sun Rising'. Their world is 'contracted thus' – 'Nothing else is', only their love. The public world is unreal: 'All honour's mimic', an illusion.[1] This sense of Gaveston and Edward temporarily escaping 'the world's great snare' (*Antony and Cleopatra*, 4.8.18) must have stimulated the imaginations of many spectators – the more so because it is shown to have profound implications for the socially stratified world of the play. As with *Tamburlaine*, the language of social rank saturates *Edward II*: the play's nobles object not just to Gaveston's influence over the king, but to his 'peasant' (1.4.7) birth: he is 'base and obscure' (1.1.100), an 'upstart' (1.4.423), a 'villain' (1.2.11), a 'slave' (1.2.25), a 'night-grown mushroom' (1.4.284 – that is, one who has jumped up the social hierarchy too quickly). Not so for Edward: when they meet (Gaveston has been away in France), the king is dismayed when his friend kneels and kisses his hand: 'Embrace me, Gaveston, as I do thee,' he insists (1.1.140). The old saying, *Amor vincit omnia* ('Love conquers all') is vindicated: social hierarchy itself is suspended. It is Gaveston who is able to see Edward as a man. Ceremoniousness is thrown off in favour of an ethic of equality. As Gaveston puts it, in a line that must have sent a thrill of delight down the spines of many non-noble spectators: 'Farewell, base stooping to the lordly peers' (1.1.18).

His is a vigorously oppositional voice. If no democrat (as we saw in his treatment of the play's Poor Men) Gaveston is yet no bootlicker. By attacking the nobility – 'Base leaden earls, that glory in your birth, / Go sit at home and eat your tenants' beef, / And come not here to scoff at Gaveston, / Whose mounting thoughts did never creep so low / As to bestow a look on such as you' (2.2.74–8) – he surely spoke for all those in the audience resentful of the establishment. Many would have relished this retort to the landed elite – those 'spacious in the possession of dirt' (*Hamlet*, 5.2.88–9). Gaveston's outburst against aristocratic snobbery surely channelled a range of social resentments; as we have seen, players and playwrights endured comparable high-handedness from Elizabethan worthies. Gaveston, indeed, is connected with the theatre, as a kind of Master of the Revels, or chief officer for Edward's entertainments, and Marlowe was himself one who, like Baldock the tutor (also of the king's party), rose on the strength of his wit. 'My gentry,' says Baldock, 'I fetched from Oxford, not from heraldry' (2.2.242–3). (Marlowe was at Cambridge.) Baldock and Gaveston both speak for the talented outsider who cannot rely on inherited status to make his way in the world (who is not a 'needy nothing', to use the phrase from Shakespeare's sonnet). They embody the merit principle. Like such playwrights as Marlowe, Shakespeare and Ben Jonson, Baldock and Gaveston must rely on their wits for what Hamlet – who complains he lacks it – calls 'advancement' (*Hamlet*, 3.2.338).

The excitement of *Edward II* for its original audience lay in the outrageous acts of insubordination the play depicts. At the end of Act One, Scene One, Gaveston roughs up a prince of the church who was 'the only cause of his exile' (1.1.178). His manhandling of the Bishop of Coventry (like the tricks Faustus plays on Catholic princes of the church) is in one sense cannily orthodox: both episodes can be explained away as anti-Catholic (*Edward II* being set in pre-Reformation England). But the extremity of Gaveston's action is the point: many in the audience must have felt he acted for them against prideful, self-aggrandizing ecclesiastics. Similarly his outrageous insults to the peers would have spoken for all those excluded from a social system run by and for the oligarchy. The shock of Gaveston's rise is all-important for the play's effect. When Mortimer Senior sees Gaveston sitting beside the king, he cries out, 'What man of noble birth can brook this sight?' (1.4.12). Part of what tragedy does in this period, then, is enable shocking sights to be seen, the unthinkable to be thought. One such unthinkable notion is the political role of the commons. Mortimer admits the 'commons now begin to pity [Edward]' (5.4.2), although earlier in the play we were told the people were discontented with Edward's rule. But simply mentioning the role of the people in politics opens up a new way of seeing.

When Gaveston turns his mind to how he will entertain the king, his language is extravagantly poetic. 'I must have,' he says,

> wanton poets, pleasant wits,
> Musicians that with touching of a string
> May draw the pliant king which way I please.
> Music and poetry is his delight;
> Therefore I'll have Italian masques by night,
> Sweet speeches, comedies, and pleasing shows;
> And in the day, when he shall walk abroad,
> Like sylvan nymphs my pages shall be clad;
> My men, like satyrs grazing on the lawns,
> Shall with their goat feet dance an antic hay.
> Sometime a lovely boy in Dian's shape,
> With hair that gilds the water as it glides,
> Crownets of pearl about his naked arms,
> And in his sportful hands an olive tree
> To hide those parts which men delight to see,
> Shall bathe him in a spring … (1.1.50–65)

Gaveston's delicate, risqué speech makes the nobles' bullying, obtuse and hackneyed vituperation all the more repulsive. When the Queen says that Gaveston 'corrupts' the king and is 'a bawd to his affections' (that is, a pander to his desires

(1.4.150–1)), the accusation is what any moralist of the period would say, and doubtless well-deserved. It is also irrelevant. The play shows up the deep cynicism and cruelty of the barons' pursuit of power (in which, later, the Queen herself participates, betraying Edward and condoning his death). In fact all the charisma and interest of the play lies with the Edward–Gaveston circle, desire being here more real than politics. As Edward says, the only value of 'kingly regiment' is that he may thereby 'honour' Gaveston (1.1.164, 163). The king may be 'brainsick' and 'wanton' (1.1.124, 131), as his enemies claim, but his choice to live as if love and beauty were more important than power politics is both scandalous and emancipating. So long, says Edward, as 'I [can] walk with' Gaveston 'What care I though the earls begirt us round?' (2.2.221–2).

The opening scene features a showdown between Edward and the truculent nobles, who are offended by the favour he extends to Gaveston. The key fact about the scene is that it is one of rebellion against monarchal authority. This dramatization of political conflict at the top of the social hierarchy is itself daring and must have had a significantly demystifying effect. The desired 'image of authority', to use Lear's phrase, was not one of self-division and conflict. Authority typically wishes to be seen as serenely above history, absolute, unified, static. But here it is represented dynamically. The effect on ordinary spectators may be likened to the demystifying effect certain types of investigative political journalism can have on voters today.

In one sense the natural reaction to Edward is to feel he has traded reality for fantasy, 'regiment' for trivial poetic fantasies and distractions. But this gets things the wrong way round. The play suggests that scholarship, art, love and desire are the true realities, not 'empery'. The urge to find some truth outside the prison of power politics is common in tragedy: in *Lear*, this is humble fellow feeling; in *Hamlet*, friendship, art and the speculative intellect; in *Antony and Cleopatra*, love, sensuality and the imagination. In *Edward II* the alternative to sterile power politics is sexual pleasure, poetry and wit. So when, in this context, Mortimer Senior declares that 'with my nature war doth best agree' (1.4.365) the line seems a confession of disability. Marlowe redefines charisma: no longer is it dependent on the traditional militaristic virtues, but on sensitivity to the aesthetic and love.

God has no part in this quarrel between king and nobles. The Queen claims the rebels' victory indicates that God is on their side: 'Successful battles gives the God of kings / To them that fight in right and fear his wrath' (4.6.19–20). (The end of the play sees the Queen committed to the Tower by the new king, her son Edward III.) The assertion in any case is empty, Edward refuting it in the next scene. It is 'hell and cruel Mortimer' who will separate him from Spencer, not 'the angry heavens' as Spencer supposes. 'The gentle heavens,' insists Edward, 'have not to do in this' (4.7.73–5). The play naturalizes political life, renders it not a matter of Providence but of amoral nature, force and cunning. Exposing the sordid reality of politics is one of the most important functions of tragedy in this period. It is a mistake to think of the genre in blandly 'artistic' terms, as if the dramatists' principal concern was to create beautiful structures. Tragedy communicated ideas. And its electrifying effect was a result of its addressing the sort of topics *Edward II* takes up.

11

Arden of Faversham

Tragedy's sensitivity to social hierarchy and inequality is illustrated in the anonymous *Arden of Faversham* (a play in which it is now reasonably supposed Shakespeare had a hand in). *Arden* is one of a group of Renaissance tragedies that adapted the tragic genre to the lives and worlds of well-to-do but not aristocratic characters. The play is based on an account of an actual crime, the murder of Thomas Arden by his wife Alice and her lover Mosby. Arden is one of those who cleaned up during the English Reformation, coming into possession of the lands of the dissolved Abbey of Faversham (1.4).[1] The play provides an ambiguous view of its hero. The servant Michael speaks of his 'kindly love and liberal hand' and the 'many good turns' his master has done him (3.177, 199), yet he is also depicted as financially unscrupulous, the character Greene claiming Arden has 'highly wrong'd' him in a deal over the Abbey's lands (2.97), and that

> Desire of wealth is endless in his mind
> And he is greedy-gaping still for gain.
> Nor cares he though young gentlemen do beg,
> So he may scrape and hoard up in his pouch. (1.474–7)

Likewise the poor sailor Dick Reede accuses Arden of 'wrongfully' depriving him of 'a plot of ground' intended to maintain Reede's wife and children while he is at sea (13.13,

12). Reede's curse – that the land that his enemy 'by force
and violence held from [him]' (Epilogue, 11) be 'ruinous and
fatal' to Arden (13.34) – is duly borne out: it is on this very
spot that Arden's murderers throw his body, the 'print' of
which is visible 'Two years and more after the deed was done'
(Epilogue, 12, 13).

The world of the play is consumed by social rank. Arden
despises the low-born Mosby, who was once a tailor (or
'botcher', as Arden puts it (1.25, 320)) but now 'bravely jets
it' in the 'silken gown' of a nobleman's 'steward' or head
servant (1.29, 30). Arden is proud of his status as 'a gentleman
of blood' (1.36), taunting Mosby as 'a velvet drudge, / A
cheating steward, and … base-minded peasant' (1.322–3).
Mosby rejects this attempt to fix his identity as forever determined by his past – 'Measure me what I am', he (with some
dignity) retorts, 'not what I was' (1.329) – but distinctions
based on rank seem inescapable, contaminating even Alice
and Mosby's relationship. When they quarrel she too throws
in his face his 'peasant' and 'base' background (1.198), later
regretting she had ever been so enchanted as to lose her honest
name by conducting an affair with 'a mean artificer' (8.77).
When Alice subsequently seeks a rapprochement with Mosby,
he responds by mocking the whole system of class snobbery
bent on keeping people like him in their place:

Oh no, I am a base artificer,
My wings are feather'd for a lowly flight.
Mosby? fie, no! not for a thousand pound.
Make love to you? Why, 'tis unpardonable;
We beggars must not breathe where gentles are.
    (8.135–9)

Nevertheless, what comes through all this is the attempt of
two people to live authentically outside social constraints.
Mosby is aware he would have done better to have married
the 'honest maid' of a handsome 'dowry' whom he forsook
for Alice (8.88, 89), yet he commits to Alice nonetheless.

Alice herself tears up the prayerbook that had temporarily prompted her to end the affair – an astonishingly rebellious, even blasphemous, moment that asserts the value of human love and desire over religious piety. Mosby's endearments, she declares, supplant even Scripture itself:

> I will do penance for offending thee,
> And burn this prayerbook, where I here use
> The holy word that had converted me.
> See, Mosby, I will tear away the leaves,
> And all the leaves, and in this golden cover
> Shall thy sweet phrases and thy letters dwell,
> And thereon will I chiefly meditate
> And hold no other sect but such devotion. (8.115–22)

Her 'penance' is owed not to God, but to Mosby – it is against *him*, and against their love, that she has sinned, and she vows forthwith to 'hold no other sect but such [earthly] devotion'. The whole episode is an audacious reversal of the old idea of the corrupting effect of poetry (including, of course, theatre): where earlier figures such as Dante's Paolo and Francesca find themselves in hell after succumbing to passion while reading an Arthurian romance,[2] Alice is led astray by her prayer book, the 'holy word' itself.

The burning of the prayer book at one level only confirms Alice's wickedness. Yet the overall impression that *Arden of Faversham* conveys is that of two people desperate to live their own lives but hemmed in by social-moral policing (Alice elsewhere rues 'narrow-prying neighbours' who 'blab', and 'the biting speech of men' (1.135, 139)). Condemned to death at the end of the play, Alice and Mosby are fittingly repentant. But this is a paltry thing by comparison with their erstwhile attempt to live according to their own desire: what has Arden, declares Alice powerfully to Mosby, 'to do with thee my love, / Or govern me that am to rule myself?' (10.89–90), the latter line perhaps reminding us of a similar sentiment in the mouth of Salome in *The Tragedy of Mariam* (see her speech on divorce at 1.4.41–52; see note 21, p. 217). Arden, Alice says to Mosby, must 'leave to live that we may love, / May live, may love; for what is life but love?' (10.92–3). Mosby's response is similarly vaulting, and the text does not invite us to register, as somehow ridiculous, the distance between the speaker's humble social identity and the height of his rhetoric: 'let our love be rocks of adamant, / Which time nor place nor tempest can asunder' (10.103–4). The murder of Arden is admittedly a dingy and sometimes comical affair (the two bungling hitmen, Black Will and Shakebag, make sure of that). But the play nevertheless allows as well for another, more passionate story to emerge, in which two lovers, defying the powerful social constraints of their 'time' and 'place', attempt to seize their freedom.

12

Hamlet

Part of the energy of tragedy in this period is its cynical, debunking tone, which is itself intellectually liberating. Often such a tone is to be found in the mouths of villainous, if charismatic, characters – Marlowe's Tamburlaine and Barabas, Shakespeare's Iago and Richard III, and so on. But a deflating rhetoric is common in good characters as well. When the courtier Osric appears towards the end of *Hamlet*, the Prince cannot forego a little fun with him. 'Dost know this water fly?' he asks Horatio, who does not: 'Thy state is the more gracious' (or blessed) Hamlet says, 'for 'tis a vice to know him. He hath much land, and fertile. Let a beast be lord of beasts, and his crib shall stand at the king's mess. 'Tis a chuff, but, as I say, spacious in the possession of dirt' (5.2.82–9). Landed wealth, says Hamlet, gives its possessor far more importance than he or she would deserve if merit alone were to be the basis of such distinctions: Osric is one of those 'needy nothing[s] trimmed in jollity' Shakespeare complained of in Sonnet 66, people lacking innate talent who nevertheless chose their parents well. This corrupt principle extends so far in Hamlet's world that, as David Bevington glosses the line, 'If a man, no matter how beastlike, is as rich in livestock and possessions as Osric, he may eat at the king's table'. 'Merit' doesn't come into it. (Recall that injured or neglected merit is one of the reasons lying behind Shakespeare's despair in the sonnet, as it is Hamlet's in 'To be, or not to be'.) Osric

is the sort of greasy bootlicker who thrives in courts or, for
that matter, modern bureaucratic and corporate organiza-
tions. (The 'gentleman usher' Dondolo in *The Revenger's
Tragedy* is the same type. He, too, is full of what he takes
to be 'golden words' (*Hamlet*, 5.2.131), the main function
of which is to mark him off from ordinary folk. When he
enters to tell Castiza that Vindice wishes to speak with
her, he adopts Osric's over-refined and roundabout manner:
'Madonna, there is one, as they say, a thing of flesh and blood,
a man I take him by his beard, that would very desirously
mouth to mouth with you' – to which Castiza's response is a
baffled 'What's that?' Dondolo will not use 'ordinary words'
because a 'gentleman-usher scorns to use the phrase and fancy
of a servingman' (2.1.10–13, 18–19, 21–3).) When Hamlet
declares the weather cold, Osric instantly agrees, and when
the Prince says it is hot, he promptly falls into line (5.2.95–
101). Hamlet finds Osric's orotund manner ridiculous, and the
Prince's deflation of courtly rhetoric has a strongly egalitarian
thrust to it. Hamlet's social identity, indeed, is interestingly
ambiguous: in a literal sense he is of course a member of the
elite, and yet when he alludes to himself as 'so poor a man
as Hamlet' (1.5.193) there is a poetic and ethical truth to the
phrase: he stands, after all, radically *apart* from Claudius's
court. At the very least his speech, in its frequently downright,
salty, proverbial manner, does connect with what F. P. Wilson
called 'the diction of common life'.[1]

Hamlet is one of the best-loved Shakespearean heroes
partly because he can speak the speech of the common people,
mix it with ordinary folk. His talk is wonderfully irreverent.
One of the oddest moments in the play occurs when, with
Horatio and Marcellus, he refers to the Ghost of his father
as 'boy', 'truepenny', 'this fellow in the cellarage', 'old mole'
(1.5.159, 160, 171): suddenly the august figure of the Ghost
dwindles to something comical. It is typical Hamlet, cutting
pretentiousness down to size; the same playfully levelling
spirit makes him refer to Polonius, a king's counsellor no
less, as 'That great baby' (2.2.382). The dislike of Polonius is

part of a general distaste for pomposity. When the counsellor shows the actors visiting Elsinore off to their lodgings, Hamlet cannot resist a parting shot: 'Follow that lord,' he tells them, 'and look you mock him not' (2.2.544–5). It is the same critical spirit that paints Claudius as 'A king of shreds and patches' (someone whose splendour is all a sham (3.4.106)), and compares him to a 'cutpurse' or common thief who has stolen the crown 'from a shelf ... / And put it in his pocket' (3.4.102, 103–4). Notwithstanding the trappings of monarchy, Claudius is a burglar like any other. In *Othello* Iago looks through appearances to make everything seem as nasty as his own character (his comment on Desdemona is typical: 'the wine she drinks is made of grapes' (2.1.254–5)); Hamlet, by contrast, looks through appearances to see things as they really are. People love Hamlet because he is one of the greatest plain-speakers and truth-tellers in literature.

Hamlet has a knack of seeing, as T. S. Eliot said of Webster, 'the skull beneath the skin'.[2] In a complicated joke about kingship, he tells Rosencrantz that the 'The king is a thing – / ... / Of nothing' (4.2.29–31). The joke probably turns on the legal fiction that the king had two bodies, one natural and corporeal, the other official and immortal, but the basic point is dismissive: Claudius is a nobody. When the king demands to know where Polonius is (Hamlet has killed him), the Prince replies he is 'At supper' – meaning he is being eaten (by 'politic worms') rather than eating. The gist of this is that 'a king may go a progress', or royal procession, 'through the guts of a beggar' (4.3.17ff., 31–2). Pomp and ceremony will not keep one out of the grave. We are all food for worms, in the end, kings as much as anyone else.

Affectionate, uninhibited interaction with the Players indicates Hamlet's unsnobbish nature. (The whole episode is probably one more of those fantasy-moments on the part of the dramatists in this period, royalty warmly addressing actors as friends and colleagues rather than as 'base grooms' (*Edward II*, 2.5.71).) There is nothing stand-offish or superior in Hamlet's interview with the actors. He greets them warmly and sincerely: 'You are welcome, masters; welcome, all. I am glad to see thee well. Welcome, good friends. Oh, old friend! Why, thy face is valanced [i.e., fringed, with a beard] since I saw thee last' (2.2.421–3); later still the Players are 'friends' and 'old friend' and 'good friends' (2.2.535, 537, 546). As far as Hamlet is concerned these men are united with him by love of poetry and wit. His egalitarianism contrasts markedly with Polonius's superciliousness. When Hamlet orders Polonius to 'see the players well bestowed', adding 'Do you hear, let them be well used' (2.2.522–3), Polonius says stiffly that he will 'use them according to their desert' (2.2.527–8). Hamlet immediately puts Polonius back in his box: 'God's bodikin, man, much better. Use every man after his desert, and who shall scape whipping? Use them after your own honor and dignity' (2.2.529–31). Hamlet demands that the counsellor treat the Players just as he would wish to be treated – and points out, in good Protestant fashion, that all of us (including the great) are sinners anyway, well deserving of a sound thrashing ('there is no health in us', as the *Book of Common Prayer* says, and salvation comes from God not our conduct). The Prince's egalitarian streak is everywhere apparent. After Hamlet has encountered the Ghost at the end of Act One, his companions respectfully wait for him to leave first. But Hamlet brushes such stuffiness aside: 'Nay, come, let's go together' (1.5.199). All his interactions with Horatio and the others are similarly informal.

Hamlet loves Horatio for his integrity. He assures him in a heartfelt speech that he does not flatter him when he says that he is 'as just a man' (3.2.53) as any he has encountered. After all, 'Why should the poor be flattered?' (3.2.58): Horatio cannot offer Hamlet 'advancement' (3.2.56) and has no 'revenue' other than his 'good spirits to feed and clothe' him (3.2.57–8). As Hamlet expatiates on this theme of flattery, we get closer to his passionately egalitarian values:

No, let the candied tongue lick absurd pomp,
And crook the pregnant hinges of the knee
Where thrift may follow fawning. (3.2.59–61)

The self-interested obsequiousness of court life disgusts Hamlet just as much as its ridiculous pomposity.

There is one arena, however, in which Hamlet *is* a snob: art. He recalls that the Player once spoke a speech to him, but fears it 'was never acted, or if it was, not above once', because 'the play ... pleased not the million; 'twas caviar to the general' (2.2.434–6). It is not obvious that Hamlet's target here is the common folk. We should bear in mind Ben Jonson's remark, that the literary opinions of 'the sordid multitude' and 'the neater sort of our gallants' are much the same, 'for all are the multitude, only they differ in clothes, not in judgement or understanding'.[3] It is not as if Osric embodies good taste. As for Polonius, 'He's for a jig or a tale of bawdry, or he sleeps', Hamlet observes (2.2.500–1). Shakespeare is careful to show how aesthetic evaluation is corrupted by social distinctions. Polonius enthusiastically compliments Hamlet on the speech he recites ('''Fore God, my lord, well spoken, with good accent and good discretion' (2.2.466–7)), but the humble Player's speech meets with a lordly yawn: 'This is too long' (2.2.498). In his advice to the actors, Hamlet derides 'the groundlings' (the spectators who paid for cheaper admission and stood in the open area round the stage) 'who for the most part are capable of nothing but inexplicable dumb shows and noise' (3.2.10–12). But what seems most to frustrate Hamlet is not the groundlings themselves but their incapacity for thought (predictable enough given their lack of education). And we might take note of that 'for the most part': some at least of the groundlings, it seems, *are* capable of more. The main point to grasp, however, is that Hamlet dislikes stupidity, wherever it is found, among 'absurd pomp' or the people. This is in itself important. It takes us back to the theme of freedom: Hamlet stands for thought, not a passive, uncritical, slavish mode of existence. And of course an uncritical person, content to live a beast-like existence and lacking in what Hamlet calls 'discourse of reason', is the type that tyrants have always preferred. The point connects with Hamlet's general critique of lust. What is objectionable about lust is the way it reduces humans to animals, driven by 'appetite' (1.2.144) and incapable of reflecting upon or restraining their actions. Such gross appetitiveness is part and parcel of tyranny: tyrants are driven to seize what they desire (power, wealth, women), and, likewise, they rely upon the unthinking acquiescence of others (Gertrude, for example). The connection between unfettered sensuality and tyranny is one Shakespeare (along with other Renaissance writers) keeps returning to.[4] What Hamlet admires in art is thought: art is the antithesis of empty shows that pander to the lust for spectacle. Hamlet's aesthetic commitments stand for freedom and against bread and circuses.

When Hamlet meets the grave-digger in Act Five he displays a certain status-consciousness. Momentarily wrong-footed by the captious and logic-chopping First Clown, he comments to Horatio, with some exasperation, 'How absolute the knave is! We must speak by the card, or equivocation will undo us. By the Lord, Horatio, this three years I have took note of it: the age is grown so picked that the toe of the peasant comes so near the heel of the courtier he galls his kibe' (5.1.137–41). Hamlet's joke is piquant. The age has become over-refined and thrusting. Now even the ordinary folk play the language-games of the upper echelons, and press so hard behind their betters that they chafe at the blisters on their masters' heels. But what is also of note in this scene is Hamlet's relaxed and friendly demeanour with the First Clown. He begins with an exchange of banter, which puts them on an equal footing. When he asks the Clown whose grave he is digging, and gets the reply 'Mine, sir' (5.1.119), he comes back with 'I think it be thine, indeed, for thou liest in't' (5.1.122, punning on 'lie'), and on it goes. Characteristically, Hamlet does not stand on ceremony: he relishes this wit-combat with a plebeian.

13

Othello

'Her voice,' Lear says of Cordelia, 'was ever soft, / Gentle, and low, an excellent thing in woman' (*King Lear*, 5.3.277–8). Lear does not mean Cordelia was weak. In the opening of the play she stands up to her father with enormous strength of will. But unlike her sisters, Cordelia is 'gentle'. When she meets Lear after her return to Britain she is without righteous vindication, and only wishes to look after him.

Something similar might be said of Desdemona. She is the absolutely dutiful wife and, like Cordelia, argues that on marriage a woman transfers her primary allegiance from father to husband. 'My noble father,' she addresses Brabantio before the Duke and Senators,

> I do perceive here a divided duty.
> To you I am bound for life and education;
> My life and education both do learn me
> How to respect you. You are the lord of duty;
> I am hitherto your daughter. But here's my husband,
> And so much duty as my mother showed
> To you, preferring you before her father,
> So much I challenge that I may profess
> Due to the Moor my lord. (1.3.182–91)

This is close to Cordelia's criticism of her insincere sisters when they proclaim their total love for their father:

Why have my sisters husbands if they say
They love you all? Haply, when I shall wed,
That lord whose hand must take my plight shall carry
Half my love with him, half my care and duty.
Sure I shall never marry like my sisters,
To love my father all. (1.1.99–104)

Both Desdemona and Cordelia speak of their 'duty' to the principal men in their lives (father, husband); both understand themselves as subordinate to these men. Importantly, however, neither *sounds* submissive. Both speak eloquently, logically, authoritatively. Both are wrathfully cast off by their fathers yet are uncowed and do not give in. Both plays open with quiet yet conscious and determined acts of *rebellion*. As Iago points out, Desdemona 'deceive[d] her father' in marrying Othello (3.3.220); Brabantio earlier uses the same words of her (1.3.296). She has undermined patriarchal authority: 'Fathers, from hence trust not your daughters' minds' (1.1.174).

What Cordelia and Desdemona *say*, then, about 'duty' is less important than what they *do*, their acts of defiance. Desdemona herself testifies to her wilfulness. Her 'downright violence and storm of fortunes' (1.3.252) – a line David Bevington glosses as 'My plain and total breach of social custom' – shows how much she desires Othello. She speaks openly about her desire, pointing out to the Senators that if she is not permitted to travel to Cyprus with her new husband she will be 'bereft' of the 'rites' of love (1.3.260). Her desire is emphasized in a subtle touch of dialogue:

A SENATOR [to Othello]
You must away tonight.

DESDEMONA
Tonight, my lord? (1.3.280–1)

Shakespeare explicitly endorses female sexuality: Desdemona is taken aback at the thought that she will miss out on her first night with Othello.

Shakespeare reserves an anti-sex rhetoric for the play's villain. Iago, rather in the manner of the Stoic philosophers of Greece and Rome, articulates a doctrine of rational self-control. Roderigo claims he cannot help being in love with Desdemona: 'it is not in [his] virtue' (that is, power) 'to amend it' (1.3.321). But Iago insists that "Tis in ourselves that we are thus or thus' (1.3.322–3): ultimately who we are is always a question of our free choice. Roderigo may *feel* as if he has no choice in the matter, but his pursuit of Desdemona is simply a consequence of his having decided that sexual pleasure is the most important thing in life. 'But we have reason,' lectures Iago, 'to cool our raging motions, our carnal stings, our unbitted' (or unrestrained) 'lusts' (1.3.332–4): we have the ability, should we exercise reason, to control desire. This cold, ascetic doctrine is the antithesis of what Desdemona and Othello live for – they have chosen love. Desdemona's elopement was a matter of 'downright violence'; Othello thinks 'Chaos [would] come again' (3.3.100) should he ever fall out of love with her. None of this is the language of what Theseus, in *A Midsummer Night's Dream*, calls 'cool reason' (5.1.6). Yet we are hardly supposed to prefer Iago, one of Shakespeare's ugliest creations, to these wilful lovers.[1]

The key fact about Desdemona is her elopement with a black man. Brabantio is convinced magic was involved: his daughter could not deliberately have married this 'extravagant and wheeling stranger / Of here and everywhere' (1.1.139). And this is Iago's opening: he can play upon the scandalous nature of Desdemona's choice. He does not need to do much work here, but can rely on attitudes towards such behaviour widely accepted in Venice – though not universally: it is remarkable that neither the Duke nor Senators share Brabantio's horror at the marriage (but then they have important business to transact with Othello – the defence of Cyprus against the Turks). Shakespeare here and elsewhere in the play invites us to notice how the same action, Desdemona's marrying Othello, can be understood in starkly different ways. Our sense of reality is always shaped by the attitudes we bring to it. What Shakespeare does in *Othello* is show the potentially lethal effect of certain ways of describing reality.

Iago exploits the racist view that sex between a black man and white woman is essentially unnatural. Desdemona's action is 'a gross revolt' (1.1.137) against the natural order. Mixing races is mixing species. Othello is likened to an Arab or African horse: 'your daughter [is] covered with a Barbary horse', Iago cries out to Brabantio (1.1.114). Will Brabantio have his grandsons neigh? His kinsmen horses? (1.1.114–16). Everything about the relationship is awry, bestial: 'Even now, now, very now, an old black ram / Is tupping your white ewe' (1.1.90–1). Social classes are mixed up too, Iago painting a sordid picture of the elopement itself: 'your fair daughter', he says to Brabantio, has been 'Transported with no worse nor better guard' than 'a knave of common hire, a gondolier' (1.1.125–8). All is topsy-turvy, religion itself violated. If the marriage stands, says Brabantio, 'Bondslaves and pagans shall our statesmen be' (1.2.101).

Hence Brabantio believes Desdemona cannot have *chosen* marriage. She must have been 'bound' by 'chains of magic' (1.2.66); nothing else could send her to 'the gross clasps of a lascivious Moor' (1.1.129). She might have married any of the 'wealthy curled darlings of our nation' (1.2.69) – an unfortunate choice of words on Brabantio's part as it does make them sound rather insipid. She cannot voluntarily have elected to incur 'a general mock' (1.2.70) – no one will approve her action – by running away 'to the sooty bosom' of Othello (1.2.71), 'a thing' not of 'delight' but 'fear' (1.2.72). Only 'witchcraft' can explain a case of 'nature so preposterously ... err[ing]' (1.3.64, 66) – 'preposterous' having here the sense of 'back-to-front', 'inverted'. Nature has been wrenched from its normal trajectory. This idea of what nature wants, and of the *un*naturalness of Desdemona's desire, is picked up later by Iago when he says that, in nature, like tends to like. And the key point is that this is what Othello *himself* deep down already fears. He cannot quite believe that his and Desdemona's union is natural. Of course consciously he does not doubt, as he says, that 'Desdemona's honest' (3.3.241). But then, unbidden, the old primitive idea of 'nature' reasserts itself in his mind: 'And yet,' he muses, 'how nature, erring from itself – ' (3.3.243). Iago doesn't let him finish the sentence before drawing out the nasty conclusion:

> Ay, there's the point! As – to be bold with you –
> Not to affect many proposed matches
> Of her own clime, complexion, and degree,
> Whereto we see in all things nature tends –
> Foh! One may smell in such a will most rank,
> Foul disproportion, thoughts unnatural. (3.3.244–9)

By nature, Desdemona should have chosen her husband from someone of her own country ('clime'), race ('complexion') and rank ('degree'). That 'Against all rules of nature' (1.3.103) she has instead fallen 'in love with what she feared to look on' (100), as Brabantio puts it, indicates that something else – 'a will most rank', or lust – is determining her actions. Once he has articulated what lies barely acknowledged in Othello's own mind, Iago's work is done. Any trivial piece of evidence – a handkerchief – can be dragged in to convince Othello of Desdemona's infidelity. Othello believes Iago's slanders because they chime with a set of tacit assumptions he holds about how the world is.

One such assumption is that a chaste white woman could not love a black man. 'Haply, for I am black,' Othello muses, 'And have not those soft parts of conversation / That chamberers have …' (3.3.279–81) – 'chamberers' being courtiers with refined, polished manners. Othello is black, a rough soldier, a 'stranger' or foreigner: how could a pure woman love him? And Othello does think blackness a defect. Consider his statement that his 'name, that was as fresh / As Dian's visage, is now begrimed and black / As mine own face' (3.3.402–4). Diana is the goddess of chastity and the silvery shining moon; blackness is grime and filth.

Another assumption Shakespeare highlights in the play is that women are less rational, more subject to the passions (notably the erotic ones) than men. The idea that women, given half a chance, would betray their husbands was standard in the age, and lies behind all the cuckold jokes in Renaissance literature – the idea that any man might be about to sprout horns from his head, legendary sign of the humiliated deceived husband. Othello grimly alludes to this motif when he complains to Desdemona of 'a pain upon [his] forehead' (3.3.300). The same view of women emerges when he exclaims, 'Oh, curse of marriage, / That we can call these delicate creatures ours / And not their appetites!' (3.3.284–6). Or, as Iago says, with no doubt a nod and a wink to the men in the audience, 'There's millions now alive / That nightly lie in those unproper beds / Which they dare swear peculiar' (4.1.68–70) – countless husbands lie in beds that are not truly theirs but which they would swear blind are.

But these understandings of blackness and women do not go unchallenged. The Duke tries to calm Brabantio with the observation that 'If virtue no delighted beauty lack, / Your son-in-law is far more fair than black' (1.3.292–3) – it is Othello's high moral character and valour that makes him attractive. Othello himself points out he is descended 'From men of royal siege' or rank (1.2.22). Iago's description of him as an 'extravagant and wheeling stranger / Of here and everywhere' is promptly and romantically redescribed by Othello: he speaks instead of his 'unhoused free condition' (1.2.26 – though later still Iago will call him 'an erring [i.e., wandering] barbarian' (1.3.358)). Iago himself admits that 'The Moor is of a free and open [i.e., frank and unsuspecting] nature' (1.3.400). To the Herald Othello is 'our noble general' (2.2.11). The play required its original audience to revise their prejudices against Moors and barbarians – the true devil of the play is not black but white.[2]

Nor is the Iago line on women unchallenged: Desdemona is actually faithful. And there is the all-important voice of her waiting-woman Emilia, an extraordinarily outspoken character. She dies braving Iago's tyranny by telling the truth: 'So speaking as I think, alas, I die' (5.2.260). Emilia provides an alternative view on women. She attacks male selfishness and hypocrisy, and protests sexual exploitation: men 'are all but stomachs, and we all but food; / They eat us hungerly, and when they are full / They belch us' (3.4.106–8). And she offers an eloquent rebuttal of the claim that women cannot be trusted. Yes, 'wives' do 'fall', but for all that are no worse than the men. Often they fall because of their husbands' infidelity and ill-treatment; or because of the 'peevish jealousies' men are subject to, 'Throwing restraint upon us'; or because husbands 'strike' women; or because they unjustly reduce their allowances (4.3.89–94). Men and women are cut from the same cloth. Husbands deceive their wives because of weakness and desire for pleasure (4.3.99–102). Well, don't women have 'affections, / Desires for sport, and frailty, as men have?' (4.3.103–4). Given the time and place in which it was written, Emilia's is a remarkable argument for equality and mutuality between men and women. Wives 'have sense' – sensory perception and appetite – just like men: 'They see, and smell, / And have their palates both for sweet and sour, / As husbands have' (4.3.97–9). The whole speech is extraordinarily close in content to Shylock's equally powerful statement about the humanity of the Jews in *The Merchant of Venice*, in which he claims that Jews are no different from Christians (3.1.55–63). So here too a reigning description of women as unfaithful is challenged from within the play itself.

Othello shows us how certain dominant modes of understanding human beings (Moors and women, in this case) can constrain and even destroy them. Both Othello and Desdemona, for all their acting against convention, are imprisoned and ultimately destroyed by these assumptions. (Perhaps, in a way, even Iago is: bizarrely, he seems to imagine that Othello may have had an affair with Emilia and that Michael Cassio too has designs on her – see his suspicion that 'the lusty Moor / Hath leaped into my seat' and the remark on 'fear[ing] Cassio with [his] nightcap' (2.1.297–9, 309).) *Othello* shows how murderous particular ways of describing experience can be. Tracing the corrosive, inexorable power of such descriptions on even the most intimate of personal relationships, the play is genuinely tragic, in the traditional sense of that word: it demonstrates the constraints placed on the actions and desires of its protagonists. But in so doing it also demonstrates that these constraints are *no more* than descriptions – cultural fictions like the showy 'lendings' that make Lear a king. In other words, Iago's appeal to 'nature' is a double-edged sword – in the end, the play's challenge to any moderately reflective spectator is to understand that what he or she thinks of as 'natural' may in fact be a matter of cultural invention. We are always free to question the descriptions of reality that we inherit, to open ourselves to better or truer ones.

14

King Lear

King Lear displays an extraordinary speculative freedom: it is
a laboratory for testing out new ideas. Characters repeatedly
ask general questions, and make general statements, about the
nature of the world they find themselves in – about the divine,
nature, justice, evil. 'Is there any cause in nature that makes
these hard hearts?' asks Lear (3.6.76–7): does the evil in the
world of the play come from nature itself, so that there is no
hope of things ever being different, or is there some other way
of looking at this problem? *Lear* debates the key question raised
in Part One of this book: what portion of human suffering is
fated or unavoidable, and what somehow chosen by us?

In many respects, the play mounts a powerful case for the
ineradicable nature of human misfortune. Suffering is part of
'the mystery of things' (5.3.16). Humanity is 'bound / Upon
a wheel of fire' (4.7.47–8). Suffering will always exist, no
matter what social order obtains. The play shares much of the
profound pessimism of Greek tragedy: existence *is* suffering.
'When we are born,' says Lear, 'we cry that we are come / To
this great stage of fools' (4.6.179–83).

Yet it also stages a debate about the nature of existence
– shows human beings actively thinking about their world,
choosing how they will understand it, and, therefore,
themselves. At least three ideas about the universe are entertained. The first is that the gods love justice, punish the wicked
and reward the good: when Albany hears that Cornwall's

servant has slain his master in an attempt to stop him blinding Gloucester, he exclaims 'This shows you are above, / You justicers, that these our nether crimes / So speedily can venge!' (4.2.79–81). Gloucester, for his part, believes 'The winged Vengeance' will punish Lear's bad daughters (3.7.69) and Albany prays that 'the heavens' will dispatch 'visible spirits / ... to tame these vile offenses' (4.2.47–8). A second view is that there are no gods, and faith in them is, to quote Edmund, 'foppery' or foolishness (see 1.2.121). What matters is getting ahead; anyone believing in pity, justice or the sanctity of law is naive. There is malicious irony in Gloucester's trusting that the 'ever-gentle gods' (4.6.219) prevented his falling to his death. (Edgar tells him his 'life's a miracle' (4.6.55).) We know he didn't fall from Dover Cliffs: it was all just a therapeutic-theatrical ruse of Edgar's to make Gloucester think life was worth going on with, that he should not commit suicide (4.6.220–1). Equally ironic is Albany's prayer 'The gods defend her!' (5.3.261), followed immediately by Cordelia's dead body being brought in. A third view is that the gods do exist but relish human agony. Gloucester contradicts himself. 'As flies to wanton boys,' he had said earlier, 'are we to th' gods; / They kill us for their sport' (4.1.36–7). And if, with Lear, we believe 'the great gods' sent 'this dreadful pother' or storm to punish the wicked, there is the problem, as Lear recognizes, that it assaults, along with criminals, the innocent poor ('houseless poverty': 3.2.49–50; 3.4.26). So where is justice?

When Gloucester ruminates on Edgar's supposed plot to kill him he invokes an orderly, integrated universe. The human, natural and divine spheres are part of a cosmos or general order. The 'eclipses' he has noticed are linked to other calamities: the cooling of love and friendship, civil wars, treason, conflicts between father and son (1.2.106, 109–12). Edmund and the other villains think this is claptrap. They stand instead for what Gloucester calls 'the wisdom of nature' (1.2.107) – a materialistic-naturalistic-proto-scientific outlook. There is no larger whole. What happens in cities, countries, families is not conditioned by an overarching divine or extra-human pattern.

The world has no moral meaning – the heavens look upon our lot with blank indifference. Goneril mocks her husband Albany as 'a moral fool' (4.2.59). The position is presented by its proponents as realism, but issues in nihilism. All is chance, the ceaseless play of material and human forces. Morality and spirit have nothing to do with it. 'Good' and 'evil' refer to nothing 'out there', beyond human language, customs and conveniences. Regan, Goneril, Edmund are rationalists: what they want, Regan insists, is simply to 'mingle reason' with Lear's 'passion' (2.4.236) – to introduce some clear thinking into the situation. But 'reason' for them is a cold and heartless thing. Like Machiavelli, they see the world solely in terms of power interests.[1] (W. H. Auden described such a brutally rationalistic outlook in his poem 'The Shield of Achilles': 'That girls are raped, that two boys knife a third, / Were axioms to him, who'd never heard / Of any world where promises were kept, / Or one could weep because another wept'.)[2] There is a rationalistic way of understanding the world that dismisses goodness, beauty, truth as pious fictions. For the wicked characters, nature is 'red in tooth and claw', as Tennyson put it.[3] For Lear, Gloucester, Kent and the others it is, on the contrary, full of moral meaning. The question Shakespeare seems especially interested in is what effect such doctrines have on *conduct*: what *Lear* highlights is that electing to see the world in such and such a fashion will have direct consequences for how you act in it. When Edmund declares that his goddess is Nature he liberates himself to behave in particular (immoral) ways. Lear's nature is different. He appeals to Regan, saying that she, unlike Goneril, 'know[s] / The offices of nature, bond of childhood' (2.4.178–9): that is, the duties towards parents that nature imposes upon children everywhere. The tortured Gloucester calls on Edmund to 'enkindle all the sparks of nature / To quit [or avenge] this horrid act' (3.7.89–90). For Lear and Gloucester 'nature' means 'filial love': love is actually an objective part of the natural order. It is of the essence of things that children will honour, love, obey their parents.

All this comes into focus in the scene when Goneril and

Regan insist on reducing (or, as we might put it today, 'ration-alizing') Lear's retinue of a hundred knights. Of course Lear does not, strictly speaking, need these knights. Goneril and Regan can supply his material wants. For Lear, however, the knightly entourage adds meaning and dignity to life. Goneril and Regan are blind to such symbolism, which doesn't connect with anything real or objective for them. The two daughters count down, with arithmetical rigour, just how many followers he needs – 100, 50, 25, 10, 5, 1 ... the inevitable conclusion being he needs none at all. 'Oh, reason not the need!' Lear cries out (2.4.266), in one of the great speeches: even beggars keep something about them that isn't of *purely* utilitarian value, something that (by its very non-utility perhaps) reminds them they aren't animals but people. If you don't give human beings 'more than nature needs', he points out, you make 'Man's life [as] cheap as beast's' (2.4.266–9). Deep down, human existence is a matter of meaning. This is unintelligible to Goneril, Regan, Edmund and Cornwall, who really *do* think human beings are animals (always a handy belief to hold if you want to exploit or kill large numbers of them). The play depicts an intellectual revolution in which the wicked characters strip away old constraining belief systems so as to act in any way they wish. Choosing to see the world in a certain way licenses them to live in it accordingly.

As we saw in Part One, tyranny is a major concern. How large is a king's prerogative? Is it unlimited? Must he listen to counsellors? What if he behaves tyrannically – may his subjects resist? These were burning issues in early and mid-seventeenth century England, which saw growing conflict between Crown and Parliament. In the 1640s, tension between Parliament and Charles would erupt into Civil War, concluding with Charles's execution in 1649. *King Lear* debates questions that would over time lead men and women into bitter political and religious conflict.

Lear is about tyranny and the consequences of kingly arrogance. (Lear is a victim, but we must not forget his own tyrannical conduct: the ruination of the realm is a direct result of his absolute insistence on 'divid[ing] / In three our kingdom' (1.1.37–8).) The play shows in horrific detail what follows upon the morally anarchic lust for power of certain members of the ruling elite. Certainly here, as in many other plays of the period, 'The Prince of Darkness [i.e., the devil] is a gentleman' (3.4.141): it is the factionalism and lack of restraint of the elite that brings the country to the apocalypse. But the problem goes deeper still, into the texture of everyday life. Selfishness and materialism have reigned unchecked. Lear finds more compassion and help 'hovel[ed] … with swine and rogues forlorn' (4.7.40) than he does in the great 'hard house' (3.2.63), now under the control of Cornwall, to which Kent applies unsuccessfully for entrance (3.2.65–6). This image of a stony-hearted class of rich men is pervasive. (We have encountered Lear's 'great image of authority', that of the farmer's dog chasing away a beggar desperate for food and shelter.) In Lear's revolutionary speech on the law's injustice he recognizes that 'Through tattered clothes small vices do appear; / Robes and furred gowns hide all' (4.6.164–5). The law aids and abets wealthy criminals but punishes the misdemeanours of the poor. The 'rascal beadle', or corrupt parish officer, whips the very 'whore' he 'hotly lusts to use' (4.6.160, 160–2). Lear's conclusion is that 'None does offend' (4.6.168) – all of us are rascals and no one should be singled out for retribution. The weight of Lear's tirade in this extraordinary scene is directed against the hypocrisy and outrages of the rich. Edgar puts paid to the objection that Lear is mad and that we cannot take what he says seriously: 'matter and impertinency [i.e., sense and nonsense] mixed, / Reason *in* madness!' (4.6.174–5, my emphasis).

The egalitarian theme continues, in a different key, when Lear and Cordelia are reunited. Lear grasps how unreal are all distinctions of title and rank. Earlier he acknowledged the central truth that, in nature, we are equal. Kings are no different from lesser men. Now he understands how his enemies 'flattered [him] like a dog' (4.6.96–7). Everyone slavishly agreed with him, he notes of these toadies, said 'ay and no to everything that I said ay and no to' (4.6.98–9). He knows now all that was sham. He might be a king, but even he can't stop the rain drenching him or the cold wind making his teeth chatter (4.6.100–1). 'They told me I was everything. 'Tis a lie', he realizes: 'I am not ague-proof [i.e., able to withstand illness or fever]' (4.6.104–5). It is no exaggeration to say that this is a revolutionary position. Lear strips monarchy of its mystic quasi-magical foundation. There is nothing in nature separating a king from a beggar: both are needy vulnerable creatures. The Fool reminds Lear of the distinction between the 'titles' he has 'given away' and the one title he was 'born with' like the rest of us: 'fool' (1.4.146–68).

The implication of this line of thinking is shattering. If kings are no better than beggars, what is the basis of their authority? This disenchanting view of power is memorably articulated in the conversation with Cordelia just as she and Lear are taken off to prison. There, Lear imagines, they will be able to live together happy and alone. Liberated from the pretensions of court life, they will be able to

> laugh
> At gilded butterflies, and hear poor rogues
> Talk of court news; and we'll talk with them too –
> Who loses and who wins; who's in, who's out –
> And take upon 's the mystery of things,
> As if we were God's spies; and we'll wear out,
> In a walled prison, packs and sects of great ones,
> That ebb and flow by the moon. (5.3.12–19)

From the perspective of eternity, court politicking appears tawdry and silly; vain and gaudily attired courtiers are 'gilded butterflies'. And from their secluded seat of retirement (their prison cell), Lear and Cordelia will be able to listen to all that court gossip about who's up and who's down without caring about it – will be 'God's spies', blissfully detached but understanding observers of the human comedy, this great stage of fools. In a sense their life will be more real and substantial as they 'live, / And pray, and sing' (5.3.11–12) in their 'walled prison' than the lives of court politicians ('great ones'), men whose fortunes 'ebb and flow by the moon', are continually unstable and vulnerable. Considerations such as these make their prison, as Hamlet says of death, 'a consummation / Devoutly to be wished' (3.1.64–5).

As with other plays discussed in this book, the play worries away at this whole problem of rank. It is perhaps going too far to claim that *Lear* is a 'democratic' play. The king and Kent are themselves outraged at the offhand behaviour of the servant Oswald towards Lear. Kent abuses Oswald as a 'slave', a 'beastly knave', with no right to 'wear a sword' (the privilege of a gentleman: see 2.2.70, 73). 'I'll teach you differences' (that is, distinctions of status) he threatens Oswald (1.4.88), before thrashing him for pretension and impudence. When, disguised as the 'poor' man Caius, Kent first meets Lear, he tells the king he wants to serve him because Lear has 'that in [his] countenance which I would fain call master' (1.4.19, 27–8). In other words, Kent sees in Lear's appearance and bearing what he calls 'Authority' (1.4.30) – which suggests that kingliness is somehow a quality inscribed onto the very body of Lear, as if the right to rule was a natural faculty rather than a mere conventional title anybody might enjoy. Still, Oswald is no democrat either. When he encounters Edgar disguised as a 'most poor man' helping Gloucester, he abuses him as 'bold peasant', 'slave' and 'villain' (4.6.224, 234, 239, 249). Having himself climbed up the greasy pole he kicks those further down. Lear and Kent are no democrats, but it is a stretch to liken their status-consciousness to the social-climbing Oswald's. Oswald is only out for himself. He is 'duteous to the vices of [his] mistress' Goneril (4.6.256), Edgar tells us. This is not how Kent acted *vis-à-vis* Lear. Rather than pandering to his master's vices, Kent tried to curb them. This is what ideas like hierarchy and duty mean to the good characters in the play: relations of love, honourable, thoughtful and free service, care. Unlike the

independent-minded Kent, if it suits Oswald to pander to the
bad impulses of his master that is precisely what he will do.

The overall impression, however, of elite life conveyed by
King Lear is summed up in the phrase Shakespeare's Titus
uses to describe the Rome of the emperors: 'a wilderness of
tigers' (*Titus Andronicus*, 3.1.54). As many have noticed,
Lear is replete with animal imagery. Elite life is a scene of
gangsterism. Everything in the kingdom is weighted against
the have-nots: as the Fool says, in a socio-economic understanding of the goddess Fortuna, 'Fortune, that arrant whore, /
Ne'er turns the key to th' poor' (2.4.51–2). The image of the
cold hungry beggar locked out from the great house is central.
'Shut up your doors, my lord,' says Cornwall to Gloucester
once the king has left the castle in high rage, ''tis a wild night. /
… Come out o'th' storm' (echoing Regan's earlier counsel to
Gloucester to 'Shut up your doors' (2.4.310–11, 306)). Edgar's
disguise is a vehicle for highlighting the extent and depth of
the suffering in the kingdom: 'Who gives anything to poor
Tom?' he asks plaintively: 'Tom's a-cold' (3.4.50, 57). Tom
stands in for the persecuted and destitute thousands of
Lear's realm and, of course, Elizabeth's and James's. He is
'whipped from tithing to tithing', or parish to parish, 'and
stock-punished and imprisoned' (3.4.133–4). Loyalty in this
competitive world of power-seekers is virtually unknown,
as the Fool acerbically observes: 'That sir which serves and
seeks for gain, / And follows but for form, / Will pack [i.e.,
be off] when it begins to rain / And leave thee in the storm'
(2.4.76–9). The Fool and Kent do not follow this example of
sleazy followers who are only out for themselves and merely
pretend to serve their masters – but they are the exception to
the rule. (Iago in *Othello* embodies this aggressive individu-
alism too: he despises the 'duteous' and 'honest' servant, who
'Wears out his time, much like his master's ass', serving a lord
who, 'when he's old', straightaway dismisses him. He instead
is one of those who, 'throwing but shows of service on their
lords, / … / Do themselves homage' (*Othello*, 1.1.47, 51, 49,
50, 54–6).) The Fool's mordantly cynical advice reflects the

general wisdom: 'Let go thy hold when a great wheel runs down a hill lest it break thy neck with following; but the great one that goes upward, let him draw thee after' (2.4.70–3).

Edgar, Lear, Kent and Gloucester all experience what it is like to be poor and vulnerable, and Kent is put in the stocks like any common offender. It is true that, as Lear confesses, he has 'ta'en / Too little care of this!' (3.4.32–3) – failed to notice the injustice, poverty and inequity in his kingdom. The best characters in the ruling elite are not free of culpability for the state of the kingdom, and their moral progress depends upon the extent to which they come to identify with the lot of the outcast and immiserated.[4] When Edgar says to his father Gloucester that he is 'A most poor man, made tame to fortune's blows' (4.6.224), this is in one sense a fiction. But in another sense it is true: Edgar has come to learn what it might feel like to be a 'poor man' made submissive because of a run of bad luck.

Lear continually opens up the question of what to do in the face of an illegitimate government. The play endorses armed resistance towards a barbaric and violent tyranny when we witness the country liberated by the French forces under Cordelia. And the common people are starting to turn against the rapacious elite: the Servant who tries to stop the torture of Gloucester is a straw in the wind – people are openly standing up to the Cornwall faction. (As we saw, Regan suspects that the public sight of the blinded Gloucester 'moves / All hearts against us' (4.5.12–13).) Gloucester's torture and mutilation sees him repeatedly accused of treason: 'the traitor Gloucester', 'your traitorous father', 'the traitor Gloucester', 'the traitor', 'So white, and such a traitor?', 'the traitors / Late footed in the kingdom', and so on (3.7.3, 8, 23, 28, 38, 45–6). When Oswald is about to murder Gloucester he abuses him as an 'old unhappy traitor' and 'a published traitor' (4.6.231, 235). For Regan he is 'that blind traitor' (4.5.39). But the very people accusing others of treason are the worst characters in the play, a fact even minimally attentive audience members would have found food for thought; and, of course, accusations of treason were not unknown in the world outside the playhouse. An audience is being asked to decide for itself who are and who are not the true traitors. In this respect alone the play fosters a critical attitude towards power.

With its shocking descent into cruelty and anarchy, *King Lear* seems an irredeemably bleak work. Since the Second World War it has probably displaced *Hamlet* as the play speaking most powerfully to us today.[5] Its depiction of a world torn apart by extreme political violence and naked will-to-power resonates with an age that has known the tyrannies of Hitler, Stalin, Mao and countless others. It ends with an exhausted and ruined country. But a shred of hope can be picked from the ashes. Edgar has learned lessons in the netherworld of the poor that will make him a different sort of king from Lear. One could not speak freely in Lear's court; in the new kingdom people will be able to 'Speak what [they] feel, not what [they] ought to say' (5.3.330). Throughout people bravely resist tyranny: Gloucester is tortured, we should remember, because he is in league with the French forces helping Lear; he has sent the king to Dover in an attempt to save him. In the end, such resistance makes us feel all is not lost: 'When hell is denounced from within, it ceases to be hell'.[6]

15

Antony and Cleopatra

In *King Lear*, freedom figured as both an existential problem (is suffering ineradicable, simply a part of human life itself?) and a political and social one (has the elite ruled for the sake of its own selfish interests, 'ta'en / Too little care' of and oppressed the ordinary people of the kingdom (3.4.32–3)?). In *Antony and Cleopatra*, Shakespeare once again takes up the question of the nature and conditions of human freedom – but here freedom is understood differently, as a problem of the relation between our public and private selves. Privileging the private sphere as the realm of greatest human freedom (here imagined as a space for friendship, sensual pleasure and erotic love), the play operates along lines that we would recognize as 'modern', in the sense of a commitment to individuality and the pursuit of private, or personal, preferences.

The first lines of the play highlight the excessiveness of the Roman general Antony's behaviour in Egypt, where he devotes himself to a life of sensual pleasure with the gorgeous 'eastern star' (5.2.308) Cleopatra: 'Nay,' laments Antony's follower Philo, 'this dotage' (or foolish affection) 'of our general's / O'erflows the measure' (1.1.1–2). Antony's passion for Cleopatra exceeds the classical ideal of moderation. 'There's beggary,' or little value, 'in the love that can be reckoned' (1.1.15), Antony asserts: he loves Cleopatra infinitely and beyond any form of calculation. Cleopatra teasingly says she will 'set a bourn' (or limit) to how far she is to be loved by Antony (1.1.16); but Antony avers she will need to find a new universe ('new heaven, new earth') to confine this love (1.1.17). Antony is hopelessly, irrationally in love with this woman whose 'tawny front' (1.1.6), or dark face, Philo asserts in his casually racist way, hardly merits his master's attentions. This great military commander now serves 'a gypsy's lust' (1.1.10), is nothing other than 'a strumpet's fool' (1.1.13). This is all presented in the harshest terms: what Antony's friends feel about their commander's romance is, above all, embarrassment: Antony is failing himself, publicly sullying his good name.

Again and again the play returns to this theme of Antony's shame – and Antony himself, it must be admitted, is one of his most vehement critics. He fully grasps how Cleopatra has charmed him, and wonders at his seeming inability to alter course. He is frightened of losing himself, or the better part of himself, in this sexual obsession.[1] 'These strong Egyptian fetters I must break,' he resolves, 'Or lose myself in dotage' (1.2.122–3). But it is no use: he is overwhelmed by Cleopatra's appeal. The issue the play raises, then, is the nature of desire and the self. What is it to want something that (so we believe) we do not *really* want? That one might 'lose' oneself, or not live up to one's best self, is a complex notion (Antony speaks of his 'worthiest self' (4.12.47)). Philo raises this problem of self-division early on when he says that 'sometimes ... [Antony] is not Antony', that he fails to display 'that great property', or unique characteristic (1.1.59, 60), usual with him. As far as Cleopatra is concerned, however, Antony is *most* Antony when he is a lover and bon vivant rather than soldier and politician. She interprets a momentary absence as a regrettable lapse from his pleasure-seeking ways: 'He was disposed to mirth, but on the sudden / A Roman thought hath struck him' (1.2.87–8). Here Antony's *Romanitas*, his sense of duty and masculine honour, appears as an extraneous, and therefore dubious, piece of social conditioning; his *real* character is mirthful. Romanness here is equivalent to what Jean-Paul Sartre called 'the spirit of seriousness' (580) – that is, the mistake of identifying one's self with one's external social function or office, as if one has no choice or freedom in the matter: one *is* a general, a Roman, a public man and so on. The play raises the possibility that, as Pompey's friend Menas suggests, we may be in important respects 'ignorant of ourselves', and as such 'Beg often our own harms' (2.1.5, 6), desire the things that harm us. Heirs of a philosophical tradition going all the way back to Socrates, we tend to equate our 'worthiest self' with reason (this is the same tradition that, as discussed in Part One, sees tyranny as consisting of a lack of self-government on the part of the tyrant). But Antony 'would make his will', or sexual desire, 'Lord of his reason' (3.13.3–4). This account, of course, still leaves open the question whether or not such desires are just as real and authentic as more wholesome or socially acceptable ones: perhaps Antony *should not* desire to spend his days with Cleopatra (a ruinous course of conduct) but equally, perhaps, he really *does* desire so to spend them. Perhaps Antony is more Egyptian than he realizes? There is an important ambiguity in that '*would make* his will ...': the active phrasing conveys an element of choice, as if Antony is not, in fact, helplessly borne along by sexual instinct (like an animal) but at some level freely elects to pursue his scandalous lifestyle.

Nevertheless, Antony does not want to own up to the possibility that he is, at heart, a hedonistic Egyptian. His failure to render Caesar the help he promised him he dismisses as a case of his temporarily lacking self-awareness: 'poisoned hours had bound [him] up / From [his] own knowledge' (2.2.96–7). At such hours Antony lacked self-knowledge – another case, it appears, of Antony not being Antony.[2] As far as he is concerned he really *is* a Roman, and identical with all the duties that go along with Romanness – the rest is just an epicurean excursion from his 'worthiest self'. The play frequently provides a morally outraged perspective on both Antony and Cleopatra, which fits well with this notion of high and low selves. After the sea-battle of Actium, when Cleopatra flees with her ships and Antony impulsively follows, his friend Scarus can barely believe his master's conduct: 'I never saw an action of such shame', he laments: 'Experience, manhood, honor, ne'er before / Did violate so itself' (3.10.22–4). It is Antony's *self-violation* that horrifies Scarus – but as the play goes on we are likely to wonder if he is misconstruing what is going on here: Antony might be never so much himself as when fully an Alexandrian.

For the truth is that, while the play gives expression to such conventional sentiments as Scarus's, it is far more excited by reckless convention-breaking. All the poetry, glamour and splendour of the play is on the side of libertarian abandonment. Romanness seems by comparison drab and prim. *Antony and Cleopatra* in this regard might be said to effect a Nietzschean 'revaluation of all values'.[3] Nietzsche looked forward to a day when the values the moral tradition had taken for granted would be downgraded, and attitudes and modes of behaviour conventionally stigmatized would be celebrated. Perhaps the most notable example of a revaluation of values occurs at the beginning of the play, when Antony delivers a speech that turns received ideas upside down:

> Let Rome in Tiber melt and the wide arch
> Of the ranged empire fall! Here is my space.
> Kingdoms are clay; our dungy earth alike
> Feeds beast as man. The nobleness of life
> Is to do thus ... (1.1.35–9)

Probably Antony kisses or embraces Cleopatra here. But the gist of what he is saying is clear: a sensual hedonistic lifestyle is true 'nobleness' – certainly more noble than the political life of republics and kingdoms. It is hard to emphasize how breathtaking a claim this must have seemed to many of Shakespeare's auditors. Courtly and aristocratic culture in Europe was heir to a long tradition of classicizing or Christian thought that paired certain concepts, prioritizing one term over the other. Thus soul would be privileged over body, reason over the passions, public life over private existence, and so on. But it is such well established hierarchical pairs that Antony violently upturns. The lover's life is *nobler* than that of the prince or captain. It is not ruling a well-ordered and extensive empire that counts – let that fall, let Rome herself melt into the Tiber; far better to devote oneself to love and happiness in Egypt. Antony reverses the traditional claim of the European medieval and Renaissance aristocracy that a life dedicated to great affairs – government and war, the court and the camp – is preferable to the (sub-human) pursuit of pleasure. Actually, asserts Antony, kingdoms and empires are in the end just earth, which sustains animals and plants as well as men. Being 'spacious' or rich in the 'possession of dirt', as Hamlet describes the ridiculous aristocrat Osric, is not the alpha and omega of human life. For genuine nobility, one has to 'do thus' – make love.

In this brief speech, then, Antony, like Marlowe's Edward and Calyphas, son of Tamburlaine, breaks with the classical, medieval and Renaissance assumption that war and high political office – life in the council chamber, assembly or senate, or on the field of honour – were the properly human pursuits. For Antony, a truly human life involves expressing one's capacity for pleasure, play and erotic fulfilment. The remarkable fact about both Antony and Cleopatra is that through sheer force of personality they make what would normally be seen as boorish or immoral behaviour beautiful and attractive – even exemplary. We saw earlier that, according to the priggish and businesslike Caesar, Antony is 'the abstract [i.e., epitome] of all faults': at Alexandria he 'fishes, drinks, and wastes / The lamps of night in revel' (1.4.9, 4–5). He has lost all sense of due hierarchy: rather than keeping aloof from the common people, he has been spotted drinking 'with a slave' (1.4.19) and consorting 'With knaves that smells of sweat' (1.4.21). And there is a bizarre confusion of sex roles: according to Caesar, Antony 'is not more manlike' than Cleopatra, she not 'More womanly' than he (1.4.5,

7) – and then there was the time when, during their love-making, Cleopatra put on Antony's sword, and he donned her headdresses and garments (2.5.22–3). As to Cleopatra, she is, if possible, even more out of step with normal standards. To begin with she does not meet the Elizabethan canons of beauty: she is black, or, as she imagines it, 'with Phoebus' amorous pinches black' (1.5.29) – in her fancy the Sun is her lover and has turned her black from embracing her. (The Elizabethans preferred fair beauties.) What is emphasized is Cleopatra's promiscuity: she is made for sex. Enobarbus jests that it will be 'death' (1.2.150) to the women if Antony and he leave for Rome, but then puns lewdly on the word (as already noted, 'die' could mean 'achieve sexual climax'): Cleopatra 'hath such a celerity [i.e., speed] in dying' (1.2.42, 151). Her affair with Caesar is common knowledge: 'he plowed her, and she cropped' (2.2.238). So sensual is the lifestyle of her court that even the eunuchs have 'fierce affections' (or desires) and think about 'What Venus did with Mars' (1.5.19) – as if the eunuchs themselves are freed by the force of imagination from the constraints of their bodily natures. Cleopatra might be able to 'guess what temperance should be' but she does not 'know … it' (3.13.123–4). All of this ought to be held up for our disapproval. Instead the play makes it beautiful: the justly famous lines that describe the unearthly beauty of Cleopatra as she sailed in her barge on the Nile convince us that her sexual appeal is so wonderful that, again, the normal rules (fidelity, continence) don't apply (see 2.2.201ff.). The usual assumption that a wife ought to be chaste does not apply either. Antony's Octavia, Enobarbus tells us, is 'of a holy, cold, and still conversation' or demeanour (2.6.124–5). But such a dull virtue is of no interest to Antony, who 'will to his Egyptian dish again' (2.6.128). Cleopatra makes chastity seem unpalatably bland.

While the play builds a case against Antony and Cleopatra, all of this material in the end becomes yet one more reason why they should be wondered at – only very extraordinary or charismatic people could turn such demerits to advantage.

The judgement of the play is unequivocal: there has never been, never will be again, people like Antony and Cleopatra. It is petty-minded to submit a charge sheet against them: they brush it off. What would be ugly or base in others is beautiful in them. This sort of thinking, of course, raises problems for morality: it is the rogue's excuse for bad behaviour – and yet we probably recognize too that the identity of the person behind a given action frequently enters into our judgement of it. We have seen how the 'holy priests' are moved to 'bless' Cleopatra even when she is in a state of sexual arousal. Similarly it doesn't matter what mood Antony is in, he looks good anyway: whether he be 'sad or merry, / The violence of either [him] becomes, / So does it no man else' (1.5.62–4). The ability to make passions of any kind attractive sets Antony and Cleopatra apart. Cleopatra may be merely a 'lass', and therefore like any other woman as far as her human needs go, but she is also 'unparalleled' (5.2.316): even making allowance for her abundant narcissism, irrationality, lack of courage, and inconstancy she remains great. Upon hearing a report of Antony's death, she acknowledges her vulnerability and dependence: she is 'No more but e'en a woman, and commanded / By such poor passion as the maid that milks / And does the meanest chares' (4.15.78–80). Given how preoccupied Shakespeare's age was with social rank, this statement is a remarkable assertion of a universal human bond uniting queens with milkmaids (it is the sort of sentiment we find in *Lear*). Egalitarianism, in fact, is a feature of Alexandrian life. Cleopatra may act viciously towards the bearers of bad news (see her treatment of the hapless Messenger), but her court is also full of warmth, affection and easy humour: there is nothing stuck-up or frigidly grandiose and ceremonial about it. Similarly Antony is an instinctive democrat, more comrade and soldier than prince: soldiers and servants are devoted to him. The night before the deciding battle with Caesar witnesses a remarkable scene in which he gives heartfelt thanks to his attendants, addressing them as his 'good fellows', 'honest friends' and 'hearty friends' (4.2.21, 30, 39). The whole scene is moving, not least because the social distinction between master and slave falls into abeyance. (Antony's kindness towards and respect for his servants – he says that while following him 'kings have been [their] fellows' (4.2.14) – can bring to mind Hamlet's democratic manner with the Players.) At the same time, a *natural* aristocracy asserts itself: Antony and Cleopatra simply are *by nature* more wondrous than anyone else round them – but the important point is that this is a natural rather than social distinction. The play drives home the point that, as Cleopatra puts it, ''Tis paltry to be Caesar' (5.2.2). In context what she means is that Caesar is as subject as anyone else to the twists and turns of fate: he is 'but Fortune's knave' or servant (5.2.3). The only real freedom from Fortune lies in death: in this regard suicide is the passage to absolute liberty. But the contempt expressed for Caesar is part of the play's general disavowal of politics and power, which does indeed come to seem 'paltry' by comparison with the ecstatic and love-filled life Antony and Cleopatra make for themselves. Like Donne's lovers, or like Edward II and Gaveston, their world is 'contracted thus' – into the space of a bedroom. Kingdoms are 'clay'.

16

The Revenger's Tragedy

The first words of *The Revenger's Tragedy* capture its scabrously satiric mood: 'Duke, royal lecher' (1.1.1). Almost certainly a pastiche of Shakespeare's *Hamlet*, Middleton's play follows the revenge mission of Vindice against an Italian duke and his family, the Duke having ravished Vindice's beloved Gloriana some years earlier. (Vindice carries round her skull to remind him of his duty.) Unlike Hamlet, however, Vindice is not unequivocally separated from the immoral atmosphere of the court. He may be a disenfranchised critic of his world but, as Hippolito remarks, 'This our age swims within him' (1.3.23); his cynicism and bloodthirstiness make him almost as perverse as those he punishes (consider his ruse to kill the Duke by having him kiss Gloriana's poisoned skull).

Like *Hamlet*, *The Revenger's Tragedy* anatomizes elite sexual depravity. The Duke's sons Supervacuo and Ambitioso plan to kill the dukedom's heir (their brother Lussurioso – though Supervacuo plans to murder Ambitioso once Lussurioso is out of the way (3.1.13–15)). When Vindice learns that Lussurioso wishes to find a 'pander', he is unsurprised: 'his heat is such, / Were there as many concubines as ladies / He would not be contained, he must fly out' (1.1.82–4). And the Duchess, Vindice has pointed out, would 'do' (or have sexual intercourse) with the Devil (1.1.4); she herself later expresses regret at having an 'old cool Duke' for a husband, 'as slack in tongue as in performance' (1.2.74–5). Spurio, the Duke's bastard son, nevertheless claims he had 'a hot-backed', or lustful, 'devil' for a father (1.2.163). The Duchess begins an affair with Spurio to avenge her husband's permitting the execution of his son, the rapist Junior (the crime was a mere matter of 'flesh and blood' (1.2.47), casually explains Junior).

The palace is 'accursed', Vindice points out (1.1.30), but as with the 'ulcerous place' Hamlet speaks of, its corruption is masked. 'How go things at court?' Vindice asks his brother Hippolito. 'In silk and silver,' Hippolito replies, 'never braver' (or finer, 1.1.51–2). The carnivalesque violence of Vindice's revenge would have appealed to those ordinary spectators who resented the decadent and selfish elite, or to those frustrated intellectuals or courtiers who, like Hamlet, lacked 'advancement', or to those who found the servility of life under a monarchy unbearable. The bastard Spurio's wish that 'all the court were turned into a corse' (or corpse) expressed the feelings of many (1.1.36). Certainly the play assumes there are 'ill-contented' persons to be found at court (1.1.77): discontent is as common as the nobleman's consumption (1.1.127). Characters like the aptly named Supervacuo are an instance of the 'needy nothing' Shakespeare's sonnet complains of. This is not a story about an unusually debauched crime family – the Duke and his ilk are typical. Virtuous figures such as Castiza, or Vindice's recently deceased father, or the victim of Junior's rape, the wife of Antonio, who kills herself (1.4), are presented as shining exceptions who prove the rule (even Castiza's own mother is prepared to prostitute her to Lussurioso). As with *Hamlet*, something is rotten in the *state* of Italy, not merely some individuals. Just as Edmund, in *King Lear*, affirms that 'men / Are as the time is' (5.3.31–2) – so that it is futile to stand against the prevailing corruption – so Vindice declares that his decision to disguise himself merely makes him 'a man o'th' time; / For to be honest is not to be i'th' world' (1.1.94–5).

A principal theme is the corrupting effect of money, the 'Indian devil' because made from gold from the Indies (1.3.87). When Vindice discovers his mother will prostitute his sister he excoriates women and money ('Were't not for gold and women there would be no damnation' (2.1.250)). He can remind us here of Shakespeare's Timon, who famously declares that gold can corrupt any moral distinction and 'bless th'accurst' (*Timon of Athens*, 4.3.35). Lussurioso guesses that Gratiana will become a bawd to her daughter because she herself complains of her 'poor estate' (2.1.107) – and Lussurioso could never marry Castiza because 'her blood and ... fortunes / Are both too mean' (1.3.103–4). Middleton makes clear the large role inequality of rank plays in the story. Gratiana is in part vulnerable to Lussurioso's determination to bed her daughter because of that 'poor estate'. As Castiza wryly observes, 'Were not sin rich there would be fewer sinners' (2.1.6). The economic critique is pursued in the crucial interview between Gratiana, the disguised Vindice and Castiza. 'Angels' (that is, gold coins) are devils (2.1.85–8), perverting everything they touch. The issue of lack of 'advancement' at court is key: the word is used repeatedly (2.1.112, 4.4.100, 4.4.135), and Gratiana cannot believe that Castiza would 'Deny advancement, treasure, the Duke's son' (2.1.155).[1] Vindice, testing incognito his sister's virtue, paints a vivid picture of the luxury awaiting Castiza if she will only give herself to Lussurioso:

> O, think upon the pleasure of the palace,
> Secured ease and state, ...
> ...
> Banquets abroad by torch-light, musics, sports,
> Bare-headed vassals ...
> ...
> Nine coaches waiting – hurry, hurry, hurry! (2.1.193–200)

The world of the elite is depicted in all its sordor. Great court ladies embody its decadence. Virtue, insists Vindice to Castiza, is for naïve and simple homespuns, who watch while 'those / Poorer in face and fortune than herself / Walk with a hundred acres on their backs' (2.1.208–10). Chastity is 'the poorer profession', which is why it is seldom followed: 'That's accounted best that's best followed' (2.1.223–4). Only 'mean' and 'ignorant people' worry about chastity, Gratiana informs Castiza: 'The better sort,' she adds, 'cannot abide it; / And by what rule should we square out our lives, / But by our betters' actions?' (2.1.145–8). Only a 'foolish country girl' would bother with 'Chastity' (2.1.81–2): who would want to be 'poor' and 'despised' for that (2.1.78, 79)?

Plays such as *The Revenger's Tragedy* delegitimate elite culture, revealing the infected sore beneath the silk and velvet. It is true the play is in some ways crudely misogynist, but the real target is the vanity of *court* women, great ladies whose greed demands that nature and the common people be racked to gratify their desires. As Vindice remarks, 'many an infant starves / For [a great lady's] superfluous outside' (3.5.86–7), that is, for her cosmetic adornment. It is the superficiality and self-indulgence of court life that is singled out for criticism, not women *per se*. Pampered 'Mighty women that sleep soft' (4.3.11) embody a morally bankrupt order. The play is bent upon exposing noble vice: Castiza, had she given way to her own mother's urgings, would have become a typical aristocratic lady, 'A drab', or prostitute, 'of state, a cloth o' silver slut' (4.4.72). Of course, although she is just such a 'drab of state', the Duchess (like the secretly lecherous lady in *King Lear* who shakes her head at the very name of lust) cannot bear to defile her lips with the word 'strumpet' (2.3.24).

As in *Hamlet*, or *King Lear*, *The Revenger's Tragedy* introduces us to a scene of grossly disordered rule – 'great folks' riots' (3.5.15). (It is crucial to notice that what tragedy on the whole does *not* do is show the 'riots', or moral disorders, of the *common* people: it is invariably the *elite* that is the source of the mayhem the plays describe.) When the Duke supposes Lussurioso is about to slaughter him, he begs him not kill him straightaway, as his 'great sins' will require 'months' of penitence if he is to work them off his account (2.3.9–12). All the Duke's sons bear a murderous hatred towards each other, since each is a political rival of the other. The court is also a place of morbid perversity. The Duke is an aged lecher (one thinks here of Hamlet's nasty vision of aged female lust in his speech to his mother) and even he recognizes the rank unnaturalness of desire at his advanced years: 'Age hot is like a monster to be seen' (2.3.129).

The Revenger's Tragedy is one of the wildest receptions of Shakespeare's art ever written. It pushes the morbidity and violence we find in Shakespearean tragedies to the limit and displays a deeply cynical and amusing tone throughout. But its farcical tone should not blind us to the serious critique that runs through it. It is intensely preoccupied with inequality and illegitimate rule. It is about the vulnerable, those who 'curse fates' and are 'full of want and discontent' (4.1.47). Vindice is a victim of outrageous tyranny. Lussurioso gloats in his ability to 'rear up towers from cottages' (4.1.54) – he can easily make the poor rich if they agree to serve his turn. Other human beings are mere raw material for him and his ilk. Vindice is part of the court, but speaks as an embittered outsider, indignant at the depredations of the great: when Lussurioso asks him what he is thinking of, he replies that he thinks of 'how a great rich man lies a-dying and a poor cobbler tolls the bell for him … when to all men's hearings he whurls and rattles in the throat, he's busy threatening his poor tenants; and this would last me', adds Vindice, 'now some seven years' thinking' (4.2.68–9, 74–7). Such grievous exploitation and oppression of the vulnerable is the permanent background of tragedy in the period.

17

The White Devil

The White Devil opens with Count Lodovico learning he has been banished from the court, and complaining bitterly of the dangers of having great men as one's enemies. But of course Lodovico himself is no ideal courtier, but a drunkard and murderer, and his follower Gasparo points out he has consumed such a mountain of caviar that his provendor is now 'lord of two fair manors' (1.1.20). In keeping with the proverbial ruthlessness of court life he has been abandoned by 'Those noblemen / Which were invited to your prodigal feasts, / Wherein the phoenix scarce could scape your throats' (1.1.21–3): the image is one of outrageous self-indulgence, the phoenix being a fabulously rare bird. So Lodovico is a victim of great men, but also himself part of the grotesquely luxurious scene he denounces so bitterly. As for the Duke Bracciano, Lodovico sums him up in a few lines: the Duke seeks to 'prostitute / The honor' (1.1.41–2) of Vittoria Corombona, the wife of Camillo (Lodovico himself is in love with Bracciano's wife Isabella). The whole of the opening scene is a denunciation of so-called greatness. These great men are wolves (1.1.8–9).[1] They strip others of their possessions and then kill them: 'Great men sell sheep thus to be cut in pieces / When first they have shorn them bare and sold their fleeces' (1.1.62–3). Vicious ruthlessness in getting one's own way is everything.

The ideal or commonwealth conception of kingship is barely present, other than as a standard to show how far short of it come the courts of Rome and Padua. Vittoria connives with Bracciano in the murder of her husband Camillo, the upshot of which is a string of bloody revenges. Cornelia, Vittoria's mother, asserts that courts should be a school of virtue, but the sentiment is barely heard amid the jostling for power, sex and money: 'The lives of princes,' she argues, 'should like dials move, / Whose regular example is so strong / They make the times by them go right or wrong' (1.2.287–9). Princes and the ruling elite are there to set a moral example. Even a corrupt polity can go right by following their model. Of course none of this is in evidence, the courts are sinks of vice. One of the most interesting perspectives on the play's action is provided by Flamineo (Vittoria's brother) who assists her in her adulterous affair with Bracciano (and helps murder Vittoria's husband Camillo along with the Duke's wife Isabella). Flamineo makes clear to his mother, who is shocked at his pandering to the Duke's corrupt desire, that the reason he does so is need – like Bosola in *The Duchess of Malfi* it is poverty that drives him to this ruthless work: Flamineo hopes one day to 'bear [his] beard out of the level of [his] lord's stirrup' – that is, not to have to walk beside his lord's horse as a wretched servant (1.2.313–14). 'What,' exclaims Cornelia indignantly, 'Because we are poor, / Shall we be vicious?' (1.2.314–15). Flamineo gives the realist's viewpoint: those lacking 'preferment' (1.2.329), what in *Hamlet* and *The Revenger's Tragedy* is called 'advancement', cannot afford the luxury of morality. As he bitterly points out to his mother, 'Pray, what means have you, / To keep me from the galleys, or the gallows?' (1.2.315–16). (Webster's villain Bosola, we will see, did it hard in the galleys too.)

The perspective here is interestingly social: instead of a purely moral account of the character (Flamineo is a villain, such people will always exist), we get a structural one – it is the system that is corrupt and corrupting, and it is not villains who need correction so much as the system that creates them. Flamineo expands on this theme of the abuse of the poor by the rich later in the play (foreshadowing here the complaint

of Bosola about the ill-usage ex-soldiers suffer at the hands of
their masters). Flamineo asks his brother Marcello what he
has been rewarded with for his military service to 'the great
duke': 'What hast got?' (3.1.39, 41). The answer, naturally,
is nothing: Marcello's 'wealth', comments Flamineo, is like
that of all 'captains', that is, 'a poor handful, / Which in
thy palm thou bear'st, as men hold water' (3.1.42–3). (One
might compare the bitter complaint of the soldier Iago: when
the 'honest' but 'old' servant has worn out his life for his
master, 'For naught but provender', or food, he is promptly
'cashiered' – dismissed from service. Iago is adamant this
doleful fate is not going to be his; as he says, 'In following
[Othello], I follow but myself' – it is his 'own peculiar [i.e.,
personal] end' that counts (*Othello*, 1.1.51, 50, 60, 62). As
with Flamineo, Iago offers us a vision of a cruelly neglectful
and selfish world. Villains are made as well as born.)

This theme of the selfishness and ruthlessness of 'greatness'
is, as John Russell Brown suggests, a principal concern. As the
Conjuror (employed by Bracciano to poison his wife Isabella)
remarks, 'great men do great good, or else great harm'
(2.2.57). It is harm that the great do in *The White Devil*. As
the banished Lodovico puts it in an extraordinarily cynical
speech:

> Oh, the art,
> The modest form of greatness, that do sit
> Like brides at wedding dinners, with their looks turned
> From the least wanton jests, their puling stomach
> Sick of the modesty, when their thoughts are loose,
> Even acting of those hot and lustful sports
> Are to ensue about midnight ... (4.3.145–51)

Part of the malicious pleasure of the play is in watching such
'wretched eminent things', as they are called by Webster in
The Duchess of Malfi (5.5.131), suffer the brutal punishments
they so richly deserve. The abuse, torment and strangling of
Bracciano is not cursorily depicted but takes some considerable

amount of stage time and is meant to be relished. Plays such as this offer a certain sadistic compensation to their audiences: one might not be a great man – but given the fates of such types would one want to be? At the end, magnates are abandoned by their flatterers: 'As heretofore they have unpeopled towns, divorced friends, and made great houses unhospitable, so now, O justice, where are their flatterers now?' (5.3.42–5). And it is taken for granted how heartless the rulers are: Bracciano is described as the kind of leader more concerned about the cost of a siege than about how many of his subjects die in the prosecution of it (5.3.61–4). At his death Bracciano goes mad; he abuses those around him as having 'Bought and sold offices, oppressed the poor' – but 'I ne'er dreamt on it' he claims (5.3.84–5). Yet this is the pot calling the kettle black. Like King Lear, he must acknowledge his own role in injustice: 'Indeed I am too [i.e., too much to] blame. / For, did you ever hear the dusky raven / Chide blackness? Or was't ever known the devil / Railed against cloven creatures?' (5.3.87–90). In fact Bracciano is not uniquely devilish: again and again the play points to a systemic violence and oppression. Once he is dead we are told that 'The people have liberty to talk / And descant on his vices' (5.3.202–3). Flamineo disapproves: how terrible that princes are 'censured by their slaves' (5.3.204). But the point is that the whole play has taken this kind of liberty of speech, if in a highly oblique and coded way. As Flamineo says in words that must have rung true for many an Elizabethan and Jacobean writer, 'To reprehend princes is dangerous, and to overcommend some of them is palpable lying' (5.3.67–8). It is dangerous to criticize princes directly – but the theatre doesn't need to in order to get its message across.

18

The Duchess of Malfi

Webster's inspiring play, so bold and heterodox on so many fronts, sketches early on the love between the Duchess and her steward (clerk or secretary) Antonio Bologna. Part of the play's challenge to the existing order is the sympathy with which it treats this relationship, despite the vast gap between the two. The relationship is a social fantasy on Webster's part: a low-born man (and intellectual, like Webster and the other writers discussed in this book) wins the hand of an aristocratic woman. (In that regard the play has some resemblance to *Faustus*: we observed how in Marlowe's play a scholar of humble background rises to celebrity status among popes and emperors – and noted how he has his revenge on a dim and arrogant knight who insults him (B-Text, Act Four, Scene One).) Even more unorthodox is Webster's endorsement of the Duchess's sexual desire. She is obliged to woo Antonio – not, as we might expect, the other way round – because of his deference to her rank ('The misery of us that are born great! / We are forced to woo, because none dare woo us' (1.1.442–3)). The Duchess speaks unembarrassedly of 'violent passions' (1.1.446). Webster does not represent female desire as somehow polluted: in the figure of the Duchess the play celebrates its free expression. Of course, once her appalling brothers – Ferdinand, Duke of Calabria (a monster Antonio sums up as 'A most turbulent and perverse nature' (1.1.169)) and the Cardinal – uncover her relationship with Antonio they slander her as a whore. In fact the Duchess is the embodiment of virtue, honour, intelligence and sensitivity. Webster sympathizes with her desire for erotic and emotional freedom and models in her a virtue oriented towards nature and authenticity and away from courtly artifice. The Duchess's own convention-breaking behaviour only augments our admiration. The approach is comparable to Shakespeare's treatment of another maligned heroine, Desdemona: everything about Desdemona's behaviour – her rebellion against her father, her love for (outrageously, as far as Brabantio is concerned) a black, 'extravagant and wheeling stranger' – would, by the standards conventional at the time, tarnish her character. But none of this applies, the play finding her rebellious and unorthodox conduct an essential part of her goodness. We are here close to an idea of virtue that looks ahead to Romantic and modern notions of the noble outsider and authentic, necessarily rebellious, individual.

As we have seen, the frequent and evident injustice of elite rule is a major theme of English Renaissance tragedy. The attitudes and actions of 'These wretched eminent things', as they are alluded to at the end of Webster's play, are held up for fierce disapproval – an extraordinary fact in itself when we recall that many if not most of the spectators of these plays hailed from commonplace backgrounds. Snobbery is a main theme. The love between Antonio, a 'base, low fellow … of no birth' (3.5.118, 120), and the Duchess is an unconscionable scandal in the eyes of her tyrannical brothers (the word 'tyranny' figures heavily). The Duchess must not consider marrying anyone lacking 'the addition, honor' insist the Duke and Cardinal – that is, the all-important aristocratic title (1.1.298). Ferdinand rages that Antonio is 'A slave that only smelled of ink and counters' ('counters' were for doing sums), a man who 'nev'r in's life looked like a gentleman / But in the audit time' (3.3.72–4). But this is a perverse irrelevant understanding of Antonio, who is a man of surpassing *natural* virtue. Bosola is the sort of villain who at times speaks the truth. He wheedles out of the Duchess her marriage to Antonio and, in doing so, gives expression to the perennial theme of innate 'virtues' as opposed to the prestige of breeding or 'pedigrees' (3.2.262). The Duchess has elected 'to prefer [i.e., give advancement to] / A man merely for worth', rather than observe instead the 'shadows' of 'wealth and painted honours' (3.2.276–8) by choosing a husband of noble blood. Bosola can scarcely believe his ears: such respect for character, without regard for social rank, is unheard of in 'this ambitious age' (3.2.275). Scholars will take heart from it. The Duchess has demonstrated that 'preferment' (Hamlet's 'advancement' again) can still 'Arise from merit', so 'the neglected poets' will forever honour her generous deed (3.2.282–95, 290–5). When Bosola glances at the Duchess's affair with Antonio, slyly noting that 'grafting' is 'a pretty art' (2.1.148 – he means the confusion of social distinctions involved in her affair), the Duchess's retort is witty: ''Tis so: a bett'ring of nature' (2.1.149) – mingling high and low breeds (or social groups) can improve rather than corrupt them. As soon as Bosola learns the truth of the affair he reveals his intelligence to the Cardinal and the Duchess's fate is sealed. But the contrast has been established between Antonio's natural virtue and the atrociousness of the established rulers. The brothers take the same attitude to Antonio that the haughty barons took to the King's minion Gaveston in *Edward II*: the Duchess's crime is to have fallen in love with someone of mean birth. But, as Webster makes clear in the extended parable of The Dogfish and the Salmon, virtue is a matter of character not birth. This is the Duchess's view: 'Man is most happy,' she opines, 'when 's own actions / Be arguments and examples of his virtue' (3.5.121–2). Bosola disdains this as a 'barren, beggarly virtue' (3.5.123). But the parable refutes this snobbery: when the grand Dogfish (or shark) rebukes the humble Salmon for daring to stray from her 'shallow rivers' into 'our high state of floods' (3.5.129, 132), the latter pointedly inquires what good high rank is if it causes one's destruction? The fisherman (and the cook!) will be sure to rate the Salmon higher than her 'dogship' (3.5.134, 135–40). The 'moral' is that 'Men oft are valued high when they're most wretch'd' (3.5.142).

The world of the play is governed – or, rather, egregiously misgoverned – by an immoral ruling faction (like Hamlet, the Duchess is a comparatively powerless, marginalized figure). The moral tone is set early on when the old courtier Castruchio retails his wife Julia's joke about 'a captain she met, full of wounds' (1.1.109–10): the captain was 'a pitiful fellow, to lie, like the children of Ishmael, all in tents' (1.1.111–12). ('Tents' are surgical dressings; 'children of Ishmael' may refer to the Arabs or, if this is a mistake for 'Israel' in the early printed copy of the play, the reference may be to the Jews – both peoples being in any case tent-dwellers.) It is a sufficiently heartless sally to make about a man suffering from war wounds and one can only wonder what disabled veterans in Webster's audience made of it. The opening of the play introduces us to a scene of degraded servility. Ferdinand bridles at his courtiers laughing at a joke of Silvio's: 'Why do you laugh?' he demands, suddenly full of menace. His 'courtiers', he observes, should be like 'touchwood [i.e., tinder]: take fire when I give fire, that is, laugh when I laugh, were the subject never so witty' (1.1.124–6).

The decadence of court life is assumed, but its sleaze only sets off the Duchess's virtues. 'For her discourse,' says Antonio, 'it is so full of rapture / You only will begin then to be sorry / When she doth end her speech' (1.1.190–2). Significantly for a tale of passion, Antonio draws attention to her 'divine ... continence' (1.1.199), which forms a stark contrast to the Cardinal's and Duke's *lack* of self-government. (As we have noted, intemperance is characteristic of tyrants: the carnivorous sexuality of Edmund, Regan and Goneril in *Lear* indicates that these 'murderous lechers' (*King Lear,* 4.6.279) will stop at nothing to gratify their desires.) Webster redefines 'discourse' or thoughtfulness. The Duchess's intense love for Antonio is rational and pure, sexual passion not in itself evil. Like *Antony and Cleopatra* and *Romeo and Juliet,* the play provides a liberated view of erotic desire. Love and sex are not opposed to reason: the Duchess is a thinker. Conversely, there is something obsessive about the Duke's demand that his widowed sister not remarry. He instructs Bosola not to 'ask the reason' why the Duchess should not marry again (1.1.259). One suspects he does not know why either – he is just borne along on a stream of perverted desire. Webster presents the Duchess's desire for love as wholesome and legitimate. There is a marked contrast here to the harsh treatment of Gertrude in *Hamlet*; one wonders whether Webster invented his Duchess in response. For Hamlet, that an older woman should feel sexual desire is repellent: 'You cannot call it love, for at your age / The heyday in the blood is tame, it's humble, / And waits upon the judgment' (3.4.69–71); see also his attack on 'the matron's' lust (83ff.). But in Webster anti-widow rhetoric is given to villains: it is Ferdinand who claims 'They are most luxurious [or lecherous] / Will wed twice' (1.1.299–300), while the Duchess herself wittily subverts the opposition to remarriage: 'Diamonds are of most value,' she remarks, 'that have passed through most jewelers' hands' (1.1.301–2).

As in *Hamlet*, spying is pervasive, further evidence of the Duke's and Cardinal's tyrannical rule. Bosola is a 'quaint invisible devil, in flesh: / An intelligencer' (1.1.262–3); flatterers offer their 'firstborn' sons as 'intelligencers' to the powerful (3.2.237). A related theme is the 'scurvy politician' (*Lear*, 4.6.171) or grubby political insider. When the Duchess receives a letter from Ferdinand asking her to 'Send Antonio' because the Duke 'want[s] his head in a business', she is alert to the 'politic equivocation': Ferdinand does not want Antonio's 'counsel' but his life (3.5.28–30). The 'politic skill' of the Cardinal and Ferdinand is held up for contempt. ('Politician' is a cursed word in the period, connoting ruthlessness, intrigue, anything but public service – compare the exchange in *The White Devil*: 'the famous politician; whose art was poison ... and whose conscience murder' (5.3.158–9).)

Bosola is part of this political machine, but that is an effect of poverty. A practiced deceiver, he is, in another sense, too honest for the world in which he finds himself, brutalized rather than a born devil. Incredibly, Ferdinand will not reward him for the murders of the Duchess, her waiting-woman Cariola, or her children (4.2.290ff.), and he has already spent two years as a galley slave, for some obscure crime committed for the Cardinal, who subsequently discarded him: 'I have done you / Better service than to be slighted thus' Bosola complains (1.1.29–30). He is the instrument, not inventor, of crime – Ferdinand's 'creature' (1.1.289). His brutality ('Whose throat must I cut?' (1.1.251)) is an indictment of his world. Once dismissed from the Duke's service he feels as if he has awoken from a dream (4.2.326–8). The reality is he has 'served ... tyranny' (4.2.332). A melancholic like Hamlet, Bosola resents those in power, but equally he does not want to play their shabby game. As Ferdinand says to him, 'You envy those that stand above your reach, / Yet strive not to come near 'em' (1.1.281–2). Bosola is a savage critic of the world of place-getting, power and wealth, the 'who's in, who's out' scene Lear also comes to despise. As he says, 'place and riches oft are bribes of shame' (1.1.292).

One of the most remarkable things in Webster's tragedy is the Duchess's defiance of family and social code: 'If all my royal kindred / Lay in my way unto this marriage / I'd make them my low footsteps' (i.e., rungs of a ladder – 1.1.342–4). Just as Shakespeare endorses the desire of Romeo and Juliet, so Webster admires the Duchess's determination to enjoy the pleasures of this world, above all love. Her wilfulness is aware and deliberate – 'So I, through frights and threat'nings, will assay / This dangerous venture' (1.1.348–9) – a completely conscious defiance of convention and of the prejudice and tyranny of her own brothers. There is the enormous thrilling heroism of will: 'For I am going into a wilderness / Where I shall find nor path nor friendly clew [i.e., guiding thread] / To be my guide' (1.1.360–2). The Duchess must find her own way, can rely on no precedent. We need to appreciate how radically libertarian this rhetoric was in its cultural context: the authority of family, and the power of men over women, were almost universal assumptions. All that is thrown to the winds. The devaluing of the world of family and of social

and political propriety in favour of love is starkly presented
in the Duchess's indifference to the rite of marriage. 'What
can the church force more?' she demands (1.1.489). With
her maid Cariola as witness, Antonio and she in effect marry
themselves. The defiance of institutions is astounding. 'How
can the church build faster?', that is, more securely, the
Duchess asks. All that matters is their 'fixed wishes' (1.1.492).
Desire is the reality, not marriage. 'We are man and wife,'
declares the Duchess, 'and 'tis the church / That must but echo
this' (1.1.493–4). The free, living, individual will is primary,
not the dead social institution.

Just as surprising is her defence of 'violent passions'
(1.1.446). The traditional formula, borrowed from classical
thinkers such as the Stoics, was that reason should govern
emotion. The Duchess defends passion. 'This is flesh and
blood, sir,' she says to Antonio, ''Tis not the figure cut in
alabaster' that 'Kneels at my husband's tomb' (1.1.454–6).
(The phrasing recalls Gratiano's defence of love in *The
Merchant of Venice*: 'Why should a man whose blood is warm
within / Sit like his grandsire cut in alabaster?' (1.1.83–4),
alabaster being the stone used for the effigies on tombs.) She
urges Antonio to wake up to the truth of his desire: 'Awake,
awake, man!' (1.1.456). She wants to rouse her lover to an
authentic desire freed of social forms and conventions. It
is the kind of moment often seen in Renaissance tragedy,
the emancipation from oppressive custom. 'Off, off, you
lendings!' cries Lear in the storm (3.4.107): he strips himself
to penetrate to the real (pre-social) human beneath. English
Renaissance tragedy also peels away 'lendings' to reveal the
actual truth of men and women as desiring beings. 'Farewell
compliment!' (that is, convention), cries Juliet to Romeo
(2.2.89). 'I do here put off all vain ceremony,' says the
Duchess, 'And only do appear to you a young widow, / That
claims you for her husband, and, like a widow, / I use but half
a blush in't' (1.1.457–60). The Duchess is without shame. As
with Romeo and Juliet, or Antony and Cleopatra, the lovers'
truth is what matters, not society: 'Truth speak for me!'

exclaims Antonio (1.1.460). Once again, we are reminded of Donne's lovers and their 'contracted' world. 'Do not think,' says the Duchess, of her brothers, 'All discord, without this circumference [i.e., outside their marriage-bonds], / Is only to be pitied and not feared' (1.1.469–71). Love is what matters, not power or social standing, Donne's 'honour'.[1] Desire is more substantial, domestic life more important than palaces and fame. When the Duke imprisons the Duchess, Bosola testifies that she bears herself 'Nobly' (4.1.2). Yet at the same time imprisonment increases desire: 'this restraint, / Like English mastiffs that grow fierce with tying, / Makes her too passionately apprehend / Those pleasures she's kept from' (4.1.12–15). Webster actually links here desire for pleasure with nobility.

A charming exchange demonstrates the happy free sexuality of the pair. There is a light-hearted joke about 'Laboring men' (3.2.18 – i.e., labouring in bed). 'When were we so merry?' (3.2.54) the Duchess asks Antonio and her maid. Webster wants us to enjoy a scene of natural affection and, of course, freedom from hierarchy. The Duchess is eloquent about her right to a sexual life: 'Why should only I' she demands of Ferdinand, 'Of all the other princes of the world, / Be cased up, like a holy relic? I have youth, / And a little beauty' (3.2.140–3). She wants to claim her rights as an ordinary woman, not be hampered by ceremony or social expectations as to what a prince can or cannot do. Why should she not seize happiness, and marry, while she can? From the point of view of the modern reader, her desires seem natural and reasonable. In the world of the play, however, such opinions are daringly rebellious.

A critique of artifice is central to *The Duchess of Malfi*. As in other Renaissance texts (for example *Hamlet*), cosmetics convey falsehood. 'Painting' conceals 'an old morphewed [or scabbed] lady', syphilitic and corrupt (2.1.31–2). It is wrong to take such imagery as straightforward misogyny (though it is in part that). It should instead be read as of a piece with the genre's insistence on truth, reality and nature as against artfulness and hypocrisy. Ferdinand cares only for 'Reputation' (3.2.137). The image of the grand but diseased woman, with a pure outward appearance, emblematizes a corrupt polity. The play champions liberation. There is a new naturalness in the relations of Antonio and the Duchess, marked by her urging him not to remove his hat in her presence (2.1.119–27 – compare Edward's 'Embrace me, Gaveston, as I do thee' in *Edward II* (1.1.140)). Both ultimately wish to be free of custom and hierarchy. As the Duchess puts it poignantly later in the play, when all their plans have come undone, 'The birds that live i'th'field / On the wild benefit of nature live / Happier than we; for they may choose their mates, / And carol their sweet pleasures to the spring' (3.5.18–21). Freedom is happiness.

One of the remarkable things about the Duchess is the loyalty she inspires in 'poor men'. Her servants remain true (3.5.3). Like Hamlet she has the common touch. In general, however, this is a ruthlessly competitive world. 'From decayed fortunes every flatterer shrinks,' observes Antonio mordantly (3.5.10). Cariola cannot decide whether a 'spirit of greatness or of woman' drives her mistress (1.1.505). Actually the play redefines greatness. It is a woman's ordinary desire for love and happiness that is great, not the sham sick perverse greatness of place, honour, title and so on. The Duchess displays 'a fearful madness' (1.1.507), at least as measured by this world. But in fact 'discourse' or rationality illumines everything she says and does. It is Ferdinand and the Cardinal who are mad. Likewise sexual corruption is a major theme, but it is not the Duchess's sex life that is questionable. Castruchio's Julia, who casually notices Bosola's 'excellent shape' (5.2.124), conducts an affair with the Cardinal. Ferdinand attacks the Duchess crudely. She is 'loose i'th' hilts, / ... a notorious strumpet' (2.5.3–4); in a moment of wild fantasy he imagines her enjoyed by 'some strong-thighed bargeman' (2.5.43). (He wants to 'boil' the Duchess's and Antonio's 'bastard to a cullis' or broth (2.5.72).) The belief that women can never be trusted (2.5.31–3) is highlighted as an absurdity.

Outside observers bring home the savagery of the ruling clique. The First Pilgrim comments that 'the Cardinal / Bears himself much too cruel' (3.4.27–8). The Pope has seized the Duchess's territory with no 'justice' except the Cardinal's 'instigation' (3.4.35–6). When Ferdinand later runs mad, believing himself to be a wolf, the symbolism is complete: the ruling elite are wolves to everyone else (see Act Five, Scene Two). Bosola, no stranger to violence, can hardly endure witnessing the tortures the Duchess's brothers subject her to and pleads in vain for mercy to be shown (4.1.118–19, 4.2.255). Like other plays discussed in this book, the play exhibits a deep scepticism towards glory and high rank. Looked at from afar these things are impressive enough, but examined up close turn out to be fantasies: 'Glories, like glowworms, afar off shine bright, / But, looked to near, have neither heat nor light' (4.2.140–1). Ambitious princes are 'wholly bent upon the world' rather than 'heaven' (4.2.156–7, 153). The play undertakes a revaluation of values. The Duchess's concern for the ordinary needs of her children ('look thou giv'st my little boy / Some syrup for his cold' (4.2.199–200)) is more real than her brothers' vain pursuit of power. The gates of 'princes' palaces' are 'highly arched'; Heaven's require you to get down on your 'knees' (4.2.229–31). The arrogant pride of these great ones is damnable; and the point of view is that of Hamlet in the graveyard. Greatness is illusory, 'bubbles blown in th'air' (*The Duchess of Malfi*, 5.4.68). There is something fantastical about such eminence as the Cardinal's: 'like a huge pyramid' it 'end[s] in a little point, a kind of nothing' (5.5.92, 94). And 'great men' are not really great unless they are also 'lords of truth' (5.5.136, 137).

19

The Changeling

The centre of interest of Middleton's and William Rowley's play is De Flores, servant to the wealthy gentleman Vermandero and in love with his master's daughter, Beatrice-Joanna. The play shows us the consequences of illicit love when Beatrice uses De Flores to assassinate her betrothed, Alonzo de Piracquo, so she can marry the nobleman Alsemero. When De Flores carries out this deed, he demands his reward: to sleep with Beatrice.

Beatrice despises De Flores for his repulsive appearance. But the drama also turns upon the outrage of a man of humble rank desiring a great lady. De Flores (the name puns on his 'deflowering' of Beatrice) is in fact a 'gentleman' whose 'hard fate has thrust [him] out to servitude' (2.1.48–9). He is used to the maltreatment dished out by 'great men': when Beatrice says he may keep the ring on the finger of her dead fiancé Alonzo, he grabs the opportunity: 'Well, being my fees, I'll take it; / Great men have taught me that, or else my merit / Would scorn the way on't' (3.4.46–8). What enrages him, however, is Beatrice's assumption he can be bought off with a 'salary' (3.4.63). It is interesting to speculate what kind of impact this taut scene, between a despised servant and superior gentlewoman, would have had in the public theatre. As far as Beatrice is concerned, De Flores falls into that category of more or less invisible beings whose function is to supply her wants. But here we have a serving-man insisting on due reward for his extreme service to her: sex. 'Do you

place me,' he demands, 'in the rank of verminous fellows /
To destroy things for wages? Offer gold? / The lifeblood of
man! Is anything / Valued too precious for my recompense?'
(3.4.64–7). He won't be sent off with a few pennies. The
play shows us a member of the ordinary folk (for, despite his
gentle beginnings, that is what in effect he is) demanding what
he sees as justice: 'Justice,' he points out to Beatrice, 'invites
your blood to understand me' (3.4.100). But understanding a
functionary or tool like De Flores is precisely what Beatrice is
trained not to do.

Of course De Flores' demand is outrageous. Yet one can't
help imagining some members of the audience rather taking
his side: must it not have been delicious to see this holier-
than-thou woman of the elite brought down a peg or two
– actually made to confront the desire of the sort of person
she normally disdained to notice? De Flores is startled when,
prior to Beatrice's request for his help in ridding her of her
troublesome fiance, she addresses him by name: 'Ha, I shall
run mad with joy! / She called me fairly by my name, De
Flores, / And neither "rogue" nor "rascal"' (2.2.70–2) – both
of those derogatory terms having in Middleton's and Rowley's
day a much stronger social meaning than they do now, and
conveying the notion of low status. The scene when De Flores
demands his reward is full of social resentment: finally, a great
lady is forced to listen to the wishes of someone she disdains.
In his exchange with Beatrice, De Flores assumes a bold
freedom: 'I have eased you / Of your trouble,' he points out
with relentless logic: 'think on't. I'm in pain, / And must be
eased of you' (3.4.97–9). Once the murder has been committed
there is nothing separating them: they are equal in sin. And it
is not as if De Flores does not want the 'gold' Beatrice tries
to palm him off with: he needs it, 'piteously' (3.4.112). But he
wants 'pleasure' more than 'wealth', and only she can provide
that (3.4.115). Beatrice can no more speak of 'modesty', De
Flores insists: she is 'A woman dipped in blood' (3.4.126).
Of course she clings to her sense of social distance: 'Think
but upon the distance that creation / Set 'twixt thy blood and

mine, and keep thee there' (3.4.131), she says. But in a chilling speech De Flores dismisses this mystifying rhetoric of 'blood' and 'birth':

> Look but into your conscience; read me there;
> 'Tis a true book, you'll find me there your equal.
> Push, fly not to your birth, but settle you
> In what the act made you; you're no more now.
> You must forget your parentage to me.
> You're the deed's creature; by that name
> You lost your first condition, and I challenge you,
> As peace and innocency has turned you out
> And made you one with me. (3.4.133–40)

Beatrice must acknowledge that she is what she has chosen to do; she cannot hide behind false social distinctions such as 'birth' and 'parentage', but has instead made a new identity for herself, one 'equal' with De Flores'. We cannot but feel that Beatrice does not deserve this treatment, that she is not by nature evil, that it was love (for Alsemero) that made her perform this crime – and one must not forget how she emphasizes the disability of being a woman: she is obliged by her father to marry someone other than the man she loves. To be a man, Beatrice declares, would be 'the soul of freedom' (2.2.111): 'I should not then be forced to marry one / I hate beyond all depths; I should have power / Then to oppose my loathings' (2.2.112–14). Had Beatrice had 'freedom', been able to switch her affection from Alonzo de Piracquo to Alsemero, all would have been well, and she wouldn't have required De Flores' services. But as it is, the play rubs her face in the dirt of what she has become: morally speaking, she is now no different from her tormentor. In upturning the power relation in this way the play is a wish-fulfilment fantasy. If only more of these haughty great ones could be so humiliated! Finally exposed as a murderess and adulteress, Beatrice must admit to her own father her commonness: he must not touch her, she will defile his blood; he must cast his blood from him,

'Let the common sewer take it from distinction' (5.3.162). Social distinction is nothing in the face of mortal sin: *The Changeling* places the illusions of social hierarchy in the balance with eternal verities of sin and salvation.

20

'Tis Pity She's a Whore

Ford's play is a perverse *Romeo and Juliet*. (The play probably contains an allusion to Shakespeare's Friar Laurence, who assists Romeo, in the sympathetic Friar who is Giovanni's ally.) In Shakespeare's play the impediment to the lovers' union was social, the feud between the houses of the Montagues and Capulets. In Ford the barrier is natural, the lovers being brother and sister. But, as with Edmund's audacious speech on bastardy in *King Lear*, the play questions this very distinction between nature and culture. Is the incest taboo natural or cultural? Plays like Ford's explain why the theatre's opponents saw it as debauching public morals. Even today, when 'tolerance' is a shibboleth of respectable opinion, the play's theme is shocking.

Of course it frames its exploration of right and wrong with a moralistic condemnation of its misguided hero and heroine. But even its title leaves open the possibility of approval – if it is a pity Annabella is a whore, that is because in and of herself she is remarkable and pure-minded. 'With admiration [i.e., wonder] I beheld this whore', a short dedicatory poem by Thomas Ellice to the early printed copy says. Annabella is 'Gloriously fair, even in her infamy' (lines 1, 10). The play troubles moral distinctions – evil should be ugly not 'fair' and the wonder the heroine inspires threatens to overwhelm a moral response.

The play centres upon an intellectual. Like Hamlet and Faustus, Giovanni is a 'miracle of wit' (1.1.47): 'the university applaud[ed]' his 'learning' and 'speech' (1.1.50–1). Florio, Giovanni's father, rather disapproves of his son's 'overbookish humor' (2.6.128) – Giovanni is a scholar and therefore prone to melancholy. Unlike Edmund in *Lear*, he is not an outright villain: the university was impressed with his 'government', or conduct, and 'behavior' (1.1.51). As Marlowe does in *Faustus*, the play connects the advanced thinking of 'forward wits' such as Giovanni with social and moral transgression. On the basis of *Faustus* and *'Tis Pity* alone we can say the critics of the Elizabethan and Jacobean drama had it right: there is indeed something astounding about thousands of spectators watching a play that renders incest glamorous and interesting.

From the outset the play emphasizes the risks of wild intellectual speculation – the 'lawless and incertain thought' we have noted previously. The Friar is shocked at Giovanni's confession of his love for his sister, blaming this perversion of an essentially good young man on the taste for disputation he acquired in his studies. The problem with intellectuals and their 'Nice [i.e., finicky] philosophy' (1.1.2) is that they are tempted to deny God because they can come up with clever arguments for His non-existence: such renegades, who

>   presumed
> On wit too much, by striving how to prove
> There was no God, with foolish grounds of art [i.e.,
>   learning],
> Discovered first the nearest way to hell,
> And filled the world with devilish atheism. (1.1.4–8)

The problem with clever ideas and arguments is that they are just as likely to lead to hell as heaven. For the Friar it is better 'To bless the sun than reason why it shines' (1.1.10).

For Giovanni, advanced thought is a way of legitimating unhallowed desires. His speech against the incest taboo resembles Edmund's against the prejudice disadvantaging children born out of wedlock. Giovanni has contempt for mere convention, what Edmund in *King Lear* calls the 'plague of custom':

Shall a peevish [i.e., petty] sound,
A customary form from man to man
Of brother and of sister, be a bar
'Twixt my perpetual happiness and me? (1.1.24–7)

The incest taboo is a mere 'customary form'. It has no
foundation in nature. Actually there is nothing *more* natural
than incest. Are not kin, the product of 'one father' and 'one
womb', bound 'by nature', 'blood' and 'reason' to love one
another 'So much the more'? (1.1.28–34). Giovanni scorns
the usual pieties. When Annabella's father marries her off to
the nobleman Soranzo, he finds this diminishes his pleasure
not a whit: the notion that sharing one's beloved with another
man is unthinkable is simply a myth of 'Busy opinion', foolish
popular wisdom (5.3.1). Instead, Giovanni declares, since the
marriage 'I find no change / Of pleasure in this formal law
of sports' (5.3.6–7). The 'formal law' surrounding love is
not Giovanni's concern and does not affect his 'sports' with
Annabella, which are entirely *outside* forms and laws.

It is not, however, reason, or its perversion, that drives
Giovanni to offend against common standards, but desire.
Like *Romeo and Juliet*, and *Antony and Cleopatra*, *'Tis Pity*
depicts willing submission to romantic desire: in the end, for
Giovanni, nothing is more important than love itself. What
we are encouraged to admire in Shakespeare's tragic lovers is
their willingness to offend against any 'formal law' in order
to satisfy their desire. This libertarian defence of 'extremes' of
passion (*'Tis Pity*, 1.1.42) is one of the most radical features
of Renaissance tragedy. The Friar's 'counsel', although it
seems to come 'As from a sacred oracle', is powerless in the
face of desire: it would be easier, declares Giovanni, 'to stop
the ocean / From floats [i.e., tides] and ebbs than to dissaude
my vows' (1.1.40–1, 64–5). The Friar speaks the language
of self-denial, of God's will not man's: 'acknowledge what
thou art,' he urges Giovanni, 'A wretch, a worm, a nothing'
(1.1.75–6). But Giovanni and Annabella stand for the human
will to grasp pleasure and happiness through the fulfilment

of one's desires, however these outrage social convention. In any case, reasoning against desire is hopeless: as Giovanni tells Annabella, he has 'Reasoned against the reasons of [his] love, / Done all that smooth-cheeked Virtue could advise', but has 'found all bootless' or unavailing (1.2.226–8). Giovanni cannot disavow the 'reasons' of his own desire. And the battle for Annabella's consent is not difficult – she is already in love with her brother: 'For every sigh that thou hast spent for me, / I have sighed ten' (1.2.248–9).

The worldliness of Giovanni's outlook is another way Ford challenges received ideas. (Of course the play cannot explicitly endorse such a viewpoint, but it does put it into public circulation.) The Friar tries to argue Giovanni out of his conviction that loving Annabella is not wrong. The young man has been infected by the impieties of ancient naturalistic philosophy:

> Oh, ignorance in knowledge! ...
> ...
> Indeed, if we were sure there were no deity,
> Nor heaven nor hell, then to be led alone
> By nature's light – as were philosophers
> Of elder times – might instance some defense.
> But 'tis not so. Then, madman, thou wilt find
> That nature is in heaven's positions [i.e., doctrines] blind.
>   (2.5.27–34)

But the speech opens up the possibility that the Friar is in fact wrong, and the Greek and Roman materialist or naturalistic philosophers right. The prestige of classical culture is a factor here; and if those philosophers were right, then it makes sense to follow nature, not heaven (including if one 'naturally' desires one's sister). The point about the passage is that simply by arguing against atheism the Friar raises it as an option – and gives it a weighty intellectual lineage. Giovanni's response to the Friar is equally daring: the Friar only thinks the way he does because he is old: 'Your age o'errules you' – overmasters the Friar; 'Had you youth like mine, / You'd make her love your heaven, and her divine' (2.5.35–6). The Friar believes what he says because he is an old man without interest in sex. But Giovanni is young, and Annabella the most beautiful woman he has ever seen. When he and she face death he finds the thought of heaven and hell a delusion. Annabella insists those things are 'most certain', but Giovanni's response is a dismissive 'A dream, a dream!' But then he mocks the concept of heaven by inquiring whether, if they are in 'this other world' they will be able to 'kiss one another, prate [i.e., chat], or laugh, / Or do as we do here?' (5.5.35–41). On the one hand this makes light of the whole notion of posthumous existence, which turns out to be not another and better type of being (e.g., union with God) but a simulacrum of earthly life. But if heaven is like earth, that presumably means earth is our true heaven.

Scandalously, the play raises the possibility that betraying one's desire may itself be a sin. In this way (the same can be said for Marlowe) it anticipates the critique of morality advanced by Nietzsche in the nineteenth century. Nietzsche claimed that a slave class – people miserably lacking in courage and self-assertiveness – had devised conventional morality in order to justify their own timidity. Giovanni takes a similar view: 'Keep fear and low fainthearted shame with slaves' he says (1.2.160). It is not 'lust' but 'fate' that drives him towards Annabella (1.2.158–9) – but it would perhaps be more accurate to think of the play as asserting that one's desire or basic project in life, to use the Sartrean phrase evoked in Part One – for example, love and sexual pleasure – *is* one's 'fate', and that freely embracing this 'fate' and remaining true to it is the sign of courage, authenticity, integrity. When it appears that Annabella's and Giovanni's affair has been discovered, Giovanni is defiant: 'Are we grown traitors to our own delights?' (5.3.37). He means that they have been found out, but the phrasing is nonetheless suggestive: perhaps the true immorality is betraying or resisting one's 'delights', lazily following the law or public morality rather than one's most basic desire. And the concept of 'betrayal' does connote something like (culpable) choice – so one's 'delight' or desire is indeed always a question of choice, and of staying true to that choice, even as it *feels* like 'fate' or compulsion or necessity.

Giovanni raises the amazing possibility that in future times his and Annabella's love will be celebrated, even as other examples of incest are condemned. And this will happen simply because of the force and intensity of their passion:

> If ever aftertimes should hear
> Of our fast-knit affections, though perhaps
> The laws of conscience and of civil use [i.e., social custom]
> May justly blame us, yet when they but know
> Our loves, that love will wipe away that rigor
> Which would in other incests be abhorred. (5.5.68–73)

Giovanni is saying that their love is so extraordinary it will suspend moral law. As with Antony and Cleopatra, the normal expectations don't apply – only moralistic pedants would suppose they do. As Nietzsche believed, laws are not for all. And people in the future will recognize this, and bless the 'fast-knit affections' of Giovanni and Annabella. Giovanni is never brought to any repentance. At the end of the play he owns up to his sexual relationship with his sister, expressing not a hint of shame: 'nine months I lived / A happy monarch of her heart and her' (5.6.44–5). And even the Cardinal at the end of the play is given some ambiguous words on the affair, acknowledging Annabella's exquisite and gifted character as much as her depravity: 'Of one so young, so rich in nature's store', that is, in the gifts of nature, 'Who could not say, 'Tis pity she's a whore?' (5.6.160–1).

Conclusion

Tragedy, I have argued, focuses on the ways in which human life is subject to certain (often desperately severe) limits – most obviously the limit of death itself. But it also stresses that the way one conducts oneself in relation to such limits is always a matter of choice. The concept of freedom, then, is fundamental to the genre. English Renaissance tragedy shows people heroically refusing merely to submit to the circumstances in which they find themselves, and instead actively and consciously choosing a life in regard to them. This is perhaps the main reason why the plays remain inspiring: while realistic about the inevitable constraints on, and costs of, freedom, they nevertheless affirm human agency as a supreme value.

Indeed even death itself becomes in these plays an occasion for thinking critically about one's world rather than merely passively accepting it. Death is not just an absolute natural phenomenon, but has social and political meaning as well. It is the great leveller, exposing the futility and vanity of distinctions of social rank.

When Gaveston is forced to confront his own death at the hands of his noble enemies, he makes comic play of the snobbery that concerns itself even with the method of execution. The Earl of Warwick insists the low-born Gaveston will be 'hang[ed]' from the 'bough' of a tree (*Edward II*, 2.5.24), fit end for such an upstart. But Gaveston's jaunty retort captures the absurdity of the nobles' obsession with rank: 'I thank you all, my lords. Then I perceive / That heading is one, and hanging is the other, / And death is all' (2.5.29–31). *Death is all*: beside it, the social distinctions

that are the whole cause of the conflict in the play fade
into insignificance; death shows the meaninglessness of such
purely conventional differences between human beings. As
Cornelia says of her dead son Marcello, in *The White Devil*,
'His wealth is summed, and this' (that is, his grave) 'is all
his store. / This poor men get, and great men get no more'
(5.4.110–11). *The Changeling* likewise highlights the fleeting
character of rank distinctions: Diaphanta (Beatrice's waiting
woman) remarks that 'Earth-conquering Alexander, that
thought the world / Too narrow for him, in the end had but
his pit-hole' (4.1.61–2). Or as Bosola puts it to the Duchess of
Malfi just before he has her strangled, 'Much you had of land
and rent; / Your length in clay's now competent' (4.2.177–8).
In *Edward II*, when the scholar Baldock, another of the
king's unlordly companions, faces his death, he expresses a
philosophic distance on life and, by implication, on worldly
hierarchies. Addressing another favourite of the king, 'Reduce
we all our lessons unto this' Baldock preaches: 'To die, sweet
Spencer, therefore live we all; / Spencer, all live to die, and rise
to fall' (4.7.109–11). This kind of metaphysical perspective,
focused on mortality and cognizant of the vanity of all human
striving, renders the power politics and obsession with social
rank in the play tawdry and absurd. When Zenocrate views
the 'bloody spectacle' of the bodies of Bajazeth, Emperor of
Turkey, and Bajazeth's queen Zabina, she reflects likewise
on the absurdity of worldly glory: 'Those that are proud
of fickle empery / And place their chiefest good in earthly
pomp, / Behold the Turk and his great emperess!' (*1 Tamb.*,
5.1.338, 351–6) – though the spectacle also has a lesson for
Tamburlaine: his pursuit of 'slippery crowns' too (*1 Tamb.*,
5.1.355), Zenocrate implies, is likewise rendered meaningless
by this spectacle. In *The Revenger's Tragedy*, death is a 'terror
to fat folks', that is, the wealthy. 'Be merry, merry,' says
Vindice to Gloriana's skull: those now in 'three-piled flesh'
(the metaphor is from the luxurious cloth used for courtiers'
garments) will at length be 'As bare as this; for banquets,
ease and laughter / Can make great men, as greatness goes

by clay, / But wise men little are more great than they'
(1.1.44–9). Social superiority, Vindice asserts, is 'great' only
in a superficial sense: the lowly wise man is greater than the
heedless man living a life of luxury.

The most famous example of the essential egalitarianism
of tragedy occurs in *Hamlet* in the graveyard scene. Here all
social ambition turns to dust. The scene opens with a logic-
chopping exchange between two peasants digging a grave for
Ophelia and inquiring as to whether 'Christian burial' should
be accorded her given that she is guilty of suicide (5.1.1–29).
The Second Clown points out 'the truth' of the matter: if
Ophelia 'had not been a gentlewoman, she should have been
buried out o' Christian burial' (5.1.23–5). So social rank
matters even in graveyards. And yet in the end these distinctions amount to nothing at all, Hamlet demonstrates. The
skull the First Clown throws up out of the grave 'might be
the pate of a politician', Hamlet muses, 'now 'o'erreach[ed]'
by the low-born gravedigger (5.1.77–9); or it might be the
skull 'of a courtier … Lord Such-a-one' (5.1.82–4); but now
it is merely 'my lady Worm's' skull, 'knocked about the
mazard' (or head) 'with a sexton's spade' (5.1.88–90). Finally
Hamlet notes of another skull pitched up by the gravedigger
that here might be 'the skull of a lawyer' and 'a great buyer
of land' – but now the many deeds of conveyance for his
land purchases 'will scarcely lie in this box' – that is, fit into
his coffin (5.1.98–9, 104, 111). So much for the clever and
grasping lawyer's vast tracts of land. The theme is further
developed when Hamlet addresses Yorick's skull: 'Now get
you to my lady's chamber,' he urges the skull, 'and tell her,
let her paint an inch thick, to this favor [or appearance]
she must come' (5.1.192–4). The fact of mortality leads
Hamlet to further wide-ranging reflections: 'imagination',
he says, might 'trace the noble dust of Alexander' until it
finds it 'stopping a bung-hole' (or opening of a cask) – for
Alexander died and returned to dust and earth, and 'of earth
we make loam' (a mixture of clay and other materials), and
loam we use to 'stop a beer-barrel' (5.1.203–4, 210–12);

similarly, 'Imperious Caesar, dead and turned to clay, / Might stop a hole to keep the wind away' (5.1.213–14). Ruling-class magnificence is trivial and even laughable when seen from the viewpoint of death. Kings and conquerors are only 'earth' (5.1.210), whatever pretentious nonsense they might believe about themselves. The easily drawn, and radical, implication of Hamlet's reflections in the graveyard is that the mighty prerogatives rulers award themselves over other mortal beings are highly questionable, to say the least, and possibly illegitimate and sinful. The graveyard scene gives memorable expression to a radical egalitarian politics based on fundamental realities of human nature. The scene shows Hamlet taking up an active relation to death – thinking about its *meaning* for political and economic equality.

Tragedy focuses on death, then, but it does not follow that it simply underscores human powerlessness. Instead it invites us to reflect upon the implications of death for life. What actually follows from our saying that in death we are all equal? How should that fact about us condition the way we live? Death is the most basic limit we face but, if we choose to think about its significance, as Hamlet does so eloquently and humanely in the graveyard, it can become a means for understanding what is wrong in our world – and, perhaps, changing it for the better. (The first step in overcoming an evil is to recognize it.) Death, then, can be a ground for action, not mere acquiescence in the status quo.

Tragedy's preoccupation with agency – with what we can *do*, as against suffer – extends as well to its representation of the common people. For tragedy is not only concerned with the tribulations of socially elevated individuals – kings, princes and so on. It typically concerns communities – nations and cities. And certainly a key feature of English Renaissance tragedy is the attention it gives to the people and their distinct perspective on affairs. (This is true too of ancient tragedy – the Chorus, after all, tends to give the view of the man in the street.) In *Edward II* the rebellious nobles have to take into account popular opinion. If Gaveston, Edward's hated favourite, doesn't finally humble himself before them they will be able to rise against the king without fear of being accused of 'treason' (1.4.281): 'So shall we have the people of [i.e., on] our side' (1.4.282) they assert. And the people's support is crucial because 'when the commons and the nobles join' not even the king will then be able to save his minion (1.4.287–8). It is not that 'the people' are necessarily enlightened democrats: what they resent, we are told, is not Gaveston's careless disregard for the suffering of ordinary people but his lording it over 'the nobility' (1.4.286); and later Mortimer is convinced that 'The king must die' because 'The commons ... begin to pity him' (5.4.1–2). Nevertheless the main point is that the nobles feel the need to *take account of* (and of course to manipulate) public opinion. In *The Duchess of Malfi* Bosola takes it for granted that 'the common people curse' any 'eminent courtier' – indeed earning their hatred is a sure sign one has finally arrived, become 'one of the prime nightcaps' (that is, a rich lawyer; see 2.1.1–2, 20–1). In *Hamlet* Claudius's wariness about moving openly against the Prince is likewise explained by 'the great love the general gender' (that is, the people) have for Hamlet (4.7.19); the King cannot 'put the strong law on' him because Hamlet is so 'loved of the distracted multitude' (4.3.3,4). Saturninus in *Titus Andronicus* has a similar problem with the rebel Lucius: ''Tis he the common people love so much', he observes, noting that the people resent Lucius's banishment (4.4.73; see also 76); and the rebels have begun to 'buzz' their complaints 'in the people's ears' (4.4.7), which suggests that the plebs are a significant factor in high politics. The play concludes with 'the common voice' freely hailing Lucius as the new emperor – a moment in the play that feels like a democratic revolution (5.3.140). In *Lear*, too, Edmund thinks it prudent to have the old king imprisoned lest his distressed appearance 'pluck the common bosom on his side' (5.3.51). Regan has the same troubled thought about the blinded Gloucester: letting him live was a mistake – wherever he goes 'he moves / All hearts against us' (4.5.12–13). The plays continually show rulers attempting to manage public opinion. Claudius worries about 'the people muddied' (or confused), 'Thick and unwholesome in their thoughts and whispers / For good Polonius' death' (4.5.82–4). The bursting into the palace of Laertes and the 'rabble' (4.5.105) only confirms the impression of a political elite anxious about popular reaction to its doings. This especially 'riotous' (4.5.104) incident conveys the heady intoxicating atmosphere of insurrection. The people 'call [Laertes] lord, / And, as the world were now but to begin, / Antiquity forgot, custom not known, / The ratifiers and props of every word, / They cry, "Choose we! Laertes shall be king!" / Caps, hands, and tongues applaud it to the clouds, / "Laertes shall be king, Laertes king!"' (4.5.105–11). The passage carefully positions itself on the side of 'antiquity' and 'custom', the supports here of good order; and the people themselves are dismissed as 'the rabble' (105). But that is all to be expected, and was the usual official view of such matters; imaginatively, what sticks in the mind is that exhilarating image of a rebellious people in full cry for the right to *choose* – an exceptionally loaded word in a monarchy like that of Elizabeth and James. (One might compare the people's ringing use of 'choose' here with Cassius's resonant exhortation in *Julius Caesar*: 'Some to the common pulpits [i.e., the public platforms], and cry out / "Liberty, freedom, and enfranchisement!"' (3.1.81–2).) The description of Laertes and the people is only a glimpse of democracy in *Hamlet*, and it is over before it has begun – but it is there.

We have discussed a similar proto-democratic insurrection in *Lear* when one of Cornwall's servants attempts to protect Gloucester from mutilation by Regan and Cornwall. What comes through in the scene is the rulers' incredulity that one of their 'slave[s]' (3.7.99) should think he has the right to tell them how to behave. When the First Servant begs Cornwall to 'hold [his] hand' (3.7.75), Regan cannot believe her ears: 'How now, you dog?' she exclaims, 'A peasant stand up thus?' (3.7.78, 83). Cornwall echoes her astonishment: 'My villain?' (3.7.81, 'villain' having a sharper *social* signification in Shakespeare's age than it does now). This rebellion (and the Second and Third Servant at the end of the scene support the First's defiance of Cornwall and Regan) is an astounding moment. As with the intrusion of the 'rabble' into Claudius's chamber, we get a momentary – and inspiring – vision of popular agency. The brave loyalty to Gloucester of his old tenant in the next scene reinforces this theme of deliberate plebeian resistance to the Cornwall faction.

English Renaissance tragedy, then, very often gives us a proto-democratic sense of the people as collective and individual political actors. In *Coriolanus* the people are easily manipulated, but their reading of Coriolanus is perfectly accurate: he is 'a very dog to the commonalty' (1.1.26–7) – that is, inordinately arrogant, and that despite their initially patient treatment of him. The idea of democracy seems built into the fabric of *Hamlet* in particular, via its flirting with the elective principle (Denmark seems to be some kind of elective monarchy). When Hamlet dies he 'prophes[ies] th'election lights / On Fortinbras', affirming that the Norwegian prince 'has [his] dying voice' (see 5.2.357, 358). Earlier we learned that Claudius had 'popped in between th'election and [Hamlet's] hopes' (5.2.65), the suggestion being he has somehow finessed the electoral process. Much of this is rather obscure and no doubt not fully worked out in Shakespeare's mind – he was not a political theorist but a poet – but the very fact of an elective monarchy, of 'choosing' and voting for a ruler, must have been of extraordinary interest to Shakespeare's audience. *Titus* opens with similar material. Saturninus and Bassianus, sons of the late emperor, compete for the right to succeed him. Being eldest, Saturninus appeals to the 'Noble patricians' and principle of hereditary right or primogeniture – 'successive title', as he calls it (1.1.1, 4). Bassianus, 'a poor competitor' (63) in this debate (because youngest), addresses himself to 'Romans, friends, followers' (9), and pleads for support on the basis of merit: 'let desert in pure election shine' he urges them, 'And, Romans, fight for freedom in your choice' (16–17). As it turns out, the tribune Marcus, representing 'the people of

Rome', declares that the 'common voice' has 'In election for the Roman empery / Chosen [Titus] Andronicus' (20–3). Titus thereupon transfers his power to Bassianus: the 'successive' or monarchal principle is accordingly preserved. But, again, what must have fascinated Elizabethan spectators was simply the detailed representation of a political process that allowed the people an active role. It is the spectre of political democracy – the issue of who will win 'the people's favor' (1.1.54) – that stalks the play's opening scene, the words 'commonweal', 'commonwealth', 'election' and 'suffrage' occuring repeatedly (1.1.114, 183, 219, 228, 236, 248, 314; compare too 2.1.24 and 'the people's suffrages' at 4.3.19).

Julius Caesar also portrays the populace as political actors – a far cry from the actual position of the Elizabethan 'rabble'. Caesar is a populist who has deliberately and even theatrically courted the plebs' favour: 'When ... the poor have cried, Caesar hath wept' (3.2.93). (The play continually addresses social divisions between rich and 'poor', so making these divisions a potential object of critical reflection for a playhouse audience.) It is important to note that the play emphasizes that 'the people' do 'choose' Caesar as 'their king' (1.2.79–80). Of course from the view of the republicans this choice is a betrayal of all that is best in Rome, yet Caesar's apparent championing of the common people would be food for thought for an Elizabethan audience. More generally the concept of 'the general good' (1.2.85) is central to the play. Brutus is admitted to have acted out of 'a general honest thought' and 'common good to all' (5.5.71–2). The play thus foregrounds the idea that it is the 'commonweal' that is the proper object of politics, not mere monarchal or elite self-interest; once again, interesting material for a plebeian spectator to think with. *Timon of Athens* likewise presents the people as an actual political force. The play depicts a successful armed rebellion, led by the Athenian commander Alcibiades, of 'penurious' and 'discontented' soldiers (4.3.93; 3.5.121) against the wealthy senators, men who, from their 'great chairs of ease' (5.4.11), have routinely made their 'wills / The scope of justice' (4–5). (They have, for example, lent out money 'upon large interest' (3.5.114).) Up until now those oppressed by these wilful magnates have 'breathed' their 'sufferance vainly' (5.4.6–7), that is, voiced their sufferings to absolutely no effect. They have, indeed, been terrified into submission; but all that is now past. 'The time is flush' (8), or ripe, and those who have laboured under oppression cry out '"No more!"' (10). *Timon* represents a moment of social revolution against oppression and inequality. Athens has been dominated by 'traffic' (1.1.250), or the profit principle and selfish exploitation; but this victorious rebellion against the senators' tyranny augurs well for the city's future.

English Renaissance tragedy addressed some of the deepest and hardest questions of human life, frequently in enormously subtle, intellectually demanding language. In doing so it implicitly treated its audience as if it was, as Cassius asserts of himself in *Julius Caesar*, 'born free' (1.2.97) – that is, naturally capable of thought and judgement about what matters in life, of the activity that Hamlet calls 'discourse of reason'. Such an audience is – or ought to be – an active subject in its world, not a mindless object or slave for a privileged one per cent to exploit. The soaringly speculative character of tragedy at this time, the quality Sidney identified when he spoke of the poet 'freely ranging ... within the zodiac of his own wit', has the result that it often seems to relish challenging accepted opinion for its own sake, an orientation regularly leading it into 'lawless and incertain thought'. It is also, as we have seen, a serious art that aimed not merely to distract its audience but to make it think about what was wrong in its world, most importantly lack of freedom, justice and equality. In a world in which those good things still seem a long way off, we today could do with an art as defiantly critical and oppositional as that of tragedy in the age of Shakespeare.

NOTES

Preface

1   The classic essay on this topic of different notions of freedom is Isaiah Berlin's 'Two Concepts of Liberty', based on a lecture of 1958. See *The Proper Study of Mankind: An Anthology of Essays*, eds Henry Hardy and Roger Hausheer (London, 1998), pp. 191–242.

Tragedy and Freedom

1   Philip Sidney, *A Defence of Poetry* (1595), in *English Renaissance Literary Criticism*, ed. Brian Vickers (Oxford, 1999), p. 363.

2   Blaise Pascal, *Pensées* (1670), trans. A. J. Krailsheimer (Harmondsworth, 1966), p. 45.

3   Jean-Paul Sartre, *Being and Nothingness* (1943), trans. Hazel E. Barnes (New York, 1956), p. 439. Subsequent references are in the text.

Introduction

1   R. H. Tawney, *Equality* (1931; London, 1964), p. 168. Subsequent references are in the text.

2   See, for example, his suggestion that happiness 'needs the external goods as well; for it is impossible, or not easy, to do noble acts without the proper equipment'. See *Nicomachean Ethics*, Book One (1099a32–3), vol. 2 of the *Complete Works of Aristotle*, ed. Jonathan Barnes (Princeton, 1984).

3 Aristotle, *Politics*, Book One (1253a3–6), in vol. 2 of the *Complete Works*.

The Tragic Genre

1 Geoffrey Chaucer, 'The Prologue of the Monk's Tale', Fragment VII of *The Canterbury Tales*, in *The Riverside Chaucer*, ed. Larry D. Benson (Boston, 1987), p. 241. The lines can be glossed as: 'Tragedy is a particular kind of story, as old books remind us, about the man that enjoyed great prosperity, and is fallen out of his high rank into misery, and ends wretchedly.'

2 William Wordsworth, 'Simon Lee, the Old Huntsman', in *The Major Works* (Oxford, 1984), p. 87.

3 Compare Pascal on human life: 'Imagine a number of men in chains, all under sentence of death, some of whom are each day butchered in the sight of the others; those remaining see their own condition in that of their fellows, and looking at each other with grief and despair await their turn. This is an image of the human condition' (*Pensées*, p. 165). See also Tolstoy's powerful story about mortality, 'The Death of Ivan Ilyich'.

4 Sophocles, *Antigone*, line 833; see text, trans. Elizabeth Wyckoff, in *Oedipus the King, Oedipus at Colonus, Antigone*, eds David Grene and Richmond Lattimore (Chicago, 1954). Subsequent references to *Antigone* are in the text, and refer to line numbers.

5 Thomas Hardy, *Tess of the d'Urbervilles* (1891), ed. Tim Dolin (London, 2003), p. 397.

6 Friedrich Nietzsche, *The Birth of Tragedy and Other Writings*, eds Raymond Geuss and Ronald Spiers, trans. Ronald Spiers (Cambridge, 1999), p. 40.

7 Friedrich Nietzsche, *Writings from the Late Notebooks*, ed. Rüdiger Bittner, trans. Kate Sturge (Cambridge, 2003), p. 38.

8 Friedrich Nietzsche, *Writings from the Early Notebooks*, eds Raymond Geuss and Alexander Nehamas, trans. Ladislaus Löb (Cambridge, 2009), p. 51.

9 Ibid., p. 23.

10   Nietzsche, *The Birth of Tragedy*, p. 24.

11   Euripides, *Heracles*, lines 1315–16; see text in *Heracles and Other Plays*, trans. John Davie (London, 2002).

12   Elizabeth Cary, *The Tragedy of Mariam*, ed. Ramona Wray (London, 2012), 1.5.20. Subsequent references are in the text.

13   Bradley is struck by Lady Macbeth's 'force of will'; both she and her husband 'are sublime, and both inspire … the feeling of awe': A. C. Bradley, *Shakespearean Tragedy: Lectures on Hamlet, Othello, King Lear, Macbeth* (1904; Houndmills, 2007), pp. 284, 265–6. Compare Pascal's statement that there are certain rare kinds of evil that attaining them takes 'extraordinary greatness of soul' (*Pensées*, p. 215).

14   G. K. Hunter, 'The Heroism of Hamlet', in *Dramatic Identities and Cultural Tradition: Studies in Shakespeare and His Contemporaries* (Liverpool, 1978), p. 247.

15   The poet, courtier and soldier Sir Philip Sidney wrote in his *Defence of Poetry* that tragedy should induce a feeling of 'well-raised admiration', i.e., exalted wonder (p. 383); see also Vickers's Glossary in *English Renaissance Literary Criticism* for Sidney's phrase.

16   E. M. Cioran, *The Temptation to Exist* (1956), trans. Richard Howard (Chicago, 1998), p. 193.

17   Compare Goethe: 'All things the gods bestow, the infinite ones, / On their darlings completely, / All the joys, the infinite ones, / All the pains, the infinite ones, completely'; see *Poems and Epigrams*, trans. Michael Hamburger (London, 1983), p. 25.

18   W. B. Yeats, *Poems*, ed. A. Norman Jeffares (London, 1989), p. 412.

Tragedy: Freedom, Order and Tyranny

1   Euripides, *Alcestis*, line 782; see text, trans. Richmond Lattimore, in *Alcestis, The Medea, The Heracleidae, Hippolytus*, eds David Grene and Richmond Lattimore (Chicago, 1955).

2   Sophocles, *Oedipus at Colonus*, lines 962, 963–4; see text, trans. Robert Fitzgerald, in *Oedipus the King, Oedipus at*

Colonus, Antigone. Subsequent references are in the text and refer to line numbers.

3   Sophocles, *Oedipus the King*, line 977; see text, trans. David Grene, in *Oedipus the King, Oedipus at Colonus, Antigone*. Subsequent references are in the text and refer to line numbers.

4   Seneca, *Oedipus*, line 1019; see text in *Tragedies II: Oedipus, Agamemnon, Thyestes, Hercules on Oeta, Octavia*, ed. and trans. John G. Fitch (Cambridge, MA, 2004). Subsequent references are in the text and refer to line numbers.

5   Euripides, *Iphigenia Among the Taurians*, lines 477–9; see text in *Heracles and Other Plays*.

6   Euripides, *Trojan Women*, lines 1204–6; see text in *Trojan Women, Iphigenia Among the Taurians, Ion*, ed. and trans. David Kovacs (Cambridge, MA, 1999).

7   Euripides, *Hippolytus*, lines 189–190; see text, trans. David Grene, in *Alcestis, The Medea, The Heracleidae, Hippolytus*.

8   Euripides, *Medea*, line 1228; see text, trans. Rex Warner, ibid.

9   Martin Heidegger, *Being and Time* (1927), trans. Joan Stambaugh (Albany, 1996), p. 262.

10 Giovanni Pico della Mirandola, 'Oration on the Dignity of Man', trans. E. L. Forbes, in *The Renaissance Philosophy of Man*, eds E. Cassirer et al. (Chicago, 1948), p. 225.

11 It is important to grasp that Sartre is not arguing the absurd proposition that all human beings are continually going about, or should go about, in a state of high philosophic reflection as regards death (which even if possible would certainly be undesirable). I may not think about death from one day to the next; but in behaving in this way I will certainly have chosen, somewhere along the line, and perhaps only implicitly (by preferring to occupy myself with other goals, such as material rewards or sensual gratification or the revolutionary transformation of society) to be *the kind of person who does not think about death*. In other words, precisely by *not* thinking about death, I have adopted a definite attitude towards it (for example, that it is unnecessary to live one's life with the awareness that one day death will come). And the

same goes for any other phenomenon: *not* thinking about it is nevertheless to adopt a particular stance towards it.

12 'Ode to a Nightingale', in *The Complete Poems*, ed. John Barnard (London, 2006), p. 348.

13 For an exploration of this idea of the deterministic nature of the passions in Shakespeare, see Peter Holbrook, 'Shakespeare, Montaigne, and Classical Reason', in *Shakespeare and Renaissance Ethics*, eds Patrick Gray and John H. Cox (Cambridge, 2014), pp. 261–83.

14 'What hearts has Venus' power not subdued?' See Jean Racine, *Phaedra*, 1.1.123, in *Iphigenia, Phaedra, Athaliah*, trans. John Cairncross (Harmondsworth, 1963).

15 *On Materialism*, trans. Lawrence Garner (London, 1975), p. 50.

16 *The Eighteenth Brumaire of Louis Bonaparte* (1852), in *The Portable Karl Marx*, partial trans. and ed. Eugene Kamenka (New York, 1983), p. 287.

17 Sidney, *A Defence of Poetry*, p. 343.

18 Uguccione da Pisa, *Magnae Derivationes*, quoted in Willard Farnham, *The Medieval Heritage of Elizabethan Tragedy* (Oxford, 1936), p. 171.

19 Boethius, *The Consolation of Philosophy*, trans. Victor Watts, rev. edn (London, 1999), p. 26.

20 Euripides, *Phoenician Women*, lines 523–4; see text in *The Bacchae and Other Plays*, trans. John Davie (London, 2005). Subsequent references are in the text and refer to line numbers.

21 Seneca, *Thyestes*, lines 206–8; see text in *Tragedies II*.

22 Aeschylus, *The Persians*, lines 242–3, trans. Seth Benardete, in *The Persians, The Seven Against Thebes, The Suppliant Maidens, Prometheus Bound*, eds David Grene and Richmond Lattimore (Chicago, 1956).

23 Euripides, *Heracleidae*, lines 422–4; see text, trans. Ralph Gladstone, in *Alcestis, The Medea, The Heracleidae, Hippolytus*.

24 Euripides, *Helen*, line 1637; see text in *Helen, Phoenician Women, Orestes*, ed. and trans. David Kovacs (Cambridge,

MA, 2002). Subsequent references are in the text and refer to line numbers.

25 Euripides, *Ion*, lines 854–6; see text in *Trojan Women, Iphigenia Among the Taurians, Ion*, ed. and trans. Kovacs. Subsequent references to *Ion* are in the text and refer to line numbers.

26 Seneca, *Hercules on Oeta*, lines 657, 652; see text in *Tragedies II*.

27 Aeschylus, *Prometheus Bound*, line 358, trans. David Grene, in *The Persians, The Seven Against Thebes, The Suppliant Maidens, Prometheus Bound*, eds Grene and Lattimore. Subsequent references to *Prometheus Bound* are in the text.

28 In the 1603 printed copy of the play the theme of social conflict between rich and poor, oppressor and oppressed, is even more prominent: 'Who'd bear the scorns and flattery of the world – / Scorned by the right rich, the rich cursed of the poor, / The widow being oppressed, the orphan wronged, / The taste of hunger, or a tyrant's reign, / And thousand more calamities besides' (7.124–8); see *Hamlet: The Texts of 1603 and 1623*, eds Ann Thompson and Neil Taylor (London, 2006).

29 Compare the Chorus in Seneca's *Agamemnon*: 'Who can fully break out of bondage? / Only one who scorns the fickle gods, / who looks without gloom at gloomy Styx, / looks upon dark Acheron's face, / and has courage to set an end to life: / such a one is a match for kings, for gods. / How wretched to be unschooled in dying!', lines 604–10; see text in *Tragedies II*.

30 Aeschylus, *Agamemnon*, lines 1362, 1364–5, in *Oresteia: Agamemnon, The Libation Bearers, The Eumenides*, trans. Richmond Lattimore, eds David Grene and Richmond Lattimore (Chicago, 1953).

31 Sartre's example of this radical doctrine of responsibility is drawn from the circumstances of his own life in Nazi-occupied France: 'If I am mobilized in a war, this war is *my* war; it is in my image and I deserve it. I deserve it first because I could always get out of it by suicide or by desertion … For lack of getting out of it, I have *chosen* it. This can be due to inertia, to cowardice in the face of public opinion, or because I prefer

certain other values to the value of the refusal to join in the
war (the good opinion of my relatives, the honor of my family,
etc.). Anyway you look at it, it is a matter of a choice. This
choice will be repeated later on again and again without a
break until the end of the war' (p. 554). Compare Cassius
on the prospect of living under Caesar's monarchy: 'I know
where I will wear this dagger then; / Cassius from bondage will
deliver Cassius' (*Julius Caesar*, 1.3.89–90).

32 See the translation of La Boétie's treatise by Harry Kurz, ed.
Murray N. Rothbard (Montreal, 1997).

Freedom, Tyranny and Order in the English Renaissance

1 D. M. Palliser, *The Age of Elizabeth: England under the Later
Tudors, 1547–1603*, 2nd edn (London, 1992), p. 111.

2 See facsimile of the 1623 *Certain Sermons or Homilies
Appointed to be Read in Churches In the Time of Queen
Elizabeth I* (1547–71), eds Mary Ellen Rickey and Thomas B.
Stroup (Gainesville, 1968), pp. 69, 71.

3 See *Certain Observations Made Upon a Libel ...* in vol. 8 of
The Works of Francis Bacon, eds James Spedding, Robert
Leslie Ellis and Douglas Denon Heath (collected 1857–74;
Stuttgart, 1963), p. 178.

4 See Morris Palmer Tilley's *Elizabethan Proverb Lore in Lyly's
Euphues and in Pettie's Petite Pallace: With Parallels from
Shakespeare* (New York, 1926), p. 303.

5 Speech to Parliament of 19 March 1604 in *King James VI and
I: Political Writings*, ed. Johann P. Sommerville (Cambridge,
1994), p. 139.

6 For a vivid account, see Stephen Greenblatt, *Will in the
World: How Shakespeare Became Shakespeare* (London, 2004),
pp. 172–3.

7 The belief that drama might bring crimes to light was expressed
by the playwright Thomas Heywood, who described how a

'towns-woman' in Norfolk had, while watching a play that depicted a woman's murder of her husband, confessed that she herself 'had poisoned her husband' some 'seven years ago'. See 'A Defence of Drama' (1608), in *English Renaissance Literary Criticism*, ed. Vickers, pp. 498, 499.

8   On the topic of political disobedience in *King Lear*, see Richard Strier, *Resistant Structures: Particularity, Radicalism, and Renaissance Texts* (Berkeley, 1995), pp. 177–99.

9   *The Republic*, trans. Desmond Lee, 2nd edn (Harmondsworth, 1974), Book IX, (574e–575a). Compare Edmund Burke from a letter of 1791: 'men of intemperate minds cannot be free. Their passions forge their fetters': vol. 4 of *Works of Edmund Burke* (London, 1899), p. 52.

10   *Paradise Lost*, ed. Alastair Fowler, 2nd edn (Harlow, 1998), Book XII, lines 83–90.

11   *Basilicon Doron* (1599), in *Political Writings*, p. 20.

12   William Baldwin, 'Preface' to the 1599 edition, in *The Mirror for Magistrates*, ed. Lily B. Campbell (1938; New York, 1960), line 2, p. 63. Subsequent references to *The Mirror* are in the text and refer to pages in Campbell's edition.

13   'Kings are justly called gods, for that they exercise a manner or resemblance of divine power upon earth' – speech to Parliament dated 21 March 1610, *Political Writings*, p. 181.

14   J. B. Black, *The Reign of Elizabeth, 1558–1603*, 2nd edn (Oxford, 1959), p. 178.

15   *Paradise Lost*, Book XII, lines 26, 25, 37.

16   *The Elizabethan World Picture* (1943; Harmondsworth, 1963), p. 29.

17   King James I, *The True Law of Free Monarchies*, in *Political Writings*, p. 65.

18   Heywood, 'A Defence of Drama', p. 493.

19   To the 'young man [who] had great possessions' Jesus said, 'If thou wilt be perfect, go *and* sell that thou hast, and give to the poor': Mt. 19.21–2.

20   Compare *The Duchess of Malfi*, in which Bosola also portrays the rich as a source of disorder and corruption. Shamelessly

accusing the Duchess herself of such disorder (when, in fact, she is the embodiment of moral sanity), he makes the general satirical point that it is the degenerate rich, not the common folk (such as milkmaids), who are the source of riot and disorder: 'Thou art some great woman, sure, for riot begins to sit on thy forehead, clad in gray hairs, twenty years sooner than on a merry milkmaid's' (4.2.132–4).

21 Female frustration at the powerlessness of women is not uncommonly expressed in the plays. In *The White Devil*, the wronged wife of Bracciano, Isabella, declares 'Oh, that I were a man, or that I had power / To execute my apprehended wishes! / I would whip some with scorpions' (2.1.244–6). (Compare Vittoria later in the play: 'Oh, woman's poor revenge, / Which dwells but in the tongue!' (3.2.288–9); and Beatrice in Shakespeare's *Much Ado About Nothing*: 'Oh, God, that I were a man! I would eat his heart in the marketplace' (4.1.304–6).) In *The Tragedy of Mariam*, Salome expresses her bitterness that she is unable easily to divorce her husband Constabarus, as he could her: 'Why should such privilege to man be given? / Or, given to them, why barred from women then? / Are men than we in greater grace with heaven? / Or cannot women hate as well as men? / I'll be the custom-breaker and begin / To show my sex the way to freedom's door, / And with an offering will I purge my sin; / The law was made for none but who are poor' (1.4.41–52).

The Rhetoric of Disenchantment

1 E. K. Chambers noted the mythic unreality of the monarchs' official appearances: 'the Tudor kings and queens came and went about their public affairs in a constant atmosphere of make-believe, with a sybil lurking in every court-yard and gateway, and a satyr in the boscage of every park'; royal progresses through the realm were occasions for extravagant pageantry and 'hagiology and allegory'. See vol. 1 of *The Elizabethan Stage* (1923), 4 vols (Oxford, 1974), p. 107. Subsequent references to Chambers are in the text and refer to volume and page number.

3

NOTES

2 Michel de Montaigne, *Essays*, ed. and trans. M. A. Screech (London, 1991), p. 291. Shakespeare read Montaigne, at least in part, quoting him in his late play *The Tempest*. Subsequent references to the *Essays* are in the text.

3 A pioneering discussion of the demystificatory aspects of English Renaissance tragedy was Jonathan Dollimore's *Radical Tragedy: Religion, Ideology and Power in the Drama of Shakespeare and His Contemporaries*, 3rd edn (1984; Basingstoke, 2010).

4 Pascal makes the point that, because people see kings surrounded by 'guards, drums, officers and all the things which prompt automatic responses of respect and fear', they identify the person of the king with these trappings of power: thus they mistakenly believe that the king's power 'derive[s] from some natural force' rather than an artificial one (*Pensées*, p. 36).

5 John Donne, *Selected Poetry*, ed. John Carey (Oxford and New York, 1996), pp. 7, 8.

6 See the reproduction of the Note in Paul H. Kocher, *Christopher Marlowe: A Study of his Thought, Learning, and Character* (1946; New York, 1962), pp. 34–6.

7 See Donne's poem *An Anatomy of the World: First Anniversary*, in *Selected Poetry*, p. 163.

8 Ferdinand in *The Duchess of Malfi* makes a related point: 'though our national law distinguish bastards / From true legitimate issue, compassionate nature / Makes them all equal' (4.1.36–8).

9 See Keith Thomas, 'Age and Authority in Early Modern England', *Proceedings of the British Academy* 62 (1976): 204–49.

10 I quote from both the so-called A- and B-Texts of *Faustus* (printed versions of the play differing substantially from each other).

11 William Blake, 'London', in *Selected Poetry*, ed. Michael Mason (Oxford, 1996), p. 124.

12 This passage is discussed by Dollimore in *Radical Tragedy*, p. 15.

13 Pascal, *Pensées*, pp. 41, 40.

14 Cited in Jay L. Halio's edition: *The Tragedy of King Lear* (Cambridge, 2003), p. 225.

Going to the Theatre in Shakespeare's London

1   The Renaissance revival of the classics, and the screen of paganism, assisted dramatists in adopting this free-wheeling attitude towards sex. In *Edward II*, Mortimer Senior takes it for granted that 'The mightiest kings have had their [male] minions' (1.4.391); examples from classical history and myth follow.

2   Quoted in Wilhelm Creizenach, *The English Drama in the Age of Shakespeare* (1916; New York, 1967), p. 4.

3   For an account of the emergence of these so-called 'University Wits', see Chapter 3 of G. K. Hunter's *English Drama 1586–1642: The Age of Shakespeare* (Oxford, 1997).

4   See Jonson's tribute to Shakespeare, 'To the Memory of My Beloved', in *Ben Jonson: Poems*, ed. Ian Donaldson (London, 1975), p. 308.

5   For the epistle, see the text of the play in *English Renaissance Drama*, eds Bevington et al., p. 189.

6   For this college exercise of Milton's, see vol. 1 of *Complete Prose Works of John Milton*, ed. Don M. Wolfe (New Haven, CT, 1953), pp. 216ff.

7   Chambers (4.306) reproduces a letter from the Privy Council to the Master of the Revels (a censor, but also in charge of court entertainment) instructing him to read the manuscripts of plays before performance: matters of 'Divinity and State' – i.e., religion and politics – are 'unfit and undecent to be handled in plays'. A royal proclamation of 1559 instructs Elizabeth's officers 'that they permit' no 'interludes' (or plays) 'to be played wherein either matters of religion or of the governance of the estate of the common weal shall be handled or treated, being no meet [i.e., suitable] matters to be written or treated upon, but by men of authority, learning, and wisdom, nor to be

handled before any audience, but of grave and discreet persons'
(4.263).

8   The technical term for this preference for verbal elaboration
     was (in Latin) *copia*, i.e., copiousness or abundance.

9   On the likelihood that 'fixed traditions had developed for the
     expression of violent emotions, and in particular, pain and
     despair', and that 'elaborateness of gesture' was a feature of
     Renaissance acting, see Creizenach, *English Drama*, pp. 401,
     402.

10   Witness the reaction of the writer Thomas Lodge to a
     pre-Shakespearean version of *Hamlet*, and in particular to
     the 'ghost which cried so miserably at the Theatre, like an
     oyster-wife, *Hamlet, revenge*' (quoted in the Introduction to
     Harold Jenkins's edition of *Hamlet* (London, 1982), p. 83).
     Compare too the depiction of Tragedy in the anonymous play
     A Warning for Fair Women (c. 1585–99): 'a filthy whining
     ghost, / Lapped in some foul sheet ... / Comes screaming like
     a pig half sticked, / And cries *Vindicta*, revenge, revenge' (lines
     54–7): see Charles Dale Cannon's edition (The Hague, 1975).

11   Patrick Cruttwell argued that the English literature of the
     1590s saw the 'spreading and ... sharpening of the spirit of
     criticism' and satire, which takes as its target all 'abstractness
     and unreality': see *The Shakespearean Moment and Its Place in
     the Poetry of the Seventeenth Century* (London, 1954), p. 18.

12   Barbara Everett, *Young Hamlet: Essays on Shakespeare's
     Tragedies* (Oxford, 1989), p. 12.

13   Samuel Johnson, 'Note on *Hamlet*', in vol. 2 of *Johnson on
     Shakespeare*, ed. Arthur Sherbo, 2 vols (New Haven, CT,
     1968), p. 1011.

14   Sidney, *A Defence of Poetry*, p. 383.

15   See lines 2474–5 (Act Four, Scene Four) of the text in *Two
     Tudor Tragedies*, ed. Tydeman.

16   Compare Heywood's depiction of the tragic muse as the
     opponent of tyranny: 'Am I Melpomene, the buskined Muse, /
     That held in awe the tyrants of the world / And played their
     lives in public theatres, / Making them fear to sin, since fearless
     I / Prepar'd to write their lives in crimson ink, / And act their

shames in eye of all the world?' (see 'A Defence of Drama',
p. 483).

Pursuing Freedom in English Renaissance Tragedy

1   Hunter, *English Drama 1586–1642*, p. 418.

Gorboduc

1   Quotations from *Gorboduc* are by line number.

2   Thomas More, *Utopia* (1516), ed. and trans. George M. Logan (New York, 2011), p. 95.

3   Compare Webster in *The White Devil*: 'These strong court factions that do brook no checks' (5.5.14).

Tamburlaine, Parts One and Two

1   See the letter from the printer of the 1590 edition of *Tamburlaine*, Part One, reproduced in *English Renaissance Drama*, eds Bevington et al., p. 189.

The Jew of Malta

1   *Gulliver's Travels*, ed. Claude Rawson, (Oxford, 2005), p. 237.

2   'Liberal' here has a primary significance of free-spending but also connotes the idea of 'liberal arts' – studies engaged in for no practical purpose.

Edward II

1   John Donne, 'The Sun Rising', in *Selected Poetry*, p. 85.

Arden of Faversham

1   Quotations from *Arden of Faversham* are by scene and line number.

2   See Francesca's account of the 'root of love which wrought [their] fall' in the *Inferno*, Canto Five, lines 121–38. See *The Divine Comedy I: Hell*, trans. Dorothy L. Sayers (London, 1949).

Hamlet

1   F. P. Wilson, 'Shakespeare and the Diction of Common Life', in his *Shakespearian and Other Studies*, ed. Helen Gardner (Oxford, 1969).

2   'Webster was much possessed by death / And saw the skull beneath the skin': 'Whispers of Immortality', in *Collected Poems* (London, 1963), p. 55.

3   *Timber, or, Discoveries* (1640–1), in *The Oxford Authors: Ben Jonson*, ed. Ian Donaldson (Oxford, 1985), p. 539.

4   Compare the republican Milton in *Paradise Lost*, Book I, lines 500–2: 'and when night / Darkens the streets, then wander forth the sons / Of Belial, flown with insolence and wine'. The phrase 'sons / Of Belial' is a hit at courtiers.

Othello

1   For an account of the defence of the passions in works by Shakespeare and others, see Richard Strier, 'Against the Rule of Reason: Praise of Passion from Petrarch to Luther

to Shakespeare to Herbert', in *Reading the Early Modern Passions: Essays in the Cultural History of Emotions*, eds Gail Kern Paster, Katherine Rowe and Mary Floyd-Wilson (Philadelphia, 2004), pp. 23–42.

2   The Renaissance and medieval worlds often associated blackness with devilry, but Shakespeare challenged this racist assumption: 'Iago is the white man with the black soul while Othello is the black man with the white soul'; see 'Othello and Colour Prejudice', in Hunter's *Dramatic Identities and Cultural Tradition*, p. 46.

King Lear

1   'And truly it is a very natural and ordinary thing to desire to acquire, and always, when men do it who can, they will be praised and not blamed; but when they cannot, and wish to do it anyway, here lie the error and the blame'; see *The Prince*, trans. Harvey C. Mansfield (Chicago, 1998), pp. 14–15. Likewise Marlowe's Tamburlaine asserts that 'Nature, that framed us of four elements / Warring within our breasts for regiment, / Doth teach us all to have aspiring minds' (*1 Tamb.*, 2.7.18–20). The outlook is realist: men naturally seek power.

2   W. H. Auden, *Collected Poems*, ed. Edward Mendelson (New York, 1991), p. 598.

3   Alfred, Lord Tennyson, *In Memoriam*, ed. Erik Gray (New York, 2004), LVI, line 15.

4   Compare Walter Cohen's statement that both Lear and Gloucester 'emphasize the need to share the lot of the poor': *Drama of a Nation: Public Theater in Renaissance England and Spain* (Ithaca, NY, 1985), p. 334.

5   For an account of the play's post-war reception, see R. A. Foakes, *Hamlet versus Lear: Cultural Politics and Shakespeare's Art* (Cambridge, 1993).

6   John Berger, 'Against the Great Defeat of the World', *Race and Class* 40 (1998–9): 4.

Antony and Cleopatra

1   Shakespeare treats this same anxiety in the *Sonnets*: the speaker is drawn towards a woman (the so-called 'Dark Lady') he knows is unworthy of his desire but from whom he apparently cannot free himself.

2   Hamlet excuses himself similarly with Laertes: Hamlet was 'not himself' when he 'wronged Laertes' (5.2.233, 231).

3   The phrase 'revaluation of all values' was used several times by Nietzsche; see, for example, *Ecce Homo: How to Become What You Are* (1888) in *The Anti-Christ, Ecce Homo, Twilight of the Idols, and Other Writings*, trans. Judith Norman, eds Aaron Ridley and Judith Norman (Cambridge, 2005), p. 121.

The Revenger's Tragedy

1   This phrase is repeated at 4.4.135.

The White Devil

1   As John Russell Brown points out in an excellent Introduction to his edition, *The White Devil* is 'is pre-eminently about "Great Men" and the operation of privilege and authority'. It depicts 'the injustice of [the] court world' and its 'concerns' are primarily 'political'. See *The White Devil* (Manchester, 1996), pp. 3, 6, 9.

The Duchess of Malfi

1   See Donne's 'The Sun Rising'.

BIBLIOGRAPHY

Aeschylus, *Oresteia: Agamemnon, The Libation Bearers, The Eumenides*, trans. Richmond Lattimore, eds David Grene and Richmond Lattimore (Chicago, 1953).

—*The Persians, The Seven Against Thebes, The Suppliant Maidens, Prometheus Bound*, eds David Grene and Richmond Lattimore (Chicago and London, 1956).

Aristotle, *Complete Works of Aristotle*, ed. Jonathan Barnes (Princeton, 1984).

Auden, W. H., *Collected Poems*, ed. Edward Mendelson (New York, 1991).

Bacon, Francis, *The Works* (1857–74), eds James Spedding, Robert Leslie Ellis and Douglas Denon Heath, 14 vols (Stuttgart, 1963).

Berger, John, 'Against the Great Defeat of the World', *Race and Class* 40.2–3 (1999): 1–4.

Berlin, Isaiah, 'Two Concepts of Liberty' (1958), in *The Proper Study of Mankind: An Anthology of Essays*, eds Henry Hardy and Roger Hausheer (London, 1998), pp. 191–242.

Bevington, David, Lars Engle, Katharine Eisaman Maus and Eric Rasmussen, eds, *English Renaissance Drama: A Norton Anthology* (New York, 2002).

Black, J. B., *The Reign of Elizabeth, 1558–1603*, 2nd edn (Oxford, 1959).

Blake, William, *Selected Poetry*, ed. Michael Mason (Oxford and New York, 1996).

Boethius, *The Consolation of Philosophy*, trans. Victor Watts, rev. edn (London, 1999).

La Boétie, Étienne de, *The Politics of Obedience: The Discourse of Voluntary Servitude*, trans. Harry Kurz, ed. Murray N. Rothbard (Montreal, 1997).

Bradley, A. C., *Shakespearean Tragedy: Lectures on Hamlet, Othello, King Lear, Macbeth* (1904), 4th edn (Houndmills, 2007).

Burke, Edmund, *Works of Edmund Burke*, 12 vols (London, 1899).

Cary, Elizabeth, *The Tragedy of Mariam*, ed. Ramona Wray (London, 2012).

Certain Sermons or Homilies Appointed to be Read in Churches In the Time of Queen Elizabeth I (1547–1571) (1623), eds Mary Ellen Rickey and Thomas B. Stroup (Gainesville, 1968).

Chambers, E. K., *The Elizabethan Stage* (1923), 4 vols (Oxford, 1974).

Chaucer, Geoffrey, *The Riverside Chaucer,* ed. Larry D. Benson (Boston, 1987).

Cioran, E. M., *On the Heights of Despair* (1934), trans. Ilinca Zarifopol-Johnston (Chicago, 1992).

—*The Temptation to Exist* (1956), trans. Richard Howard (Chicago, 1998).

Cohen, Walter, *Drama of a Nation: Public Theater in Renaissance England and Spain* (Ithaca, NY, 1985).

Creizenach, Wilhelm, *The English Drama in the Age of Shakespeare* (1916; New York, 1967).

Cruttwell, Patrick, *The Shakespearean Moment and its Place in the Poetry of the Seventeenth Century* (London and Toronto, 1954).

Dante Alighieri, *The Divine Comedy I: Hell*, trans. Dorothy L. Sayers (London, 1949).

Dollimore, Jonathan, *Radical Tragedy: Religion, Ideology and Power in the Drama of Shakespeare and His Contemporaries* (1984), 3rd edn (Basingstoke, 2010).

Donne, John, *Selected Poetry*, ed. John Carey (Oxford, 1996).

Eliot, T. S., *Collected Poems 1909–1962* (London, 1963).

Euripides, *Alcestis, The Medea, The Heracleidae, Hippolytus*, eds David Grene and Richmond Lattimore (Chicago and London, 1955).

—*The Bacchae and Other Plays*, trans. John Davie (London, 2005).

—*Helen, Phoenician Women, Orestes*, ed. and trans. David Kovacs (Cambridge, MA, and London, 2002).

—*Heracles and Other Plays*, trans. John Davie (London, 2002).

—*Trojan Women, Iphigenia Among the Taurians, Ion*, ed. and trans. David Kovacs (Cambridge, MA, and London, 1999).

Everett, Barbara, *Young Hamlet: Essays on Shakespeare's Tragedies* (Oxford, 1989).

Farnham, Willard, *The Medieval Heritage of Elizabethan Tragedy* (Oxford, 1936).

Foakes, R. A. *Hamlet versus Lear: Cultural Politics and Shakespeare's Art* (Cambridge, 1993).

Goethe, Johann Wolfgang von, *Poems and Epigrams*, trans. Michael Hamburger (London, 1983).

Greenblatt, Stephen, *Will in the World: How Shakespeare Became Shakespeare* (New York, 2004).

Hardy, Thomas, *Tess of the d'Urbervilles* (1891), ed. Tim Dolin (London, 2003).

Heidegger, Martin, *Being and Time* (1927), trans. Joan Stambaugh (Albany, 1996).

Heywood, Thomas, 'A Defence of Drama' (1608), in *English Renaissance Literary Criticism*, ed. Brian Vickers (Oxford, 1999), pp. 474–501.

Holbrook, Peter, 'Shakespeare, Montaigne, and Classical Reason', in *Shakespeare and Renaissance Ethics*, eds Patrick Gray and John H. Cox (Cambridge, 2014), pp. 261–83.

Hunter, G. K., *Dramatic Identities and Cultural Tradition: Studies in Shakespeare and His Contemporaries* (Liverpool, 1978).

—*English Drama 1586–1642: The Age of Shakespeare* (Oxford, 1997).

James I, *King James VI and I: Political Writings*, ed. Johann P. Sommerville (Cambridge, 1994).

Johnson, Samuel, *Johnson on Shakespeare*, ed. Arthur Sherbo, 2 vols (New Haven, CT, 1968).

Jonson, Ben, *The Oxford Authors: Ben Jonson*, ed. Ian Donaldson (Oxford, 1985).

—*Poems*, ed. Ian Donaldson (London, 1975).

Keats, John, *The Complete Poems*, ed. John Barnard, 3rd edn (London, 2006).

Kocher, Paul H., *Christopher Marlowe: A Study of His Thought, Learning, and Character* (1946; New York, 1962).

Machiavelli, Niccolò, *The Prince*, trans. Harvey C. Mansfield, 2nd edn (Chicago, 1998).

Marlowe, Christopher, *Doctor Faustus and Other Plays*, eds David Bevington and Eric Rasmussen (Oxford, 1995).

Marston, John, *The Malcontent*, in *English Renaissance Drama*, eds Bevington et al.

Marx, Karl, *The Eighteenth Brumaire of Louis Bonaparte* (1852), in *The Portable Karl Marx*, partial trans. and ed. Eugene Kamenka (New York, 1983).

Middleton, Thomas, *The Collected Works*, eds Gary Taylor and John Lavagnino (Oxford, 2007).

Milton, John, *Complete Prose Works*, eds Don M. Wolfe et al., 7 vols (New Haven, CT, 1953).

—*Paradise Lost*, ed. Alastair Fowler, 2nd edn (Harlow, 1998).

Montaigne, Michel de, *Essays*, ed. and trans. M. A. Screech (London, 1991).

More, Thomas, *Utopia*, ed. and trans. George M. Logan (New York, 2011).

Nietzsche, Friedrich, *The Anti-Christ, Ecce Homo, Twilight of the Idols, and Other Writings*, trans. Judith Norman, eds Aaron Ridley and Judith Norman (Cambridge, 2005).

—*The Birth of Tragedy and Other Writings*, eds Raymond Geuss and Ronald Spiers, trans. Ronald Spiers (Cambridge, 1999).

—*Writings from the Early Notebooks*, eds Raymond Geuss and Alexander Nehamas, trans. Ladislaus Löb (Cambridge, 2009).

—*Writings from the Late Notebooks*, ed. Rüdiger Bittner, trans. Kate Sturge (Cambridge, 2003).

Palliser, D. M., *The Age of Elizabeth: England under the Later Tudors 1547–1603*, 2nd edn (Harlow, 1992).

Pascal, Blaise, *Pensées* (1670), trans. A. J. Krailsheimer (Harmondsworth, 1966).

Pico della Mirandola, Giovanni, 'Oration on the Dignity of Man', trans. E. L. Forbes, in *The Renaissance Philosophy of Man*, eds E. Cassirer et al. (Chicago, 1948), pp. 223–254.

Plato, *The Republic*, trans. Desmond Lee, 2nd edn (Harmondsworth, 1974).

Racine, Jean, *Phaedra*, in *Iphigenia, Phaedra, Athaliah*, trans. John Cairncross (Harmonsworth, 1963).

Sartre, Jean-Paul, *Being and Nothingness* (1943), trans. Hazel E. Barnes (New York, 1956).

Seneca, *Tragedies II: Oedipus, Agamemnon, Thyestes, Hercules on Oeta, Octavia*, ed. and trans. John G. Fitch (Cambridge, MA, and London, 2004).

Shakespeare, William, *The Complete Works*, ed. David Bevington, 6th edn (New York, 2009).

—*Hamlet*, ed. Harold Jenkins (London, 1982).

—*Hamlet: The Texts of 1603 and 1623*, eds Ann Thompson and Neil Taylor (London, 2006).

—*The Riverside Shakespeare*, eds G. Blakemore Evans and J. J. Tobin, 2nd edn (Boston 1997).

—*The Tragedy of King Lear*, ed. Jay L. Halio (Cambridge, 2003).

Shakespeare, William and John Fletcher, *King Henry VIII*, ed. Gordon McMullan (London, 2000).

Sidney, Sir Philip. *A Defence of Poetry* (1595), in *English Renaissance Literary Criticism*, ed. Brian Vickers (Oxford, 1999).

Sophocles, *Oedipus the King, Oedipus at Colonus, Antigone*, eds David Grene and Richmond Lattimore (Chicago and London, 1954).

Strier, Richard, 'Against the Rule of Reason: Praise of Passion from Petrarch to Luther to Shakespeare to Herbert', in *Reading the Early Modern Passions: Essays in the Cultural History of Emotions*, eds Gail Kern Paster, Katherine Rowe and Mary Floyd-Wilson (Philadelphia, 2004), pp. 23–42.

—*Resistant Structures: Particularity, Radicalism, and Renaissance Texts* (Berkeley, 1995).

Sturgess, Keith, ed., *Three Elizabethan Domestic Tragedies* (Harmondsworth, 1969).

Swift, Jonathan, *Gulliver's Travels*, ed. Claude Rawson (Oxford, 2005).

Tawney, R. H., *Equality* (1933; London, 1965).

Tennyson, Alfred, *In Memoriam*, ed. Erik Gray (New York, 2004).

Thomas, Keith, 'Age and Authority in Early Modern England', in *Proceedings of the British Academy* 62 (1976): 204–49.

Tilley, Morris Palmer, *Elizabethan Proverb Lore in Lyly's Euphues and in Pettie's Petite Pallace: With Parallels from Shakespeare* (New York, 1926).

Tillyard, E. M. W., *The Elizabethan World Picture* (1943; New Brunswick, NJ, 2011).

Timpanaro, Sebastiano, *On Materialism*, trans. Lawrence Garner (London, 1975).

Tydeman, William, ed., *Two Tudor Tragedies* (London and New York, 1992).

A Warning for Fair Women, ed. Charles Dale Cannon (The Hague, 1975).

Webster, John, *The White Devil*, ed. John Russell Brown (Manchester and New York, 1996).

Wilson, F. P., *Shakespearian and Other Studies*, ed. Helen Gardner (Oxford, 1969).

Wordsworth, William, *The Major Works*, ed. Stephen Gill (Oxford, 1984).

Yeats, William Butler, *Poems*, ed. A. Norman Jeffares (London, 1989).

INDEX